The Disciple's Handbook for the Spirit-filled Life

Living in the Power of God

Dr Bob Gordon

Sovereign World

Sovereign World Ltd
PO Box 777
Tonbridge
Kent TX11 9XT
England

ISBN 1 85240 092 7

Typeset by CRB (Drayton) Typesetting Services, Norwich
Printed in England by Clays Ltd, St Ives plc.

Contents

'Even though you have ten thousand guardians in Christ,
you do not have many fathers'
(1 Corinthians 4:15)

In memory of my father

Gilbert

whose integrity and perseverance taught me my first steps
in following Jesus

Preface

This book was first published a few years ago under the title *Understanding the Way*. The end of the first edition, a change of publisher and new developments demanded a re-print under a different title with a slightly different presentation of the material. The content is much the same except for some deletions and small changes that are not worth mentioning here. I have brought the book up to date so that it stands in line with my present ministry and reflects where I stand on most issues.

The new title *Living in the Power of God* reflects what I believe in, namely, dynamic theology. This is not a theological book in the scholarly sense of the word but it is meant to present an ordered approach to vital subjects surrounding the work of the Holy Spirit. It deals with what I would describe as some of the big themes of the faith. Themes such as our Adoption in Christ, the power of the Cross, the Word of God, the reality of Faith, the call to Discipleship, the ground of our Authority, Spiritual Warfare, ministry in the power of the Spirit, and the life and work of the Holy Spirit.

These are themes that will remain only religious theory unless we experience them in the power of the Spirit. But through the Spirit the Gospel lives. He comes, not only as the divine interpreter of truth, but its divine Energiser! It is He who makes the truth live in us. This book is about that kind of truth. Jesus said that we would know the truth and the truth would set us free (John 8:32).

Each section of the book can be read almost on its own. It's meant for that so the reader can move from one step to the next in appreciating just what great things God has done for us in Jesus and what great things He does in us by the Holy Spirit. I pray that you will be stimulated to go deeper in your own exploration of the life of God and that you will discover the height and depth and breadth and length of the riches that are ours in Christ throught the Holy Spirit.

Chapter 1

Called and Chosen

1: Following Jesus

Discipleship is a very serious business. It is a costly thing. That's how Jesus Himself looked upon it. He did not start out offering His followers a bed of roses! He made it absolutely clear from the beginning what was involved: *'Anyone who does not carry his cross and follow me cannot be my disciple'* (Lk 14:27).

After all, this is what discipleship is all about – following the Master. It is not based on a passing interest or fancy, but on a determined attitude to see this through to the end. This again reflects the attitude of Jesus towards the call to follow Him: *'No-one who puts his hand to the plough and looks back is fit for service in the kingdom of God'* (Lk 9:62).

Discipleship is commitment to the way of Jesus – no turning back! We can see just how important this idea was to Jesus Himself. 'Disciple' was His favourite word for those whose lives were closely linked with His own. The word 'disciple' occurs no fewer than 269 times in the first five books of the New Testament. It means 'one who is taught or trained', or 'one who is a learner'.

That's what we are – disciples of Jesus! We have been called to follow Him. We have been called to learn from Him, to follow His example. We have been called to become what He is, the Son of the Father in whose life the will of God is fulfilled through commitment and obedience. Jesus Himself is our great paradigm of discipleship. In the pages that follow we will look together at a number of themes that are vitally important as the basis for our discipleship.

In the Gospels, discipleship is defined in a number of ways. First, *a disciple is a person who lives continually by the Word of Jesus.* Jesus said: *'If ye continue in my word, then are ye my disciples indeed,'* (Jn 8:31, AV). The New International Version translates 'word' (*logos*) as 'teaching'. This demonstrates what, I suppose, is the real intention of the text. A disciple is not only a person who follows the occasional 'words' of the Master but is rather one who commits himself to follow through the teaching of the Master in a disciplined and committed way.

Jesus is our Master. He will speak living words to us daily through the Spirit. What we need to learn to do is follow out in our own daily lives the commands, teaching and example which He has already given us. The main thought behind discipleship is not one of inspiration, but one of instruction. We could spend the rest of our days fruitfully putting into effect (with the help of the Holy Spirit, of course) all that the Lord had left us through His own direct words and through the teaching that has been revealed in the apostolic writings.

This is one area, I believe, where there has been a massive failure in this day of so-called charismatic inspiration. We are so eager to receive direct words from the Lord that we fail to see the great reservoir of living and relevant truth which we have as the deposit of the Spirit. Disciples don't sit around waiting for inspiration. Disciples set about putting into practice what they have already been given. No truth is living truth until it is lived truth!

There is a huge need for us to move from an *emotional* base for our discipleship to a *theological* base. Too many people live their Christian lives at the level of their feelings and their own latest revelation, instead of in the light of the Word of God which has been given to us in the Scriptures. The results of this can be seen around us on every hand. Without the stable foundation of *obedience* to the Word of God as the basis of our discipleship, we are at the mercy of every subjective notion or feeling that comes along. Our lack of commitment to the Scriptures has led us into a morass of subjectivity in many areas. It certainly is a major contributing factor in our inability to distinguish truth from error.

The Holy Spirit is our guide in the things of Christ. That is what Jesus said He would do: *'He will not speak on his own; he will speak only what he hears, and he will tell you what is yet to come. He will bring glory to me by taking from what is mine and making it known to you'* (Jn 16:13–14). We would be a lot less prone to live crisis-related lives if we based our lives on the sure foundation of the Word of Jesus. Like the man who built his house on the rock, we would be well prepared to weather any storm of life that comes our way.

Second, *a disciple is a person who commits his life completely to the Master.* This commitment needs to be total! The Master cannot teach us effectively if we are only half-hearted in our commitment to Him. He must know that He can be sure of us. It is only on this basis that any effective discipling can be carried out. This is why it is so important for us to know that we are committed to the right person or people. The principle of discipling outside of Christ can be disastrous. He leads us on in love; He has no self-interest; His concern is for our total welfare and growth in God. If we committed ourselves to some other in this way, who knows where we would be led!

But then, Jesus has the right to demand this commitment of us. No one except Jesus has ever died for us. No one else ever loved us to the point of laying down his life for us. Jesus Himself knew that the way of fruitfulness was the path of total commitment, and so He points His followers in the same direction: *'If anyone would come after me, he must deny himself and take up his cross and follow me. For whoever wants to save his life will lose it, but whoever loses his life for me will find it'* (Mt 16:24, 25). The commitment that Jesus offers us is a commitment sealed in His own blood! What He wants from us is a commitment of total love, so that we will trust Him in every step as He takes our life and moulds it in accordance with His will. Paul caught the meaning of this when he wrote: *'And he died for all, that those who live should no longer live for themselves but for him who died for them and was raised again'* (2 Cor 5:15).

Third, *a disciple is one who lives in a fruit-bearing relationship with Jesus.* In His final conversation with His followers before He went to the cross, Jesus spoke of His desire for their lives. The importance of this theme can be seen in the fact that it was one of the major features in this last conversation: *'Remain in me, and I will remain in you. No branch can bear fruit by itself; it must remain in the vine. Neither can you bear fruit unless you remain in me. I am the vine; you are the branches. If a man remains in me and I in him, he will bear much fruit; apart from me you can do nothing'* (Jn 15:4, 5).

Waylon Moore writes about this same theme in his book, *Multiplying Disciples.* He catches the beauty of this idea of fruit-bearing very well:

> *Our union with Christ makes possible a life through which others can be saved. When a tree is so full of sap that it can no longer hold it, the result is fruit! When a Christian is full of Christ, others see him and hear about him and are then spiritually reborn into the Kingdom of God. Thus, new believers are one fruit of discipleship.*

I agree with Moore in the point he is making. He is arguing that while it is good and desirable to display the fruit of the Spirit of which we read in Galatians 5:22, 23, it is also necessary to see that fruit-bearing goes beyond personal holiness and enters us into areas of personal witnessing, evangelism and soul-winning. Without this sort of fruit-bearing in our lives the kingdom of God will not be expanded and the body of Christ will not grow.

Fourth, *a disciple is one who is committed to others in sacrificial fellowship.* Jesus said that this was the greatest witness to our discipleship as far as other people are concerned: *'A new command I give you: Love one another. As I have loved you, so you must love one another. All men will know that you are my disciples if you love one another'* (Jn 13:34,

35). This is no ordinary human love. It is the love which God Himself has demonstrated towards us. It is unconditional love that does not look for a return to stimulate its action. God loved us while we did not love Him: *'This is love; not that we loved God, but that he loved us and sent his son as an atoning sacrifice for our sins. Dear friends, since God so loved us, we also ought to love one another'* (1 Jn 4:10, 11). The only chance of this ever happening is if we open ourselves up unconditionally to the work of the Holy Spirit. Paul tells us that God has poured His love into our hearts by the Spirit (see Rom 5:5).

The work of God in our own day will never go forward in any great measure unless we take this particular challenge of discipleship more seriously. We need to be able to hold, without compromise, the truth which God has revealed to us, but with hearts that are filled with God's love to such an extent that we are able to comprehend all our fellow believers within the circle of our love.

Fifth, *a disciple is one who is dedicated to the fulfilment of Christ's commission*. The final command of Jesus lies in the words of what we know as The Great Commission: *'Go and make disciples of all nations, baptising them in the name of the Father and of the Son and of the Holy Spirit, and teaching them to obey everything I have commanded you'* (Mt 28:19, 20). This is the goal of our discipleship: that we shall be able to disciple others. Jesus has not sent us out to make converts. A convert may change his mind for a moment and then change it back. A disciple has made a life commitment.

We can only disciple others in those areas in which we have become a disciple ourselves. This is the aim of this book: to help each one of us review the grounds of our discipleship. I cannot pretend that it is in any way a complete study of the life of discipleship – that would need much more than one book can give -but it is an attempt to share some of those areas in which I have been challenged myself and within which I have needed to learn and to grow over the past few years.

2: Turning to God

Our experience of God lies at the heart of all discipleship. Without a deep and personal experience of God's judgement and God's mercy within our lives, discipleship becomes a mere matter of rule and rote. I say 'God's judgement' because until we have felt the impact of His wrath we will never turn away from those elements of sin and pride which prevent us from growing into the likeness of Christ. In the past few years I have become convinced that many of the problems we have to deal with in the lives of Christians today arise from the fact that they have never been allowed to feel the weight of God's judgement on their sin and bondage. As we will see, at the heart of any true work of repentance lies a deep recognition that what I am in the flesh is deeply abhorrent to a holy God. I also say 'God's mercy' because without a real experience of His forgiveness and love we would be crushed under a load of sin and darkness. The Holy Spirit comes, not only to convict us of our sins, but to point us to the mercy of God in Christ Jesus.

The cry of the Psalmist becomes the cry of every heart which is truly touched by God:

> 'Have mercy on me, O God,
>   according to your unfailing love;
> according to your great compassion
>   blot out my transgressions.
> Wash away all my iniquity
>   and cleanse me from my sin.
> For I know my transgressions,
>   and my sin is always before me ...
> Cleanse me with hyssop, and I shall be clean;
>   wash me, and I shall be whiter than snow.'

(Ps 51:1–3, 7)

A: The power of repentance

For some, the word 'repentance' may have very negative overtones. It is not like that, though. There is a right and proper sorrow involved in repentance, as we shall see, but the fruit of repentance is good and leads to an experience of God's

14

joy and forgiveness. The main idea that stands at the heart of repentance is found in the Old Testament Hebrew word *shub* (pronounced 'shoov'). It basically means 'to turn'. This is well illustrated by the Authorised Version translation of Jeremiah 31:18 *'Turn thou me, and I shall be turned; for thou art the LORD my God.'*

The act of repentance is one of the most important and fundamental factors in our walk with God. Within it are three important elements:

(a) **Repentance is cognitive.** This means, very simply, that there is something to be understood. It is *knowledge* in the widest sense of the word. The understanding that is involved in repentance will lead us to a very different understanding of ourselves. Repentance involves recognition of our sin in the eyes of a holy God! This is the sort of language Paul uses in Romans chapter 3 when he demonstrates the power of the law; it has no power to save anyone but it brings a 'knowledge of sin' (see Rom 3:20).

In repentance there is always an agent which causes this change of direction or heart. In faith terms this is the Word of God. When God's Word comes home to us in the power of the Holy Spirit it has an arresting affect within our lives. It stops us in our tracks, challenges us about our present way of life and thought and introduces us to the fact of God's right-eous demands and holiness. These are the great and deep elements of gospel preaching we need today! We don't want a gospel that is only focused on man's need; we need a gospel which reveals God's heart! Then men have a reference point against which to be judged in their own lives.

Surely the most powerful testimony of this in the Scriptures is the experience of Isaiah. In Isaiah chapter 6 we are given a profound insight into the prophet's experience. He came face to face with the majesty of God. I do not doubt that this was a deep revelation of the Holy Spirit because we cannot have such a revelation of God unless God Himself chooses to reveal Himself. The impact of this on the prophet was pro-found: *'Woe to me! ... I am ruined! For I am a man of unclean lips, and I live among a people of unclean lips, and my eyes have seen the King, the Lord Almighty'* (Is 6:5). This deep revelation of God led to a depth of self-awareness which the prophet had never experienced before. He felt the reality of his sin in the light of God's presence.

I think we should beware of thinking that such an experience is open only to Old Testament prophets. We need to be expecting God's Word to have such a convicting effect on all our hearts today. When we proclaim God's Word we ought to be looking for real signs of a deep recognition among people of their sin before God. I don't believe for one moment that this is morose. If we really understood, in this deep spiritual sense, what our old lives meant to God, we would be more ready to turn away from them in true repentance and allow the Holy Spirit to cut us off from their power and reality. This, of course, is the essence of what it means to die with Christ and be 'united with him in his death' (see Rom 6:5).

This was the experience of David in the Psalm we read earlier. He knew his sin. That is the heart of repentance. But it is not just a knowing of our sin; it is the knowledge of our sin because of a prior knowledge of the holiness of God! This, I believe, is the heart of revival. Today we readily expect God to work in the power of His Spirit in signs and wonders amongst people. I believe we are being called to look for signs of the hand of God coming down on people with such conviction that they will really turn away from their sin. It is the Holy Spirit who is at work, so we need to be ready for Him to come and manifest His nature among us. An awareness of His holiness will lead to a tremendous awareness and recognition of where we stand before Him.

(b) Repentance is emotional. This recognition of our state before God leads, of course, to a very powerful reaction within our emotions. It brings about a change of feeling. It involves a deep-felt sense of offence and regret. This was the experience of David when he knew the reality of his sin in the sight of God. He knew that his sin was an offence against God and he felt the shame and sorrow that was associated with the fact: *'Hide your face from my sins and blot out all my iniquity'* (Ps 51:9).

I will never forget the moment when I became aware of the holiness of God in this overpowering way. It was associated with what most people would describe as my baptism in the Holy Spirit, but for me it was much more! I had an encounter with God as the Holy Spirit revealed to me the greatness and the glory of God and I became aware of just how far short of that I was in my own life. I entered into something of what Isaiah must have known that day in the Temple. I felt the weight of all that was wrong in my life. It was not just a matter of particular sins, it was more a sense of sin! I felt a deep sorrow within my heart which was not relieved until I came through to the place of receiving God's forgiveness.

Paul uses a phrase in his letters to the church at Corinth which describes this feeling. It had obviously been necessary to speak to them in a stern way about their attitude towards him at some stage. This had caused them pain, but Paul knew that this pain was to their benefit: '... *your sorrow led you to repentance. For you became sorrowful as God intended ... Godly sorrow brings repentance that leads to salvation and leaves no regret, but worldly sorrow brings death*' (2 Cor 7:9, 10). Notice the contrast between godly sorrow, which is part of the Holy Spirit's way of bringing us to that place where we will receive the Word of God for our lives, and worldly sorrow, which is associated with the pain of death, tragedy and bereavement.

(c) Repentance is volitional. That is, it involves the will. Repentance is a change of mind, of heart, of purpose – in fact, of the whole direction of one's life. It is *conversion*. The Greek word *metanoia* occurs many times in the New Testament to describe this 'about turn' and means the start of a whole new life lived under the power of God.

On a number of occasions when this word is used, the clear implication is that the initiative for this act of repentance lies with God. In other words, if He had not revealed His love to us and spoken His Word into our lives, we would never have become aware of our need, or our state, before Him. This work of God is spoken of by Paul when he says: '*You show contempt for the riches of his kindness, tolerance and patience, not realising that God's kindness leads you towards repentance'* (Rom 2:4).

For every time the word is so used, however, it is used four times to speak of man's response to the grace of God. It portrays the attitude he must take if he is to receive forgiveness and describes the change that will take place when he turns to God. For example, after Peter had proclaimed the message in the power of the Holy Spirit at Pentecost, his listeners enquired urgently what they should do. *'Peter replied, "Repent and be baptised, every one of you, in the name of Jesus Christ so that your sins may be forgiven. And you will receive the gift of the Holy Spirit"'* (Acts 2:38). This work of repentance, in all its depth and power, is an element we must not leave out of consideration in ministry and evangelism. It is the root out of which everything else will grow in Christian experience.

B: The power of forgiveness

Repentance does not stand alone, however. The forgiveness of God is its spiritual twin! The experience of Isaiah would have ended in utter devastation of spirit if he had not come to know the power of God's mercy. Having acknowledged his own poor state in the presence of the God of holiness, he went on to experience the greatness of God's love: *'Then one of the seraphs flew to me with a live coal in his hand, which he had taken with tongs from the altar. With it he touched my mouth and said, "See, this has touched your lips; your guilt is taken away and your sin atoned for"'* (Is 6:6, 7).

These words from Isaiah reflect in an interesting way the witness of the New Testament, as well as the experience of every true believer. The last phrase, *'your sin atoned for'*, reflects the New Testament language. The actual word *forgiveness* is not used so often in the New Testament, apart from the Gospels, to speak of the activity of God. It is used more of what our attitude towards each other should be. Other more profound ideas are expressed, such as atonement, justification, redemption. In fact in Colossians 1:14 the idea of forgiveness is used to define what redemption is in practice when Paul says, *'in whom we have redemption, the forgiveness of sins'*. This reminds us that as far as the Father is concerned forgiveness is no easy matter. For Him it is the costliest fact in the universe!

Forgiveness stands at the heart of true discipleship. Forgiveness brings freedom. The guilt and condemnation of our hearts is removed by the Holy Spirit and we are free to grow into the full stature of our new manhood in Christ Jesus.

Consider the importance of forgiveness as a positive agent for good in your life. Even at the human level, forgiveness presents us with a tremendous challenge. It first demands that we recognise that we need to be forgiven. If someone comes up to you and spontaneously forgives you it has the effect of making you decide whether to accept that forgiveness or not. This is part of the process of repentance we have just considered.

Forgiveness as a continual reality, however, has a much greater effect than even this. We all know from our own experience, I imagine, what it is like to receive forgiveness from another human being when we do not deserve it. For the first day or so we may feel a bit fragile, knowing that we are living in the good of something we just do not deserve. Every time we see the other person concerned we read their eyes and their attitudes to make sure that we are still forgiven! The more we go on, the more we realise that this forgiveness is real and then, instead of feeling like a mouse, the effect of the forgiveness begins to be felt. We begin to feel ten feet tall. We are forgiven!

If forgiveness between human beings can have such a radical effect, imagine how much more effective is the grace of God! This is the power of God's mercy. First it humbles us, then it builds us up! *'Therefore, there is now no condemnation for those who are in Christ Jesus, because through Christ Jesus the law of the Spirit of life set me free from the law of sin and death'* (Rom 8:1).

3: Adopted as Sons

At the heart of discipleship is the idea of belonging. A disciple is not only a person who follows out of a passing interest but rather a person who commits himself to the Master. His life becomes intimately involved with the one he is following. There is the idea of choice on both sides. The Master chooses the disciples. Jesus said, *'You did not choose me, but I chose you to go and bear fruit – fruit that will last'* (Jn 15:16). This is the primary choice. Jesus went to where the men were and called them out to follow Him. He found the men He wanted and appointed them to be in this special relationship with Himself. Crowds followed Him but the twelve were chosen out: *'Jesus went up on a mountainside and called to him those he wanted, and they came to him. He appointed twelve – designating them apostles – that they might be with him and that he might send them out to preach'* (Mk 3:13, 14).

Luke's Gospel demonstrates the same truth when it reports the calling of the first disciples, Simon, James and John. It is plain that Jesus takes the initiative in going towards the men with their boats. He astounded them by His knowledge and power:

> *When Simon Peter saw this, he fell at Jesus' knees and said, 'Go away from me, Lord; I am a sinful man!' For he and all his companions were astonished at the catch of fish they had taken, and so were James and John, the sons of Zebedee, Simon's partners.*
>
> *Then Jesus said to Simon, 'Don't be afraid; from now on you will catch men.' So they pulled their boats up on shore, left everything and followed him.* (Lk 5:8–11)

This last phrase, however, highlights the second element of choice. As they were chosen, so they had to choose. We may argue what this meant in practice, because obviously they were deeply affected by this Man who had come to them and by His power and authority in the situation. Nevertheless, it remains true that they needed to respond to His choice of them.

Much the same is true in our own experience. The tremendous fact is that Jesus has chosen us! It may be difficult for us to understand why, but it is true. And His choice of us calls forth our choice of Him. We are now called to be part of His family, to be intimate within His inner circle and to allow the repercussions of this choice to become apparent in our daily lives, habits, attitudes and commitment. The very ground of our discipleship is knowing who we are in Christ. When we know who we are, we are in a place to know what we can become.

A: Children of God

Two great images are used in the New Testament to describe the relationship we have with the Father through Christ. The first is that which John presents in his Gospel. It is the picture which Jesus used when He spoke with Nicodemus about the kingdom of God: *'I tell you the truth, no-one can enter the kingdom of God unless he is born of water and the Spirit. Flesh gives birth to flesh, but the Spirit gives birth to spirit'* (Jn 3:5, 6). Earlier Jesus had told Nicodemus that unless a man was born again he could never enter the kingdom of God. This picture of new birth is a very powerful analogy because that is exactly what happens in spiritual terms when we come to Christ in faith. It is a new beginning. All the old negative factors which kept us in bondage are overcome through the power of the Holy Spirit, our sins are forgiven and we are brought into a new relationship with God: *'If anyone is in Christ, he is a new creation; the old has gone, the new has come!'* (2 Cor 5:17).

The second image is the idea used by Paul in his introduction to the Epistle to the Ephesians. This is the idea of adoption: *'He chose us in him before the creation of the world to be holy and blameless in his sight. In love he predestined us to be adopted as his sons through Jesus Christ, in accordance with his pleasure and will'* (Eph 1:4, 5). Adoption and justification are two fundamental ideas of our salvation: *'Therefore, since we have been justified through faith, we have peace with God through our Lord Jesus Christ'* (Rom 5:1). Justification is a forensic idea – that is, it has to do with the law court and with judgement. Through Christ and faith in His name we have been declared 'Not Guilty' before the bar of God as Judge. Because of our sin we are all guilty before Him, but in Christ that guilt is removed through faith: *'Therefore, there is now no condemnation for those who are in Christ Jesus, because through Christ Jesus the law of the Spirit of life set me free from the law of sin and death'* (Rom 8:1, 2).

Adoption is a family idea presented in terms of love, with God as Father. Our sin has separated us from our true Father, but God in His mercy and grace, has welcomed us home and has put us in a position in the family that we did not deserve and that was not ours according to our human nature: *'How great is the love the Father has lavished on us, that we should be called children of God! And that is what we are!'* (1 Jn 3:1). This is the heart of discipleship, because it reminds us that we do not follow out of compulsion but out of love. This sense of belonging to God's family and the great privilege we have in being united with Christ Jesus, is the motivation force in our life of holiness. It is not law but love that drives us forward in our life for Christ. There *is* a law in Christian experience, but it is no longer the letter of the law that kills, but the law of the Spirit which brings life and power.

B: The plan of adoption

This idea of adoption reveals for us the heart of our heavenly Father. Adoption, in human terms, is not an immediate thing. That is, it does not take place spontaneously. It is planned and purposed first in the hearts of those who are going to adopt the child. Over many months, perhaps years, they will live with this purpose in their hearts. It will take shape until the day the decision is made and the process is put into effect. The longer the couple wait to adopt the child, the more the expectation and longing grows in their hearts until the day arrives! Then there is such joy. The choice of their dreams is now a reality; they hold in their arms the object of their love.

So it is in heaven. The Father planned long ago to adopt us in Christ. He waited throughout countless ages to bring us to

Himself: *'He chose us in him before the creation of the world'* (Eph 1:4). The significance of this is terrific! Not one of us who has been born into God's family through faith is a chance happening! God had it in His heart before the world began! Can you see what a tremendous value this places on your discipleship? It is not a haphazard event – it is something which is part of the plan of God from before the ages began!

Today we are very conscious of the factors which affect us in our Christian lives. Sometimes we are made aware of lines of inheritance from our human parents and antecedents which affect us in the present. But there is a danger in being over-conscious about such things. The truth is that the Christian believer does not take his or her line from human parents or from events in the decades or even centuries before their birth. No – the believer's line comes from before the world began! Once we are in faith, the line of our life began way back in eternity past, in the heart of God. It dips into time in the experience of our earthly lives and it lifts right forward into the power of heaven. What a plan! If we could see this in our hearts it would release us from so many of the bondages to which we are subject and enable us to stand up in the freedom that belongs to those who know the power of their birthright.

We don't take our lineage from any human descent. We take our lineage from God's purpose in Christ Jesus before the world began. We were chosen in Him, and it is from this source that we take all the power of our new life in Him.

C: The power of our adoption

The analogy of adoption fits our experience in Christ so well. In adoption the child receives a new name. It takes the name of its new parents. It takes all the privileges and potential of its new family. So in Christ we are given a new name; *'Once you were not a people, but now you are the people of God; once you had not received mercy, but now you have received mercy'* (1 Pet 2:10).

Nowhere is the authority of our adoption in Christ made more clear than in the opening chapter of John's Gospel. John emphasises the reality of the fact that we are not children of

God's family because of any right or power we have at the human level. We are born naturally outside of God's family and life. *'Yet to all who received him, to those who believed in his name, he gave **the right** to become children of God – children born not out of natural descent, nor of human decision or a husband's will, but born of God'* (Jn 1:12, 13). The word translated 'the right' is the Greek word *exousia*, which means 'authority' or 'power'. It is a word of vested authority. This right has been won for each one of us through faith. Through it we have entered into all the rights and inheritance of being in the family of God: *'Because you are sons, God sent the Spirit of his Son into our hearts, the Spirit who calls out, "Abba, Father!"'* (Gal 4:6). In fact the Holy Spirit is described as the 'Spirit of sonship'; His task is to bring into our hearts the assurance which operates as such a strong foundation for our daily living as Christians. Such strength and power come from knowing who we are and where we belong.

D: The purpose of our adoption

Paul tells us in the same verse in Ephesians what purpose the Father has for us in adopting us as His sons: *'To be holy and blameless in his sight'* (Eph 1:4). Through adoption not only do we share in the family but we are called to share in the character of our Father. This is the real purpose and calling of discipleship, that we should become like Him in our actions and attitudes and that our lives should reflect the fact that we are children of our heavenly Father. In Jesus, God has revealed the blueprint for every son who will follow through faith. It is His purpose that we should become like Jesus in all our living and in the commitment of our lives to the Father: *'For those God foreknew he also predestined to be conformed to the likeness of his Son, that he might be the firstborn among many brothers'* (Rom 8:29). Peter reminds us that this is not only the call of God on individual lives but that God's purpose in choosing us is that we should become a body of people who reflect this same nature in our lives together: *'You are a chosen people, a royal priesthood, a holy nation, a people belonging to God, that you may declare the praises of him who called you out of darkness into his wonderful light'* (1 Pet 2:9).

E: The promise of our adoption

'Now if we are children, then we are heirs – heirs of God and co-heirs with Christ, if indeed we share in his sufferings in order that we may also share in his glory' (Rom 8:17). As children of the Kingdom we have been adopted into a tremendous promise. Salvation is not only for now; it is for ever! Time and again the New Testament stresses this eternal aspect of our sonship. It is the motivation for our service. Paul himself looked forward to the crown of righteousness that was laid up for him at the end of his course.

It is the same promise, says John, which is the motivation for holiness: *'Dear friends, now we are children of God, and what we will be has not yet been made known. But we know that when he appears, we shall be like him, for we shall see him as he is. Everyone who has this hope in him purifies himself, just as he is pure'* (1 Jn 3:2, 3). You will notice that as far as the New Testament is concerned there are no daughters of God. We are all 'sons'. The reason for this has nothing to do with sexism. It is a way of highlighting the tremendous fact that in Christ Jesus we have not only been given new life but we have also been given a completely new hope! Having received the *exousia* – that is, the authority to become children of God – we now stand within the right to receive the *inheritance* as sons of God! In fact, so powerful is this idea that Paul uses the very idea of adoption to express it. He is not contradicting the fact that we are *already* adopted in Christ. He is trying to express the fullness of this idea with relation to the inheritance which believers enter into through their relationship with Christ: *'Not only so, but we ourselves, who have the first fruits of the Spirit, groan inwardly as we wait eagerly for our adoption as sons, the redemption of our bodies. For in this hope we are saved. But hope that is seen is no hope at all ... But if we have hope for what we not yet have, we wait for it patiently'* (Rom 8:23–25).

F: The principle of our adoption

The reality of our adoption in Christ has so much to say to us about our life as disciples. The essence of this life is that we are called to work out the reality of this relationship every day and in every situation. It also helps us to see what needs to stand at the heart of our Christian living. It is not some complex book of rules or complicated doctrine, it is the simple principle of trust and openness that exists between a father and his true son.

Of course, we see this perfectly displayed in the testimony of our Lord Jesus Christ. The secret of His power was His relationship with the Father. Time and again He spoke of that and His life was an outstanding witness to the fact of it. He encourages His disciples also to walk in this relationship so that their lives will express the same simple principle. Nowhere is this made more clear than in the teaching which we normally call the Sermon on the Mount. Here Jesus introduces His followers to the secrets of the kingdom of God. He teaches them to rely on their Father and to live lives which are to His glory and honour:

Imitating the Father: '*But I tell you: Love your enemies and pray for those who persecute you, **that you may be sons of your Father in heaven.**'* (Mt 5:44, 45).

Glorifying the Father: '*In the same way, let your light shine before men, that they may see your good deeds and praise your Father in heaven.*' (Mt 5:16).

Pleasing the Father: '*But when you fast, put oil on your head and wash your face, so that it will not be obvious to men that you are fasting, but only to your Father, who is unseen; and your Father, who sees what is done in secret, will reward you.*' (Mt 6:17, 18).

Speaking with the Father: '*And when you pray, do not keep on babbling like pagans, for they think they will be heard because of their many words ... This is how you should pray: "Our Father in heaven ... '.'* (Mt 6:7, 9).

Trusting the Father: '*Therefore I tell you, do not worry about your life ... Look at the birds of the air; they do not sow or reap or store away in barns, and yet your heavenly father*

feeds them. Are you not much more valuable than they?'
(Mt 6:25, 56).

G: The practice of our adoption

God wants us to live in the good of our adoption! That is
what being a disciple is all about. It is working out in the
nitty-gritty of our daily lives the tremendous ramifications of
this truth. As we will see in a later chapter, it is absolutely no
good knowing a truth without living in it! The truth of God's
Word becomes real in us when we do it. And by the Holy
Spirit we have been given everything we need to put this truth
into effect in our daily experience. God gives us not only the
pattern, He gives us the power! *'His divine power has given us
everything we need for life and godliness through our knowledge of him who called us by his own glory and goodness'*
(2 Pet 1:3).

There is one other area in which this truth of our adoption
in Christ is of great significance. This is with regard to how
God deals with us in our lives. He treats us as sons, not as
distant relatives! This means that now and again we will know
the Father's hand of discipline within our lives as He corrects
us and reminds us of our responsibilities as sons. The writer to
the Hebrews expresses it clearly when he says:

> *Endure hardship as discipline; God is treating you as sons.
> For what son is not disciplined by his father? If you are
> not disciplined (and everyone undergoes discipline), then
> you are illegitimate children and not true sons. Moreover,
> we have all had human fathers who disciplined us and we
> respected them for it. How much more should we submit
> to the Father of our spirits and live!*   (Heb 12:7–9)

So now we are in the family of God by faith! We share in
the life of Christ and in the inheritance of the saints. We have
been given a deep motivation for holy living and we experience the transforming power of the Holy Spirit in our lives.
Because we know to whom we belong we can understand the

discipline of our Father upon our lives. Above all, we live with a deep and warm experience of the love of the Father within our hearts! *'Praise be to the God and Father of our Lord Jesus Christ, who has blessed us in the heavenly realms with every spiritual blessing in Christ'* (Eph 1:3).

4: Freedom, Fruit and Power

A: Freedom

'If the son sets you free, you will be free indeed' (Jn 8:36).
Freedom is one of the major themes of the New Testament. It
is also the complete basis of our discipleship. Before we were
in Christ we were in bondage to sin, to self and Satan. Because
of this bondage we were not free to serve God. But now
Christ has set us free! Apart from this freedom which has
been achieved for us through the cross of Calvary we could
never follow Christ or fulfil the will of the Father.

Strangely enough this freedom is obtained by means of a
paradox. It is because we bind ourselves to Christ through
faith that we are set free from all these negative forces which
prevented us from serving God. When we make the confession, 'Jesus is Lord' (see Rom 10:9) we are binding ourselves to Christ. What we confess is what we are bound to.

This is why so many dear people have no spiritual freedom
at all, because the confession of their lives is someone or
something other than Christ. This confession is not only a
matter of words; it is a matter of will and attitudes. We
confess whatever we allow to have the greatest say within our
lives. I have known people who have confessed the strangest
things. In themselves they may seem totally innocuous but
coupled with our spirits and wills they create a tremendous
spiritual power within our lives. I knew one woman, for
example, whose confession was a golf circle. Yes, she played
golf, but her big confession was not the game but all the social
life and fashion that gathered around it. Everything else in life
was made to serve that confession. It came to dominate her
life and destroyed other parts of her life that should have been
precious and fruitful. It is through these things that Satan can
and does gain footholds in the lives of human beings. The
tragedy is that most people would not recognise the truth of
what I am saying because most of our confessions fall within
the category of being normal and decent. But they separate us
from the liberty of Jesus!

This, again, is why Paul is careful to teach us what he does
about anger. It must not be allowed to dominate our spirits

because it can become the confession of our lives, and through it Satan can gain power over us: *'In your anger do not sin. Do not let the sun go down while you are still angry, and do not give the devil a foothold'* (Eph 4:26, 27). Anger that is undealt with and left to fester can soon become the confession of our lives and lead to spiritual bondage. It is the same with other factors, whether physical or spiritual. If we allow them to dominate our minds and spirits then they will rob us of that freedom which the Father has won for us in Christ Jesus.

So at the heart of discipleship is the daily confession of the Lordship of Christ. When we say, 'Jesus is Lord,' we are making a confession of faith. But confessing Christ has a very different outcome from confessing anything else in life. When we confess Jesus as Lord we are bound to Him. But being bound to Him leads to freedom, not bondage! When we are bound to Him in faith, He leads us into His won victory. Our close binding of ourselves to Him ensures that these other elements lose their power over us.

This is why the secret of discipleship is obedience. Spiritual obedience is not trying in our own strength to do what God tells us. Rather is it being obedient in making the confession, 'Jesus is Lord'. Paul works out this idea of confession and binding in his own words in Romans chapter 6:

> *Don't you know that when you offer yourselves to some-one to obey him as slaves, you are slaves to the one whom you obey – whether you are slaves to sin, which leads to death, or to obedience, which leads to righteousness? But thanks be to God that, though you used to be slaves to sin, you wholeheartedly obeyed the form of teaching to which you were entrusted. You have been set free from sin and have become slaves to righteousness.* (Rom 6:16–18)

Discipleship is freedom! It is what we are called to in Christ. Discipleship means being obedient to that freedom into which we are called. This must be the daily confession of our lips: that 'Jesus is Lord!' *'It is for freedom that Christ has set us free. Stand firm, then, and do not let yourselves be burdened again by a yoke of slavery'* (Gal 5:1). It is the fact of this freedom in which we stand that leads to the possibility of the realisation of the next step in our lives as followers of Jesus. In Romans chapter 7 the subject is freedom from the bondage of law. Paul shows us how freedom from the negative influence releases us into fruitfulness: *'So, my brothers, you also died to the law through the body of Christ, that you might belong to another, to him who was raised from the dead, in order that we might bear fruit to God'* (Rom 7:4)

B: Fruitfulness

Jesus said, *'You did not choose me, but I chose you to go and bear fruit'* (Jn 15:16). God's purpose in choosing us at all is that our lives might be productive for Him. He has brought us into relationship with His Son so that we might manifest in our lives the same features of fruitfulness which Jesus showed in His. It is as we recognise our standing in Christ Jesus and what this means for us in our daily living that we are able to bring forth the fruits of righteousness and power. Jesus Himself emphasised this fact when He taught His disciples the need to keep that relationship fresh and real:

> *I am the vine; you are the branches. If a man remains in me and I in him, he will bear much fruit; apart from me you can do nothing. If anyone does not remain in me, he is like a branch that is thrown away and withers; such branches are picked up, thrown into the fire and burned. If you remain in me and my words remain in you, ask whatever you wish, and it will be given you. This is to my Father's glory, that you bear much fruit, showing your-selves to be my disciples.* (Jn 15:5–8)

I have committed a whole later section of this book to the subject of fruitfulness because I believe it is such a vital issue among believers today. I believe that, to a great degree, our lack of fruitfulness in may areas of our life and time is due to the fact that we tend to live compartmentalised lives. We tend to label certain things as 'spiritual' and associate them with growth and maturity in Christian terms. But at the same time we leave vast tracts of our experience undiagnosed or undisciplined. The result is that we waste a great deal of time, we expend a great deal of energy over things that are of little importance, and we fail to recognise the challenge of discipleship in every compartment of our daily lives.

God has called us to be fruitful in every area of our lives. This is not only a great source of blessing to other people, it brings a great measure of reward to ourselves. The spiritual satisfaction to be gained from real fruitfulness cannot be measured. Look at some of the areas where we are called to be fruitful:

(a) A fruitful spirit. Our actions and attitudes are, as we all recognise, controlled by deep spiritual forces within our lives. Men and women outside of Christ don't know how to gain control over the negative and destructive forces of their flesh. They are not, in the words of Jesus (see Lk 12:21), rich towards God. *'But the fruit of the Spirit is love, joy, peace, patience, kindness, goodness, faithfulness, gentleness and self-control'* (Gal 5:22).

(b) A fruitful mind. In Romans 8:5–8 Paul demonstrates how badly our minds are affected by our basic nature. If we live under the dominion of our old sinful nature our minds will display the characteristics of that nature in its thinking and attitudes. This is why we need to take seriously this issue of 'putting off the old self' of which the Scriptures have so much to say. Our mind cannot be fruitful to God as long as it is being subjected to the power of the flesh: *'You were taught, with regard to your former way of life, to put off your old self, which is being corrupted by its deceitful desires;* **to be made new in the attitude of your minds;** *and to put on the new self, created to be like God in true righteousness and holiness'* (Eph 4:22–24).

(c) Fruitful in deeds. This, of course, is the very heart of James's message. He argues powerfully that real fruit will issue in good works. It is not that these works save us; they are the fruit of our salvation! Our good deeds are the sign to men around that God is at work through us. They are not the pious or goody-goody works of those who are seeking through self-righteousness to impress others. These good works are the result of real faith and are the manifestation of the Holy Spirit's action. We have been saved to produce fruit like this: '*We pray ... that you may live a life worthy of the Lord and may please him in every way: bearing fruit in every good work, growing in the knowledge of God*' (Col 1:10).

(d) **Fruitful in speech.** Surely one of the most potent verses of Scripture in the whole Bible is James 3:6 '*The tongue also is a fire, a world of evil among the parts of the body. It corrupts the whole person, sets the whole course of his life on fire, and is itself set on fire by hell.*' This is just about the biggest challenge in the book! We all suffer and we have all caused others to suffer from the fruitfulness of our tongues. Of course, Jesus was right when He said that it is out of the overflow of the heart that the mouth speaks. What comes out is only symptomatic of what is inside! The destructive effect of an uncontrolled or undisciplined tongue cannot be over-estimated. The benefits of fruitfulness in speech are not only felt by other people, they are felt within the deep reaches of our own personalities. Health, peace, harmony and happiness all come from the productive power of a fruitful tongue: '*Whoever would love life and see good days must keep his tongue from evil and his lips from deceitful speech*' (1 Pet 3:10; see Psalm 34:12, 13).

(e) **Fruitful in gift.** Today we have all become very aware of 'gifts of the Spirit'. It is clear from 1 Corinthians chapter 12 that it is the right of every believer to receive these gifts according to the will of God. But the gifts are not given for our own benefit or self-interest; they are given for the benefit of the whole body and of the other people around us: '*Just as each of us has one body with many members, and these members do not all have the same function, so in Christ we who are many form one body, and each member belongs to all the others. We have different gifts, according to the grace given us*' (Rom 12:4–6).

Paul then goes on to encourage his readers to exercise their gifts to their fullest capacity in proportion to the faith that has been given. Imagine what a different place the local church would be if every believer were exercising his God-given gifts according to the principle of fruitfulness. I often hear complaints from Christians that in their church the gifts of the Spirit are not allowed to be manifested. Usually they have in mind a very limited range of the gifts – perhaps only tongues and prophecy. But all these gifts grow together in a wonderful harmony and provide an impressive balance which covers every aspect of need within the body of Christ: *'Each one should use whatever gift he has received to serve others, faithfully administering God's grace in its various forms'* (1 Pet 4:10).

(f) Fruitful in fellowship.

How good and pleasant it is
when brothers live together in unity!
It is like precious oil poured on the head,
running down on the beard,
running down on Aaron's beard,
down upon the collar of his robes.
It is as if the dew of Hermon
were falling on Mount Zion,
For there the Lord bestows his blessing
even life for evermore.   (Psalm 133)

The Psalmist knew the fruitfulness of real fellowship. There was something in it for God (symbolised by the precious oil), and something in it for man (symbolised by the dew of Hermon). There is something tremendously enriching and strengthening about true Christian fellowship. The writer to the Hebrews recognised this when he exhorted his readers to be active in this: *'Let us consider how we may spur one another on towards love and good deeds. Let us not give up meeting together, as some are in the habit of doing, but let us encourage one another – and all the more as you see the Day approaching'* (Heb 10:24, 25).

Many of these areas we have just looked at form the substance of the subject matter of later sections of this book, where we will be able to look at them in depth and see how we might become more productive in these various areas of our lives.

C: Power

Our freedom is not only achieved for us by Christ, it is achieved *in us* by the power of the Holy Spirit. Right from the beginning of the Gospels the promise is made to believers of the indwelling power of the Spirit of God. The Father does not mean us to live in weakness but in His strength. He has made available to us *all* the power which He used when He raised Jesus from the dead! This is what Paul says:

> *I pray also that the eyes of your heart may be enlightened in order that you may know the hope to which he has called you, the riches of his glorious inheritance in the saints, **and his incomparably great power for us who believe**. That power is like the working of his mighty strength, which he exerted in Christ when he raised him from the dead and seated him at his right hand in the heavenly realms.* (Eph 1:18–20)

Here is the secret of our discipleship. It is that we are not walking or acting alone. We have at our disposal all the living power of God through His Spirit. This is the fulfilment in us of the promise of Jesus to His disciples before He left them: *'Therefore, go and make disciples of all nations, baptising them in the name of the Father and of the Son and of the Holy Spirit, and teaching them to obey everything I have commanded you. **And surely I am with you always, to the very end of the age'*** (Mt 28:19, 20).

We are given the power of the Holy Spirit for every aspect of our lives and witness. We may be weak from the human point of view but from God's point of view we have all the strength and power that we need. This, in fact, is how we might describe discipleship. It is being a living illustration of the power of God at work! In the lives of men and women who seem as nothing from the outward point of view God works with dynamic power, bringing His purposes to pass through those very lives. Paul describes us as being like common earthenware pots which hold the treasure of God to show that the power we have belongs to God and not to us (see 2 Cor 4:7).

This power, which God gives through the Holy Spirit, is more than enough to meet every need we might have in every aspect of our lives as Christians. Peter reminds us that God has given us divine power which provides *'everything we need for life and godliness.'* (see 2 Pet 1:3).

(a) It is power for our inner lives. I came home one day from my work as a university chaplain to find my wife, Hilda, sitting sobbing at the dining room table. There was nothing wrong. In fact, everything was all right! What had happened was very simple. She had got up that morning with a deep desire to find God in a new way. For many hours she sat and read through the Bible until, suddenly, the Holy Spirit lit up for her the words of Ephesians 3:16 *'I pray that out of his glorious riches he may strengthen you with power through his Spirit **in your inner being.**'*

That was exactly what she needed. She needed to know that God could give her the power to cope; that He could provide the strength needed to withstand the demands and pressure of a busy life and that, above all, He could equip her with all the spiritual power she would ever need in dealing with the many people who made demands on her life.

This is what we all need. Discipleship starts here, with our receiving deep into our own hearts and lives the resources of God. Without this power there is no way that we will ever respond to God's call to holiness or be able to fulfil His will, which He wants to show us.

(b) It is power to witness for Jesus. This is why Jesus made the disciples wait at Jerusalem until they received power from on high. Jesus knew that they could never fulfil His commission to go and make disciples of all nations apart from the indwelling power of the Holy Spirit. Without this power the first disciples would have remained behind locked doors, impotent and fearful. We can see the difference it made simply by reading the pages of the Acts of the Apostles! I think it was the late Peter Marshall who once described the transformation in the disciples as being 'changed from rabbits into ferrets'.

Jesus had told them that when they received the Holy Spirit they would receive power (Acts 1:8), and that is what happened. The word for power here is the Greek word *dunamis*. It is the word from which our English word 'dynamite' comes, and that is a fair description of what took place in Jerusalem on the first day of Pentecost. It was an explosion of the power of God!

(c) It is power to believe in God. The Gospels are full of the promises of Jesus. But so often we feel like the man who prayed, 'Lord I do believe; help me to overcome my unbelief!' The Holy Spirit creates faith in our hearts.

Before Jesus left He promised His disciples that another Counsellor would come to them. He would not speak about Himself but would declare Jesus to their hearts. Through faith in the name of Jesus they would be able to accomplish the mighty deeds of the kingdom of God: *'Anyone who has faith in me will do what I have been doing. He will do even greater things than these'* (Jn 14:12).

(d) It is power in gift and ministry. When Paul speaks of the power of the Holy Spirit in 1 Corinthians chapter 12 he makes it clear that this power is available to every believer: *'Now to each one the manifestation of the Spirit is given for the common good'* (1 Cor 12:7). We are called as disciples to be ministers of the new covenant of God's grace in Jesus. This might seem a very high-blown idea for some of us, but the fact is that we have *all* been called to become channels in our lives of the grace of God for other men and women. The Father does not leave us to do this in our own strength. He provides the strength and enabling of the Holy Spirit at every point. Not only does He provide the courage to do the job but He gives us the resources to do it, through the various gifts of the Holy Spirit which He makes available to us.

The most exciting fact of all is that He equips us not only according to the needs of the job but with regard to what we are as persons. Not all Christians are called to minister the same way, and not every believer is given precisely the same gifts with which to carry out his work for God.

Many years ago there was an old Hebrew scholar in the University of Edinburgh. His name was Duncan and he was so noted in his field of study that he was called Rabbi Duncan. Duncan is on record complaining about the tendency in the Church always to try and put the working of God into a strait-jacket. He complained that we are always trying to turn God's wonderful variety into a hideous uniformity. The wonderful fact about the gifts of God through the Holy Spirit is that they are wonderfully varied – so varied, in fact, that they are suitably fitted for the lives of every believer.

(e) It is power in spiritual warfare. This is a subject which we will learn a lot more about later. Every Christian is engaged in war. The fact that we have been born again in the power of God means that we have changed sides! We cannot expect that the old lot are going to be very pleased about this, and Satan certainly doesn't take it lying down! We need to be prepared for battle.

On a wider front, we are called *into* warfare. We are called as disciples to engage the enemy on every front. Indeed, warfare is at the heart of what it means to be a disciple, because we are those whom God has chosen to represent Him and act in the power of His kingdom here on earth. We are like the advance guard. The kingdom has not yet fully come in power – that will not happen until Jesus appears in glory. But the kingdom is presently breaking through with power, showing men and women something of what it will be like when Jesus is recognised as King over all. For the moment we are given the resources of God's power for this battle, and we do not stand alone: *'Finally, be strong in the Lord and in his mighty power'* (Eph 6:10).

5: In Understanding Be Men

> *Get wisdom, get understanding;*
> *do not forget my words or swerve from them*
> *Do not forsake wisdom, and she will protect you;*
> *love her, and she will watch over you.*
> *Wisdom is supreme; therefore get wisdom.*
> *Though it cost you all you have, get understanding.*
>
> (Prov 4:5–7)

The Authorised Version of the last part of this proverb is very much to the point. It says, *'with all thy getting get understanding'*.

There is no more important need if we are to grow into maturity than the spiritual gift of wisdom. I have found, in my own experience, that this is the gift which brings all the others into focus. Without it we are at the mercy of our feelings and other people's demands. It takes wisdom to understand ourselves, to understand the needs of other, and to understand the will of God. We may have all sorts of wonderful gifts, but without wisdom we will not know how to use them effectively. Power without wisdom, in fact, is about the most lethal mixture in the body of Christ today. There is a grave danger of seeking spiritual gifts of power without the wisdom to know how to be able to apply these things properly.

A: Wisdom in the Old Testament

There are two sides to wisdom as far as the Old Testament is concerned, and these both have a great deal to teach us for our Christian lives.

First, wisdom in the Scriptures is a very practical thing. If you look at the Old Testament, and in particular at the book of Proverbs, you will see how closely related wisdom is to the basic realities of life. It is not so much intellectual prowess as practical nous! It is much more a God-given gift of knowing what to do in a given situation and how to handle life with all its challenges and opportunities. In many ways the Old Testament is totally realistic. It knows that we have only one life and that the decisions we make and the responses we have to the circumstances of our life will determine to a huge extent whether or not that life is lived to its full and most fruitful effect. The factor which makes all the difference is whether or not we face life with wisdom:

> *Listen, my son, accept what I say,*
> *and the years of your life will be many.*
> *I guide you in the way of wisdom*
> *and lead you along straight paths.*
> *When you walk, your steps will not be hampered;*
> *when you run, you will not stumble.* (Prov 4:10–12)

But there is *another dimension* to wisdom in the Old Testament. Not only is it related to the practical affairs of everyday life, but it is also related to man's understanding of the ways of God. The books of Job and Ecclesiastes reflect this search within man's spirit for the deeper meaning of life and his own existence. But neither can be understood apart from the wisdom of God. The answer does not lie in man at the level of his own understanding. Such wisdom cannot be found in man, but is a gift from God. We are directed to this truth a number of times in Scripture: '*The fear of the Lord is the beginning of wisdom*' (Ps 111:10). Job discovered this great truth through the intensity of his own experience. Faced as he was with all the pressure and trauma of his difficulties, in the end he had to come face to face with the fact that God alone knew everything and that if he wanted to share in God's understanding of things, he needed to turn his life towards the Lord. There is no more striking and beautiful passage which speaks on this theme in the whole of Scripture than Job chapter 28:

> *But where can wisdom be found?*
> *Where does understanding dwell?*
> *Man does not comprehend its worth;*
> *it cannot be found in the land of the living.*
> *The deep says, 'It is not with me'.*

It cannot be bought with the finest gold,
  nor can its price be weighed in silver...
Where then does wisdom come from?
Where does understanding dwell?
It is hidden from the eyes of every living thing,
  concealed even from the birds of the air...
God understands the way to it
  and he alone knows where it dwells.

(Job 28:12–15; 20–23)

B: The wisdom of Christ

These two dimensions of spiritual wisdom are spoken of in the New Testament as well, and they are the very elements of spiritual wisdom we need if we are to grow and mature in the way God wants us to.

James highlights the *first* in his Epistle when he is speaking of the need for us to understand the events and circumstances of our life. We cannot live in the turmoil of trials and difficulties without spiritual wisdom, or we will be blind to the fact of God's hand in them, maturing and developing us into men and women He wants us to be: *'If any of you lacks wisdom, he should ask God, who gives generously to all without finding fault'* (Jas 1:5).

Paul emphasises the *second* dimension when he speaks to the Corinthians about the source of his spiritual understanding of the deep truths of God: *'We speak of God's secret wisdom, a wisdom that has been hidden and that God destined for our glory before time began'* (1 Cor 2:7). Paul goes on to show that this wisdom does not find its source in our own intelligence or insight but depends entirely on the work of the Holy Spirit. In fact, this is what marks the spiritual man; he is able to receive and understand deep spiritual truth. This spiritual wisdom has nothing to do with human wisdom. Human wisdom, unregenerate and unsanctified, is, in fact, at odds with God's revelation. The human mind is in rebellion against God's truth and finds it impossible to comprehend apart from the work of the Holy Spirit.

This, as we will see elsewhere, is because man's unregenerate mind is a slave to his unregenerate nature. It is not until a man is born again by the power of the Spirit that his mind is freed and renewed under the power of God's Word. Only then is he in a position to take in and understand spiritual truth. Man's wisdom has led him away from God rather than deeper into God:

> *For although they knew God, they neither glorified him as God nor gave thanks to him, but their thinking became futile and their foolish hearts were darkened. Although they claimed to be wise, they became fools and exchanged the glory of the immortal God for images to look like mortal man and birds and animals and reptiles.*
>
> (Rom 1:21–23)

C: The gift of wisdom

Spiritual understanding is very important in the life of discipleship. Understanding gives us that insight into God's Word we need if we are to apply it to our daily lives. Spiritual understanding develops awareness within the circumstances of our lives as to the real significance of things. It opens us up to the real needs of other people through the sensitivity of spirit that wisdom brings. It shows us how and when to use the other gifts of the Spirit that God has endued us with so that they are fruitful and beneficial, and not arrogant and destructive.

There are a number of important areas in which this spiritual gift of wisdom is necessary if we are to grow and mature and become fruitful in our own lives for the Lord. For example, spiritual wisdom brings:

A new understanding of self. A proper self-awareness is, I believe, crucial to a balanced development in life. Without it we are subject to the illusions which arise from having a wrong view of ourselves. This, of course, works in two directions: we can have an over-inflated view of ourselves and our capabilities, or we can under-rate ourselves. Either point of view is destructive to our proper development in life and ministry. What we need is God's view of us. Paul knew the need of this when he wrote to the Romans about the renewing of their minds: *'For by the grace given me I say to every one of you; do not think of yourself more highly than you ought; but rather think of yourself with sober judgment, in accordance with the measure of faith God has given you'* (Rom 12:3).

An understanding of spiritual truth. Paul highlights this fact when he speaks to the church at Corinth. Without the gift of wisdom we cannot comprehend the deep things of God:

> *The Spirit searches all things, even the deep things of God. For who among men knows the thoughts of a man except the man's spirit within him? In the same way no-one knows the thoughts of God except the Spirit of God. We have not received the spirit of the world but the Spirit who is from God, **that we may understand what God has freely given us**.* (1 Cor 2:10–12)

Spiritual understanding in the things of God leads to a correlative dignity and maturity in the life for God. It is this spiritual discernment of truth which prevents us from being led astray and blown about by every wind of doctrine that blows. If it was necessary in Paul's day, with its great variety of religions and philosophies, it is no less essential in ours, when every conceivable notion and religious diversion has captivated the minds of men.

An understanding of Scripture. This is, of course, vitally related to what we have just spoken of above. Without a deep understanding of the Word of God through Scripture we will not develop that deeper insight in the truth that the Father desires us to have. We are at the mercy of too many teachings and philosophies of ministry today which are quite untested by the Scriptures.

> *But as for you, continue in what you have learned and have become convinced of, because you know those from whom you learned it, and how from infancy you have known the holy Scriptures, which are able to make you wise for salvation through faith in Christ Jesus. All Scripture is God-breathed and is useful for teaching, rebuking,*

correcting, and training in righteousness, so that the man of God may be thoroughly equipped for every good work.
(2 Tim 3:14–17)

Words like these of Paul to Timothy serve to remind us how important it is to be able to appreciate the truth which God has given to us in the Scriptures and to apply it in practice to our daily living.

An understanding of God's will. Surely this is one of the most important areas of our lives, that we are living in accordance with the will of God. This is not only necessary in the long term but desirable for every action in every day of our lives. We need to know the will of God for our whole life so that our goals will be productive and profitable for God. To this end we need to ask the Father for wisdom to discern His will (see Col 1:9).

We need God's direction every day in the nitty-gritty details of our lives. This is the secret of fruitful living. Paul exhorts us to find this when he says, *'Be very careful, then, how you live – not as unwise but as wise, making the most of every opportunity, because the days are evil'* (Eph 5:15, 16).

An understanding of spiritual gifts. I have already highlighted the need for wisdom in this area because there is nothing more dangerous than gifts of power when they are exercised without understanding. Lack of the discernment and discretion which arise from spiritual wisdom can lead to havoc in the lives of others who are at the receiving end of our undisciplined power. By the same token it is this wisdom from God which enables us to discern the meaning of the gifts and, indeed, whether they are authentic gifts of the Holy Spirit or not.

It is in this context that Paul appeals for maturity in thought and attitude in 1 Corinthians 14:20. There was a need for those in leadership to receive this wisdom so that they could stop reacting in the light of their own emotions and fears and begin to act in the maturity of the Lord.

An understanding of spiritual powers. Among the gifts of 1 Corinthians chapter 12 is listed *'the ability to distinguish* *between spirits'*. In his Epistle John tells us that we need to be able to test the spirits: *'Do not believe every spirit, but test the spirits to see whether they are from God, because many false prophets have gone out into the world'* (1 Jn 4:1). Paul could declare for himself that he was not unaware of the tricks and evil schemings of Satan (see 2 Cor 2:11). Unfortunately we don't all share his capacity for discerning the true from the false.

This is an aspect of spiritual understanding and discernment that is crucial for our well-being today. The Father has not left us to our own devices. He has provided, through the Holy Spirit, resources which will enable us to tell what is true and what is false. We need to keep close to the Scriptures and the counsel of those whom we know to be wise in the faith. Then we will be far less likely to be susceptible to the devices of Satan as he tries to lead the very elect astray.

An understanding of the hope to which we are called. Spiritual wisdom leads us into an understanding, through faith, of things which are otherwise completely hidden from our minds. Yet these are of vital importance to our daily walk as believers. Paul prays for his own disciples at Ephesus that they might have this gift:

> *I keep asking that the God of our Lord Jesus Christ, the glorious Father, may give you the Spirit of wisdom and revelation, so that you may know him better. I pray also that the eyes of your heart may be enlightened in order that you may know the hope to which he has called you, the riches of his glorious inheritance in the saints.*
>
> (Eph 1:17, 18)

The importance of understanding these hidden truths is that they then become for us a tremendous means of encouragement. They provide a perspective for our lives far wider and grander than the limited and sometimes difficult context our daily experience proffers.

An understanding of the signs of the times. It is not that we are called to be date watchers with regard to the coming again of Christ. We already know that it will be at an hour when we think not. Too many cranks have led people astray with strange teachings on this subject. If anyone tells you that they know the date, don't believe them. Even Jesus said He did not know; only His Father in heaven knew the secret.

At the same time we are not meant to live in ignorance about the events around us as we see things moving towards a climax. We are to live with that urgency and preparedness that belongs to people who are aware of what is happening in their times. It is not so much that we know the day and hour of Christ's appearing; it is more that we know the fact of it and that we increasingly live our lives in the light of that fact. This is what Paul teaches the Thessalonians: *'But you, brothers, are not in darkness so that this day should surprise you like a thief. You are all sons of the light and sons of the day'* (1 Thess 5:4, 5).

We gain wisdom when we know the Lord. He is the source of all wisdom and understanding and through the Holy Spirit He desires to impart His wisdom to us. The beautiful words of Proverbs chapter 9 invite us to seek the wisdom of God and remind us in their way of James's exhortation that *'If any of you lacks wisdom, he should ask God, who gives generously to all without finding fault'* (Jas 1:5):

> *Come, eat my food*
> *and drink the wine I have mixed.*
> *Leave your simple ways and you will live;*
> *walk in the way of understanding.* (Prov 9:5, 6)

Chapter 2

Behold the Lamb!

1: The Power of the Cross

'For the message of the cross is foolishness to those who are perishing, but to us who are being saved it is the power of God' (1 Cor 1:18). The Cross of Christ stands at the heart of our Christian faith. Without it we have no faith, and apart from the truth of it Christianity becomes only another philosophy of life, a matter of words and ideas. It is clear from the Gospels that Jesus Himself knew where He was heading. He did not come to introduce us to another set of ideas about God. He came to die for us! Theologians have argued with each other for years as to whether Jesus was conscious of the fact before the event. They wonder whether He really knew that He was going to die for the sins of men. The Gospel writers don't present us with that question. Jesus's own understanding of His mission is central to the very presentation of Mark's Gospel: *'He then began to teach them that the Son of Man must suffer many things and be rejected by the elders, chief priests and teachers of the law, and that he must be killed and after three days rise again'* (Mk 8:31).

John reports Jesus saying: *'Now my heart is troubled, and what shall I say? "Father, save me from this hour"? No, it was for this very reason I came to this hour. Father, glorify your name!'* (Jn 12:27, 28). The idea of the Cross was integral, as far as Jesus was concerned, to the training of His disciples. He used the reality of the Cross to emphasise to them the need for

47

absolute commitment to the life of the kingdom. He already
knew within Himself what it meant to 'take up the cross'. For
the disciples this was, as yet, an unrealised principle. They did
not at that moment comprehend the fact that Jesus had come
to die, let alone what it would mean for themselves that they
had been called as the forerunners in the witness of the Kingdom. Nevertheless, years later when they came to write their
Gospels they remembered vividly the words of Jesus: '*If
anyone would come after me, he must deny himself and take
up his cross daily and follow me*' (Lk 9:23).

A: The agony of death

The trouble with most of us today is that we have lost the pain
of Calvary. The Cross is worn as a decoration round the neck
of thousands of people who have no idea of its true significance. In our churches the Cross is often portrayed as a thing
of beauty and creative art, which blinds us to the real horror
and agony that truly stand at the heart of it.

The first sermon ever preached by Peter, on the day of
Pentecost, had the Cross as its central theme. Peter spoke then
of the 'agony of death' which Jesus endured at the hands of
sinful men. There is no virtue in highlighting the pain and
horror for their own sakes, but we do need to enter into the
reality of Christ's suffering to some degree if we are ever to
appreciate what it meant for God to save us through the
Cross.

We have lived for so long with a domesticated idea of the
Cross. We have refined it of its horror, and in doing that we
have robbed it of its power. This came home to me some time
ago when I was living in a Roman Catholic convent for a
weekend. I stayed in a room which had an exquisite crucifix
on one wall. It was carved out of beautiful wood and was a
magnificent piece of craftsmanship. But there was something
about that crucifix which really troubled me. For two days I
could not put my finger on the reason. It was not merely the
fact that it was a crucifix.

One morning I woke up early and saw the crucifix and
suddenly it dawned on me what was wrong. It was far too

nice! The man on the cross looked as though he was a perfect specimen of humanity. There was a small spot of blood somewhere around his ribs but that was all. Apart from that he seemed as though he had stepped up on to the cross and was hanging there with ease. There was little evidence of the true circumstances of Calvary. The person who had crafted that crucifix had missed altogether the horror and the agony which were involved in the experience of Jesus.

I reached for my Bible and turning to John chapter 19 I read again the testimony of what happened to Jesus on the cross at Calvary. I felt then, and I know now, that the Holy Spirit was speaking to me about the importance of Jesus' sacrifice. The Spirit was directing me to the facts of the matter, because in them lay something of great significance for the ministry we, as Christian believers, are called to now.

The Scriptures present a very different picture of the sufferings of Christ from the one portrayed by that crucifix. They hide nothing of the shame and agony that was involved for God's beloved Son. For the writers of the Scriptures the sufferings are important, not as the fibre of a sordid story of gore and horror, but as the testimony to what God has accomplished for every one of us in the death of Jesus. It is not just the fact that He died that is important; *how* He died has the greatest significance for every one of us.

It is interesting to notice that the Old Testament prophecies concerning the death of Christ put the same emphasis on the details of His sufferings. In fact, so relevant are the prophetic Scriptures that we can see how they come to pass in minute detail in the experience of Jesus Himself. Isaiah, for example, speaks of the personal humiliation which the Saviour was to endure:

> *I offered my back to those who beat me,*
> *my cheeks to those who pulled out my beard.*
>
> (Is 50:6)

And also he speaks prophetically of horrific disfigurement which Jesus endured:

Just as there were many who were appalled at him –
  his appearance was so disfigured beyond that of any
  man and his form marred beyond human likeness.

(Is 52:14).

The spiritual and physical agonies of the Lord Jesus Christ are portrayed graphically in passages like Isaiah chapter 53 and here in Psalm 22:

Many bulls surround me;
  strong bulls of Bashan encircle me.
Roaring lions tearing their prey
  open their mouths wide against me.
I am poured out like water,
  and all my bones are out of joint.
My heart has turned to wax;
  it has melted away within me.
My strength is dried up like a potsherd,
  and my tongue sticks to the roof of my mouth;
  you lay me in the dust of death.
Dogs have surrounded me;
  a band of evil men has encircled me,
  they have pierced my hands and my feet.
I can count all my bones;
  people stare and gloat over me.
They divide my garments among them
  and cast lots for my clothing.   (Ps 22:12–18)

As I read again the Scriptures relating to the Cross I knew that I too had been living with a domesticated idea of Jesus. In the Church at large we have brought Jesus down to our size and we have diminished His death to dimensions that we can handle spiritually, emotionally and theologically. If we felt the deep horror of the Cross we would know the full extent of our sin, and this is what we recoil from within the deeper reaches of our hearts and minds.

What happened that day at Calvary was not pretty. There was no sentiment in a Roman scourging, and Roman crucifixion has been universally recognised as being the most cruel form of execution ever devised. It was a horrific, slow, painful and humiliating death:

> *Bearing shame and scoffing rude,*
> *In my place condemned he stood;*
> *Sealed my pardon with his blood:*
> *Hallelujah! What a Saviour!*   (Philip Bliss)

There was violence that day. There is violence at the heart of God's salvation. There is violence in the world, there is violence in the heart of man. This violence will never be overcome with sentiment. God meets violence with violence, but not a violence of war – a violence of love! I believe this is where we need to get back to in our own day. We need to see the depth of Calvary. We need to see that everything we can have or be flows out from this act of love. More than that, we need to recognise that if we are to live for God then we need to walk the same way ourselves.

B: The power of the Cross

The significance of the Cross does not lie in the physical sufferings for their own sake. Any man who was crucified by the Romans passed through the most excruciating and horrific sufferings. Crucifixion was recognised as a most horrendous form of execution which involved excruciating pain and personal humiliation. But Jesus did not undergo the normal routine of crucifixion. The Scriptures make that clear. Certain things happened to Him which were not normally part of the crucifixion process. For example, before He was sent to the Cross He was subjected to the public humiliation of a mock trial before Pontius Pilate, during which He was abused and beaten and disfigured. His beard was torn out and a crown of thorns was placed on His head as a gesture of mockery at His claim to be a king. Even before He appeared in public at His trial He had undergone severe sufferings in physical and mental terms. In the garden of Gethsemane He had faced the awful truth that 'this cup' was His cup and it could not be drunk by any one else. The pressure within His spirit was so intense that He bled from His brow. The blood flowed from His forehead down to the ground.

Likewise, when it came to the end things were different for Him. The soldiers came and broke the legs of the two criminals who were crucified with Him that day, but when they came to Jesus they saw that He was dead already, so they did not break His legs. Instead, they pierced His side, and blood and water gushed out. This means that Jesus had died literally of a broken heart. His heart had burst and the blood had congealed. The blood and plasma had become separated and when He was pierced they flowed out from His side.

We cannot begin to speak about the spiritual sufferings. These things are hidden from us because there is no way we could ever comprehend what it meant for God's Son to be forsaken by His Father. The cry that tore from His lips which echoed the words of Psalm 22, *'My God, my God, why have you forsaken me?'* contains depths of suffering that we will never be able to understand. But what we must see is that none of these things was by chance. Not one incident of the crucifixion of Jesus was by chance. Men took Him, but men were not in charge of the proceedings that day! This is the awesome truth of Calvary: the Father was in control! The Father was offering up His Son 'for every soul of man'! We recoil from the fact because it only serves to underline ever more clearly the extent of our guilt. But this was the testimony of Peter in that first Pentecost declaration: *'This man was handed over to you by God's set purpose and foreknowledge; and you, with the help of wicked men, put him to death by nailing him to the cross'* (Acts 2:23).

For years I failed to see the reality of this. I looked upon the sufferings of Jesus in a general sense. I knew that in some mysterious way the Father had laid my guilt upon Him and that through His sufferings, which included the physical pains of Jesus, I was set free. But I failed to recognise the *dynamic* significance of the sufferings of Christ. Isaiah prophesied, not only that the Messiah would suffer, but that he would take upon himself the sin and sickness of man:

Surely he took up our infirmities
  and carried our sorrows,
yet we considered him stricken by God,
  smitten by him, and afflicted.
But he was pierced for our transgressions,
  he was crushed for our iniquities;
the punishment that brought us peace was upon him,
  and by his wounds we are healed.   (Is 53:4, 5)

The power of the Cross for us lies in the fact that every detail of the experience of Jesus in His sufferings has dynamic significance for us at every point of our need. Ever since the fall of man Satan has kept men and women under his oppression. They have been bound in chains of sin and sickness. Depression and despair have been the hallmark of much human experience. Man has become subject to every kind of suffering and affliction as a result of his disobedience to God. On the Cross every spiritual and emotional bondage and affliction which Satan has brought to man through man's disobedience has been reversed in the power of Calvary.

C: The six woes of man

In Genesis chapter 3 we are given insight into the effects of sin. After the Fall of man through his disobedience to God we are introduced to the sad effects of this disobedience. Whereas man had lived as a free agent in fellowship with God and had been given the authority to rule over everything else on earth, he was now in bondage. Satan had the mastery over him and from that moment on the human race has been subject to all the ills and trials that result from sin. In Genesis chapter 3 we find that man has become subject to *six awful woes*, which have been the source of every pain and affliction of body and spirit that the human race has ever experienced.

The *first* of these is *guilt and condemnation*. Both the man and the woman, when they were challenged by God, tried to avoid the guilt. They passed it from one to the other. In the end only the old serpent was willing to accept the blame! This has been mankind's failure ever since. It has been the factor that has divided man from man and man from God. Not until we accept our guilt can there be any reconciliation. But our guilt before God is of such a nature that we could never atone for it ourselves. Jesus became our guilt-bearer. He bore our sins in His own body on the tree.

The *second* woe is *oppression* by the devil. Before man fell he was not subject to the dominion of Satan. Now that he is separated from God he is at the mercy of Satan. Satan has in fact become, as the New Testament says, the god of this world who rules and dominates the hearts and minds of men. But the Cross brought to an end the unchallenged power of Satan. Paul speaks of the triumph of Jesus on the Cross against the power of Satan when he writes: *'God made you alive with Christ. He forgave us all our sins ... And having disarmed the powers and authorities, he made a public spectacle of them, triumphing over them by the cross'* (Col 2:13, 15).

The *third* woe is *pain and suffering*. This is emphasised in relation to women in particular, who will know pain in child-bearing. This epitomises all the pain and affliction to which the human race is subject. Nowhere in the Bible do we hear that sickness and disease are the will of God for mankind. They are the result of sin and find their source in the work of Satan as the outcome of man's disobedience. That is not to say that God cannot use pain and suffering for His own gracious ends in our lives; it is clear that He can. But we know that these are not God's best designs for His children, and in the perfect kingdom of Jesus all such foreign elements will be thrown away. Peter makes this connection most clearly for us in the New Testament: *'He himself bore our sins in his body on the tree, so that we might die to sins and live for righteousness; by his wounds you have been healed'* (1 Pet 2:24).

The *fourth* woe is *anxiety and care*. Man was sentenced to a life of hard labour. Whereas he had lived in a garden of God's bounty, surrounded by everything he needed for life and health, now he was condemned to difficulty and effort. The very ground was cursed as a result of man's sin:

It will produce thorns and thistles for you,
 and you will eat the plants of the field.
By the sweat of your brow you will eat your food.

(Gen 3:18, 19)

It was thorns that made a crown for Jesus, and He wore it for us. He took upon Himself all the agony of spirit and the anxiety of heart that belong to man as he tries to make his own way in the world without God. What a contrast now is the way of Jesus to the curse of thorns! Because He carried it for us we are free, in the power of faith, to walk the way of the Kingdom: *'Seek first his kingdom and his righteousness, and all these things will be given to you as well. Therefore do not worry about tomorrow, for tomorrow will worry about itself'* (Mt 6:33, 34).

The *fifth* woe is *death*. Man was cut off from the source of his life because of his sin. Paul describes this graphically when he writes to the Romans: *'Sin entered the world through one man, and death through sin, and in this way death came to all men'* (Rom 5:12). This is a fact that needs no independent corroboration! Our cemeteries declare the truth of it and we all know it for ourselves. Death is the result of our sin, and the common lot of all men. Of course, the Scriptures take us one step further. If physical death was the end of it, perhaps that would not be too bad. In fact, for many it would be a welcome finale to a fruitful life. For others it would be a welcome relief from a life of pain and misery. The sober truth is spelled out by the writer to the Hebrews: *'Just as man is destined to die once, and after that to face judgement, so Christ was sacrificed once to take away the sins of many people'* (Heb 9:27, 28).

But in the death of Jesus the judgement of death has been removed. He has borne the judgement for us. We shall see later what this meant for Him. At this moment we can see what it means for us: *'Since the children have flesh and blood, he too shared their humanity so that by his death he might destroy him who holds the power of death – that is, the devil – and free those who all their lives were held in slavery by their fear of death'* (Heb 2:14, 15).

The *sixth* woe is *rejection and separation from God.* The man was cast out from the garden. And man has been a spiritual castaway ever since! It is significant that many of the spiritual hurts we have to deal with in ministry today are hurts of rejection. Man at heart is a rejected being. His sin, as the Psalmist rightly perceived, has caused a separation between him and God, the very ground of his being.

The most profound cry on the cross was a cry of dereliction: *'My God, my God, why have you forsaken me?'* Jesus became a derelict for you and me! There was nothing else that could have happened, because in taking our sins into Himself He thereby put Himself outside the boundaries of the Father's presence.

The power of the Cross lies in the fact that Jesus took *all* these elements into Himself on the Cross and broke their power. He overcame every negative factor that has ever threatened man and He broke the power of Satan, who masterminds all these forces to bring man to destruction.

D: United with Him

It is not enough to wonder at the mystery of the Cross, however. For it to be effective in our lives we need to receive it into our own lives. A few years ago a member of our Fellowship gave a prophetic word which brought this challenge home to every one of us:

> *Yes! Many hold their hands up in adoration of what I have done, that death, glorious death, supreme sacrifice; their mouths show forth praise. But I say to them, 'Come join me. You must enter into that death with me; you died with me. Don't you see that? I know that you try to please me, but of yourselves you cannot, except that you join me in death. Then you will enter into resurrection life. I tell you that no man can crucify himself, purge his sins. I alone have paid the penalty for sins.'*
>
> *Therefore we can now say, 'I can do all things in Christ Jesus. It is no longer I that live but Christ lives in me.'*

Those words made a great impact in my own life. They reveal the true heart of the work of Christ. It was in the power of the Holy Spirit that He offered Himself up for us (Heb 9:14). It is as we allow the Holy Spirit to do the same work of overcoming sin, affliction and the power of death in us that we will enter into the true victory of Calvary.

2: 'Tis Mystery All

Throughout the centuries there have been many arguments about the death of Christ. There is no disagreement about its centrality. Without the death of Jesus, Christianity is only another religion with a founder who claims to be a divine/human being with miraculous powers. We cannot escape the death of Christ: it stands central to the whole Christian proclamation. The arguments have been about how it can be that God saves fallen man through the death of Jesus. In what way is His sacrifice effective or sufficient?

Many theories have been developed over the years to try to explain how God did this amazing thing. Some have been developed which attempt to appease the human intellect, so that the Cross is understandable to reason. But this can never be. Paul was right when he declared: *'We preach Christ crucified: a stumbling block to Jews and foolishness to Gentiles, but to those whom God has called, both Jews and Greeks, Christ the power of God and the wisdom of God. For the foolishness of God is wiser than man's wisdom, and the weakness of God is stronger than man's strength'* (1 Cor 1:23–25).

The fiercest debate has raged around the question of atonement: how did God satisfy the demands of His own holy nature at the same time as manifesting the depths of His love towards mankind? Any thought that God made Jesus bear the punishment of our sins and take our guilt on Himself as our substitute seems to have caused offence to many thinkers over the years. And so, time and again they have propounded theories about the death of Jesus which seek to avoid this terrible conclusion. But the conclusion is unavoidable! In the end, there is no escaping the fact that the New Testament writers clearly proclaim that Christ was offered as the sacrifice for our sins: *'He himself bore our sins in his body on the tree, so that we might die to sins and live for righteousness; by his wounds you have been healed'* (1 Pet 2:24).

Paul highlights the depths of this even further when in writing to the Galatians he appeals to the language of the book of Deuteronomy. For him it is not only a matter of Jesus taking our sins upon Himself; rather it is a matter of Jesus *becoming* something for us! This is the depth of Calvary. It is not only something done to Jesus, it is something done *in* Him! Paul says: *'Christ redeemed us from the curse of the law by becoming a curse for us, for it is written: "Cursed is everyone who is hung on a tree"'* (Gal 3:13).

Sin for us

No Scripture highlights this fact more clearly than 2 Corinthians 5:21: *'God made him who had no sin to be sin for us, so that in him we might become the righteousness of God.'* A footnote in the New International Version suggests the alternative, 'sin-offering' – that is, that God made Christ a sin offering for us. This would echo the type of sin offering in the Old Testament. But we need to recognise that the type is only a shadow of what is to come and that this image falls short of what *actually* happened in the experience of Jesus. Every major commentator on the text agrees that the import of the words, *'to be sin for us'* is much deeper than the thought implied by the type of sin offering. He *is* our sin offering, as the writer to the Hebrews makes clear: *'Unlike the other high priests, he does not need to offer sacrifices day after day, first for his own sins, and then for the sins of the people. He sacrificed for their sins once for all when he offered himself'* (Heb 7:27). But He did something that no sin offering ever did. He became our substitute, not only by taking sin *upon* Himself but by taking our sin *into* Himself. The victory over sin, death and the power of Satan was not only worked *by* Him – it was achieved *in* Him!

This profound Scripture contains all the mystery and wonder of Calvary. How will we ever be able to comprehend what God did for us in the death of His Son? Certainly we should not err on the side of underestimating it! There are certain fundamental issues raised in the light of this Scripture which will help us to see something of the power and wonder of it all.

(a) **The difference between 'sin' and 'sinful'.** It is of fundamental importance that we understand what Paul is meaning. For too long we have lived with watered-down ideas of what it meant for Jesus to suffer. E. W. Kenyon makes such comments as, 'He actually was made sin with our sin'.

Let's be clear what this means. Nowhere in the New Testament are we taught that Jesus Himself became a *sinner*. This is what I mean when I stress the difference between 'sin' and 'sinful'. Jesus, in Himself, was not sinful. This is why we speak of Him bearing the penalty of our sin rather than the punishment for sin. He was not punished for any sin of His own: He bore in Himself the penalty for our sins. The writer to the Hebrews makes it clear on more than one occasion that Jesus offered Himself up as a perfect sacrifice without spot or blemish: '*How much more, then, will the blood of Christ, who through the eternal Spirit offered himself unblemished to God, cleanse our consciences from acts that lead to death*' (Heb 9:14). Philip Bliss captured the thought of that when he wrote the beautiful meditation on the Cross, *Man of Sorrows*. In one verse he draws the contrast between what we are in our sin and what Christ is in His offering:

> *Guilty, vile and helpless we,*
> *Spotless Lamb of God was He.*
> *'Full Atonement!' – can it be?*
> *Hallelujah! What a Saviour!*

I like what P. T. Forsyth said on this subject in his book, *The Work of Christ*: 'God made him sin, treated him as if he were sin, he did not view him as sinful. God lovingly treated him as human sin, and with his consent judged human sin in him and on him. Personal guilt Christ could never confess.'

This leads us to the heart of Calvary. It was not a simple expiation. God did not deal with the question of sin merely by observing the physical death of His Son. No, Jesus *entered into* that death! This is where I go with E. W. Kenyon and others who stress the depths of the sufferings of Christ. This was no ordinary sorrow. Physical death is the outcome of man's sin and disobedience, but it is not its only effect. Divine judgement and dereliction are the result of sin. Death toward God is the ultimate outcome of sin. Satan's oppression and bondage are the result of sin. Sickness and disease are the results of sin. For man to be delivered from the fact and effect of his sin, the Son needed to take *all this sin* into Himself. This is the most humiliating truth of this necessity. No wonder we are reluctant to carry these thoughts through to their conclusion. What a horrific claim to make with regard to the Son of God! He became sin! We need to come in awe to Calvary, to take our shoes from off our feet, for the place on which we stand is holy ground! I doubt if we will ever be able to plumb the depths of it, now or in eternity. The truth is expressed by Elizabeth Clephane in her old evangelical hymn, *The Ninety and Nine* when she writes:

> *But none of the ransomed ever knew*
> *How deep were the waters crossed;*
> *Nor how dark was the night that the Lord passed*
> * through,*
> *Ere He found the sheep that was lost.*

(b) The difference between human and mortal. Part of the problem is that we don't stop to consider the real meaning of the words we use. These two words are terms which we often confuse with each other. To be human, as far as we are concerned, *is* to be mortal. But is that the truth as far as God is concerned? When God created man, did He create man to be mortal – that is, subject to death? The answer is clearly no.

Both the book of Genesis and the Epistle to the Romans are explicit as to the source of death. Genesis 3:22 makes it clear that God expelled man from the garden to prevent him from eating the tree of life by which he could live for ever. We could argue that this Scripture assumes that man was not going to live for ever. It looks much more to me that God was cutting man off from the source of his eternal life because of his disobedience. From this point on, man became subject to death as a judgement from God and, if you take the biblical record seriously, his years became shorter the further he went away from his beginnings with God, until they were set at threescore years and ten with the terms of the Old Covenant.

Paul is very explicit on the subject when he writes to the Romans: *'Sin entered the world through one man, and death through sin, and in this way death came to all men, because all sinned'* (Rom 5:12). But the point is that Jesus Himself was not subject to man's death until He took man's sin into Himself, because death is the outcome of sin. Jesus Himself was not sinful, therefore He did not live His life under the threat of death as a necessary outcome of sin. Jesus Himself made His position clear in this regard. He was the only man who ever lived who had the authority of life in Him: *'The reason my Father loves me is that I lay down my life – only to take it up again. No one takes it from me, but I lay it down of my own accord. I have authority to lay it down and authority to take it up again. This command I received from my Father'* (Jn 10:17, 18). This is the tremendous fact of Calvary; the only One who had no need to die either spiritually or physically was the very One who took death upon Himself to break its power: *'Since the children have flesh and blood, he too shared in their humanity so that by his death he might destroy him who holds the power of death – that is, the devil – and free those who all their lives were held in slavery by their fear of death'* (Heb 2:14, 15). Charles Wesley writes with tremendous spiritual insight when he proclaims the depths of this:

> *'Tis mystery all! The Immortal dies:*
> *Who can explore His strange design?*
> *In vain the first-born seraph tries*
> *To sound the depths of love divine.*
> *'Tis mercy all! let earth adore;*
> *Let angel minds inquire no more.*

That is the truth! On the cross it was the *Immortal* who was put to death! Jesus was human but immortal. He took death upon Himself. It was not until He took human sin upon Himself that He entered into the fact of death. This was the struggle of the Garden of Gethsemane. There Jesus wrestled with the awful reality of what was before Him. No man in normal human strength could ever have faced what Jesus faced. Luke tells with great pathos what happened in the Garden:

> *He withdrew about a stone's throw beyond them, knelt down and prayed, 'Father, if you are willing, take this cup from me; yet not my will, but yours be done.' An angel from heaven appeared to him and strengthened him. And being in anguish, he prayed more earnestly, and his sweat was like drops of blood falling to the ground.*
>
> (Lk 22:41–44)

It was here in the Garden that Jesus submitted Himself completely to the will of His Father and took into Himself all the reality of man's sin. From that moment forward He was subject to death.

This is where the power of Calvary lies with us. Not when we try to understand it all, because we never shall, but when we bow before it! When we accept the mystery and the power! When we receive into ourselves the saving effect of His death in the same way that He received into Himself the awful effect of our sin! When with Paul we cry through faith: *'the Son of God, who loved me and gave himself for me'* (Gal 2:20).

(c) **Born of God, not of Adam.** Of equal importance is the debate that has gone on for years about whether Jesus was born of a virgin or not. Some write it off as an irrelevancy. For them it seems to make no difference to the Gospel. But the Gospel writers themselves are clear about it. Matthew and Luke go to pains to give a detailed account of the birth of Jesus. John records the birth of Jesus in his own way. In particular, when he speaks of what God does in the lives of those who come to know Jesus through faith, he is describing the truth about Jesus's own birth: *'born not of natural descent, nor of human decision or a husband's will, but born of God'* (Jn 1:13). Tom Smail agrees with this in his book, *Reflected Glory*. He underlines the connection between what happened in the birth of Jesus under the power of the Holy Spirit and what happens by the same Spirit in the experience of the believer: 'Both the birth of Christ and the rebirth of Christians are works of the Holy Spirit in giving a new capacity for relationship and response to God to our fallen humanity' (p 32).

The truth of the virgin birth is vital to our understanding of both the life and of the death of Jesus. It is clear from Scripture that the life Jesus lived was lived in a real body of flesh. There can be no doubt that He experienced real temptations. This was no play-acting. The grounds of His humanity were the same as the grounds of our humanity as far as this is concerned. The writer to the Hebrews makes this clear: '*For we do not have a high priest who is unable to sympathise with our weaknesses, but we have one who has been tempted in every way, just as we are – yet was without sin*' (Heb 4:15). The very last phrase makes it clear, however, that there was something about Jesus which *differentiates* Him from all other men. He was not subject to sin and had the power to overcome every temptation which came to His door. Luke chapter 4 is a magnificent exposition of this fact.

But Jesus was not born of Adam! He was born of the Holy Spirit! This is not the case of men as they are born into the world. They take their lineage from the old Adam; they take their weakness from the old Adam; they take their sin from the old Adam! Jesus is the Second Adam, the Man from heaven (see 1 Cor 15:45–49). He is like them in body but not in spirit! Men in general do not take on the likeness of the Man from heaven, that is Jesus, until they too are born of God through the Holy Spirit.

Paul expresses this truth in his own way in Romans 8:3: '*For what the law was powerless to do in that it was weakened by the sinful nature, God did by sending his own Son in the likeness of sinful man to be a sin offering.*' The crux of the matter lies in our understanding of what is meant by the term 'likeness'. Traditional Christian belief has understood it to mean that the flesh of Christ is 'like' ours inasmuch as it is flesh; 'like' and only 'like' (i.e. not the same) because it is not sinful. Others have objected to this view, saying that it does away with the reality of the temptation of Jesus and the moral victory He was able to achieve over sin as an active principle in daily living.

For example C. E. B. Cranfield in his commentary on Romans takes a different view and argues that Jesus took on Himself our *fallen* nature. He criticises the traditional view and says that 'it is open to the general theological objection that it was not unfallen but fallen human nature which needed redeeming.' Of course it is true that it is our fallen nature that needs redeeming, but it will never be redeemed in the power of fallen nature! Jesus had to overcome sin at two levels. First, at the level of daily living, where He overcame the reign of sin in the flesh by His perfect obedience to the Father in the power of the Holy Spirit; secondly, in terms of the judgement of God upon sin through which He received in Himself the punishment for sin and thereby totally atoned for it, and defeated the power of death through His own death on the cross.

Jesus was born of the Spirit and lived in the power of the Spirit. He never knew what it was to sin. In fact, Jesus lived at the level of true humanity; the humanity which God created for Adam and in which he lived until he fell through disobedience. This is what the term 'likeness' means. Jesus' humanity was like ours inasmuch as the body Jesus had was a real body of flesh. It was like ours inasmuch as it was susceptible to temptation, as was the flesh of Adam before he fell, but it was unlike our humanity, in that it was governed by the Spirit of God and never knew the reality of sin until the end. This is where we see the immensity of His offering on the cross. At this point He did something which He had never experienced before; He opened Himself to the reality and effects of sin within His own body. Not His sin, but the sins of all other men, and into Himself He gathered all its awful effects and judgement: *'God made him who had no sin to be sin for us, so that in him we might become the righteousness of God'* (2 Cor 5:21).

3: Brokenness

'The old cross is a symbol of death. It stands for the abrupt, violent end of a human being. In Roman times, the man who took up his cross and started down the road was not coming back. He was not going out to have his life redirected, *he was going out to have it ended*' (A. W. Tozer).

Recently I was reading the first chapter of Paul's first letter to the church at Corinth. The Authorised Version of verse 28 made an impression on me: '*And base things of the world, and things which are despised, hath God chosen, yea, and **things which are not, to bring to nought things that are.***'

A: Something or nothing?

I am so often aware of how much needs to change if I am to know God's power at work within me to anything like the extent He desires. Satan is always making his appeal to that inbuilt urge that we all have, to be something. Even in terms of our Christian lives that basic urge is such a strong force that it often motivates our very service for God. From the first day that I became a Christian I have wanted to be something for God. Preacher or evangelist – whatever it might be – that was my whole ambition. Something for God. Looking back, it's easy to see just how much of the flesh was mixed with that desire and how often the devil was able to play on that inward urge. The trouble is that even Spirit-filled Christians find the flesh and the Spirit to be so mixed together and the balance so loaded in favour of the flesh, that the work of the Spirit is all but annulled or dissipated. This is the tragedy of our lives. There is so much potential for God, but we give Him so little room to work. As I look back, even to recent times, I become filled with great sadness because I can see that so much of my Christian life was really the old life lived in religious or spiritual guise. I realise just how far away I am from what God desires me to be. How closed we are to the reality of God and His glory and how sullied our lives are by the self-interest and pride that dominate our experience! Sometimes this fact hits me so hard that it almost obliterates me at a spiritual level, and I have to struggle in the spirit to regain any equilibrium and feeling that anything is worthwhile.

The trouble is that God really can't use 'somethings'. It is in the lives of those who are described in Scripture as being 'nothing' that God has chosen to manifest His power and glory. The fact is that we need to die to ourselves in a very radical way. Even much of our so-called spirituality and charismatic religion has done little but develop a heightened self-consciousness in which we never rise beyond ourselves or our problems to glimpse the glory of God.

B: God's visual aid

Angie is the wife of John Hindmarsh, one of our elders. I met her one day outside my office. I could see at a glance that something had affected her profoundly. She told me what had happened and I knew straight away exactly what it was all about.

Angie had newly come in from driving her car. As she was coming here she had witnessed something that deeply upset her. A lorry had just run over a collie dog. It was a terrible mess and at first glance she imagined that the dog involved was their own pet collie, Jess. It gave her a start, but as she observed the scene an amazing thing happened to her. It was as though the Holy Spirit took over and used the incident as a visual aid for Angie, and she almost heard the voice of the Lord saying in her ear, 'That's you down there. You're dead'.

It was this that was having such a drastic effect on her when I met her. By then she knew it was not her own dog that had been killed, but that wasn't important to her. She had gone through a transformation in that moment. It was like a personal crucifixion, and it has led her to a whole new sense of God and a willingness for the release of God's power in her life. The old Angie had been very concerned with her place in life and with the status of her husband's ministry, but now she came to see that to have any true ministry we all need to die to such attitudes and be open to God. The important thing that she now realised was that it was not her points of weakness that had to be dealt with by God, but those very areas that she had considered her points of strength.

She entered into that depth of understanding that some of

us around her had been experiencing during the months before; the reality of a death deep within the spirit. Not a death of the spirit, but a deep inner awareness that if we wanted to see and know the power of God, then much that we had previously counted as valuable in our lives would need to go. God had used this grotesque incident to bring home to Angie's spirit the need for such a death within herself.

That illustrates a basic truth. We all need to come through to that point of brokenness and death until we feel there is nothing left. Only then can we begin to be open to the new thing that God wants to do within and through us. Up to that point there is still too much of the old life left that gets in the way of God.

This is exactly my own experience. It is not our weaknesses that God needs to deal with, but those facets of our personalities and experience that we often regard as our strong points. They are often the places where we don't feel the need for heavy dependence on God and in which we feel strong and self-confident.

The ways of God are deep and mysterious, and they start with the demolition and death of everything in our lives and ambitions that come from the flesh. There is no doubt that the New Testament is right when it identifies the flesh as our greatest enemy and God's biggest problem. It has continually to be dealt with and overcome. Even though we are to *reckon* it dead (Rom 6:11), there is no doubt that in real terms it is still active, and if we want to know God's power within our lives, something radical needs to change with our fleshly selves.

C: Simplicity in spirit

At about the same time something else happened that only served to reinforce the first sense of God's voice. It happened one morning as I was about to lead a seminar with the students at the college. One of them announced that he had a word from the Lord for me. Now normally I don't take very kindly to such things, partly because I have suffered a lot at the hands of people who have brought some outlandish revelation at the most inappropriate moment. But this felt different and certainly the man involved was not noted for his exuberance in things of this ilk. I waited and listened.

In effect, what he told me was that the Lord had given him an impression of a new movement of God in my life. I was to give up all my previous ideas of ministry. What God wanted to do in me was contained in one word: simplicity. That revelation had a dramatic effect in my mind, and even now I am not sure that I have fully explored its meaning. I am sure that it does not mean that God is calling me to the life of a recluse or to cease being involved in the sometimes rather complex life of ministry in a modern world. I believe it is much more related to the fact that there needs to be at the heart of things a simplicity born of God in terms of heart-trust and single-mindedness. The student who spoke the word could have had no idea at that moment about the deep things that were happening at other levels of me experience.

It was a strip-down job by God. I felt through the impact of this single word as though He had taken an X-ray scan of my insides and had pronounced judgement on some of the things I held most dear. I came face to face with the fact that most of my securities in life were completely misplaced and most of my desires were misdirected, and because of these two things most of my work for God was spoiled. Not that it was all bad or that I was a walking disaster area, but I knew the absolute truth in that moment that there were large tracts of my experience which still reflected the old selfish life and which had never been exposed to the death rays of the Holy Spirit.

There was a need for a new simplicity of spirit. That simplicity is born only of God. We make God out to be far more complicated than He is. With Him, black is black and white is white. Right is right and wrong is wrong. Because He works in complete honesty and integrity within His own nature He never gets Himself in a twist. We do because we are precisely the opposite. Instead of living in cloudlessness of spirit we allow things and circumstances to dominate our spirits and destroy that inward clarity and peace and transmit themselves to other people in destructive and fleshly ways. So often the devil is able to take our best intentions and desires and pervert them for his own ends. What starts as honest concern or love in Christ so often ends up in a twisted tangle of emotions and hurt that can ruin our lives and ministry, all because we do not let God continually have His way in our lives.

When God spoke to me through that student I felt as though I had died in the very same way as Angie. As the months have passed I know that it is true. To hear in this deep way that we are nothing and that God wants us to be nothing before He can do something with us or through us could seem to be an awfully negative thing. In fact it could crush our spirit and lead us into a tremendous sense of condemnation. And that is just what the devil would delight to do in our hearts. That is not what the Father wants, however. He wants a word or an experience like this to lead to a new fruitfulness within our lives, but for that to happen we need to receive the 'nothingness'. It needs to become real in our experience, to be felt within our hearts and understood in our minds. In fact we need to see that it was the very way by which Jesus lived and manifested the power of God. He became nothing!

> Who, *being in very nature God,*
>   *did not consider equality with God something*
>   *to be grasped,*
> *but made himself nothing,*
>   *taking the very nature of a servant,*
>   *being made in human likeness.*
> *And being found in appearance as a man,*
>   *he humbled himself and became obedient to death –*
> *even death on a cross!*   (Phil 2:6–8)

D: Spirit without measure

The words of that Scripture really hit my heart; they make a deep impact on my inner being. So often we identify His brokenness with the events of Calvary, which are the very epitome of what nothingness meant for Jesus. But here we have it; for Him it was a way of life. Brokenness became a way of life for Jesus long before He saw the cross. He really was something but He made Himself *nothing*. Here was Jesus, the man above all men, who knew the ways of God's power in an immediate and personal sense – He brought life out of death more than once during His earthly ministry; when He touched men they were made well; when He spoke, demons trembled and fled.

John the Baptist understood how this could be: *'The one whom God has sent speaks the words of God, for God gives the Spirit without limit'* (Jn 3:34). The Authorised Version intensifies John's meaning even more. It says, 'not by measure'. We can see the secret of God's power in the experience of Jesus. We receive the Spirit of God only by measure. The Father is just as willing to give us the Spirit, but the limitations of our own hearts determine the measure of the Holy Spirit in us. We are so full of garbage and self-concern that there is no room for the Spirit in any great measure. Hurts, pride, selfishness and rebellion inhibit our hearts and prevent the Holy Spirit from having room to work within us. The truth is that there were no denizens of darkness within the heart of Jesus. There was *room* for God the Father to pour the Holy Spirit into Him without measure. In our lives the space is so often filled up with emotional, intellectual and spiritual clutter.

E: Ointment poured forth

I have come to see in a completely new light the words of Paul which head this section. God has chosen the things that are nothing. Not only those who *have* nothing but those who *are* nothing. It is not a matter of social status or degree, it is much deeper than that. If we are really keen to know the ways of God's power in our lives then we need to walk the way of Jesus. It is the way of death. We need to be broken. Only after that can God put healing *into* our lives so that He can pour His healing *out* through our lives. So often what pours out is not the healing balm of God but the sheer blatant arrogance of the flesh, the old nature wrapped up in religious guise. The pride of life is dressed up to make it look godly, or the ambitions of the old self are revamped to make them sound holy.

Sometimes when I am confronted by people who want to minister to others or even to me, instead of feeling that humility of spirit and wholeness that comes from God, I am offended by the sheer brutality that hits me. This is not from God. This is the old flesh with a new dress on. It is the old pride of life vaunting itself in religious guise, and there is no more dangerous animal in the whole world. God wants to put His fragrance into our lives, but as when Mary anointed the feet of Jesus, so the jar has to be broken before the ointment of the Holy Spirit can flow out from us.

God's way seems so utterly absurd. But when you examine it you know that it is the only way. Unless you become nothing. God will never make you anything.

F: No handhold for Satan

There is another important principle here. The reason Satan could never defeat Jesus was because there was 'nothing' in Him. The way Satan can succeed with us where he failed with Jesus is just at this point. The devil wants us to live with our old 'somethings'. He can reach into our lives and lay hold of these things. These traces of the old life are the very points he latches on to, to grip us up or take us back to the old way. When he tried to reach into the inner heart of Jesus there were none of these things. In a real sense He was nothing. There was nothing for Satan to get a hold of: there was no handhold for the devil. There was nothing in Jesus to correspond to the tempting voice of the evil one, not even anything left of the heavenly greatness that He enjoyed 'before the world began'. What pride could justifiably have been there! But 'he emptied himself'. Satan could find no self-interest or self-pity to play on. There is nothing more fatal than self-pity. In Jesus there was nothing, no place for Satan to grab.

This is the depth to which God is calling us today, to see something of His purpose for our lives, to deliver us from this petty self-interest that lies behind so much of our so-called ministry. If we had been to the Cross in this degree, if we followed the likeness of the Man from heaven in this degree, how much less appeal there would be in the man from earth!

G: The mark of God

I often reflect on the experience of Jacob at the brook Jabbok (Gen 32:22–32). That is where he met with God in such a special way. Alone that night he wrestled with the Messenger of God right through until the day broke. Jacob refused to let God go until He blessed him. To stay in that struggle cost Jacob everything he was and had. It cost him his old name and it cost him his strength. No longer was he called Jacob, but Israel, because he was the one who had power with God. God smote him in the tendon of his thigh and from that day he bore the mark of this meeting with God in his body. There was a lameness about the new Jacob, but his lameness was his strength. No wonder he called the name of the place Peniel, 'face of God', for he had met God face to face and yet lived to tell the tale.

No incident more portrays how we need to meet with God, to be touched by the power of God and burned by the holiness of God. To know that God has looked into our lives and in His love has spared us – that is true brokenness. Brokenness like that is not weakness, it is the very source of strength in the spirit. After such a meeting things never look the same again. I would say in fact that this is the source of the greatest power in the whole world. There is nothing stronger than a man who has been touched by God. He has nothing left to prove and nothing more to fear. The old fight has gone, the old fire has been put out and the old aggression has been laid to rest. Inside there is an emptiness that only God can fill. It is not the emptiness of nothingness or meaninglessness, it is the emptiness of God. Outwardly there is a weakness that only God can make strong. I believe this is the way forward. For too long we have engaged in the enterprise of the king-dom of God in ways that look suspiciously like a copy of the old order of things.

The old values don't seem to matter any longer. One thing, of course, that we need to guard against is the other extreme into which we can be led by Satan – to believe that nothing at all matters any more, as though everything in life has been completely devalued by this kind of experience. Not at all. What we need to realise is that the Holy Spirit comes as God's great assayer. He is here to show us God's true values and to lead us into a new and deeper appreciation of all the good things that find their source in the creative hand of the Father – not only 'spiritual' or 'religious' things but every good and perfect gift with which He surrounds us. This brings a completely new sense of appreciation and thankfulness into life and enables us to enjoy the things that God has freely given us.

In such brokenness there is a deep sense of dislocation. Paul experienced the very same thing. He wrote: '*I have been crucified with Christ and **I no longer live**, but Christ lives in me. The life I now live in the body I live by faith in the Son of God, who loved me and gave himself for me*' (Gal 2:20). Every disciple of Jesus needs to live like that if he is to be really effective for God.

4: The Full Virtue of the Cross

I was brought up with a sober and reverent but deficient appreciation of the Lord's table. For us it was a memorial in which we rightly remembered the death and suffering of the Saviour and the benefit for us in that, of salvation and the forgiveness of sins. But the full implications of Calvary escaped many of us who approached the table in this way. I recall a tremendous sense of looking back and an equally powerful sense of being drawn forward into the coming purposes of God. Some words of an old hymn, whose source I cannot recall, characterised this attitude:

> Then we will be where we would be,
> Then we shall be what we should be,
> That which is not now, nor could be,
> Then shall be our own.

Of course, there is a great deal of truth in a sentiment like this. We all know that we are far from what the Father desires and our lives display a continual struggle between flesh and Spirit and between God's power and our weakness. At the same time we need to see the dynamic significance of the Cross for us now. We do stand between the past and the future, between what has been accomplished for us in Christ Jesus and what is yet to be fulfilled. But the glorious truth is that the Holy Spirit is here with us and it is His job to take what has been accomplished in the past and make it real for us in the present and to bring what is not yet fully accomplished home to our hearts and lives as a great motivation for faith and hope. In fact, the Cross is our guarantee that we are not left in a spiritual limbo-land. In the Cross of Jesus God has established and provided everything that we need for our lives today. In his book, *Receive Your Healing*, Colin Urquhart shares his own insight when he says:

> 'I have learned to say something like this when receiving the bread: "Lord, I believe that as I eat this bread, I have received all the virtue of Christ's body, I thank you for

the physical strength and healing I receive through His stripes. I thank you for the material provision I have for all my needs through His abundant grace."'

There are many occasions in my own life when I need to go right back to Calvary to see that every need has been met in the death and resurrection of the Lord Jesus. Satan wants us to live in unbelief and despair and to stop believing that the Father can meet our needs. But God has established His promises and principles in the Cross of Calvary. If God failed to sustain His people and meet them at every point of spiritual, physical and material need He would be denying the work He has accomplished through His Son. We don't need to find our security in our emotions when it comes to trusting God, we can look to the Saviour and what the Father has accomplished in Him. As Peter rightly says: *'His divine power has given us everything we need for life and godliness through our knowledge of him who called us by his own glory and goodness.'* (2 Pet 1:3).

It is the Father's purpose to enrich us in every way through what He has done for us in the Cross of Jesus. *'For you know the grace of our Lord Jesus Christ, that though he was rich, yet for your sakes he became poor, so that you through his poverty might become rich.'* (2 Cor 8:9).

In a practical sense we need to take our stand on the finished work of Christ at every point of our daily experience.

A: The virtue of forgiveness

Self-condemnation is a common feature of our human experience. Many Christian believers suffer from condemnation of spirit. The reality of our daily failures in our walk with God and the pressure of our interaction with other people often lead to feelings of unworthiness and inadequacy. Forgiveness is a fact from God's point of view. In Christ He has covered all our sins and when we come to Him in repentance and confession He never fails to cleanse us and give us that sense of freedom and freshness which is our right through the death of our Saviour. But the devil never likes to leave it there. He loves to play on our feelings of weakness and tries to lead us back into condemnation and bondage within our hearts. This is where we need to *receive* our forgiveness. It is the difference between what the old saints used to call legal and vital truth. Something can be true without our ever entering into the reality of the fact. Sadly, it is the case for many, that God has accomplished their full salvation in Jesus but they never realise it in their own lives. The live in fear and condemnation within their hearts instead of enjoying the full liberty of sons of God.

Satan tries to convince us that, in some way, we need to pay for our sins. But this is a total contradiction of the teaching of Scripture and the work of Calvary. Jesus has met all our debt and we need to receive our forgiveness in Him.

> *Payment he will not twice demand,*
> *First at my blessed Saviour's hand,*
> *And then again at mine!*

Thank God for full forgiveness!

> *If we confess our sins, he is faithful and just and will*
> *forgive us our sins and purify us from all unrighteousness*
> *... if anybody does sin, we have one who speaks to the*
> *Father in our defence – Jesus Christ, the Righteous One.*
> (1 Jn 1:9, 2:1)

Imagine that! Think of it as you come to the Lord's table. Close your eyes and see this great truth. Not only have you a Saviour who has died for you, but you have a Saviour who at this moment is speaking to the Father on your behalf. As you open your mouth and ask forgiveness He is naming your name before the Father of lights. That's how important we are to God! Now we can take the words of the song and make them the testimony of our own hearts and lives:

> *I am a new creation,*
> *No more in condemnation,*
> *Here in the grace of God I stand!*

B: The virtue of provision

I come back to Calvary many times when things seem tough. These are days when Satan tries to whisper in my heart that God has forsaken us. There are moments when he comes and tries to convince me that my Father does not care and that it is useless to trust in a God one cannot see. He tries to show me what a foolish and senseless thing it is to put my trust in an invisible God. He tries to get me to look at the plain, hard, materialistic facts of life and overwhelm me with the sheer audacity of trusting a living God in the middle of such a secular and scientific world.

The devil doesn't mind our believing in God as long as He is a God who does nothing. After all, belief in such a god answers the spiritual cravings of the human heart. That's why those people who reject the God and Father who is revealed in Jesus need to replace Him with a god of their own manufacture. Satan's aim is to break that relationship of trust which the Holy Spirit brings to life when we are born again through His power. It is by the Spirit that we know God as our Father and it is through Him that we come to God our Father in simple trust and faith: *'For you did not receive a spirit that makes you a slave again to fear, but you received the spirit of sonship. And by him we cry, "Abba, Father." The Spirit himself testifies with our spirit that we are God's children'* (Rom 8:15, 16).

But what has the Cross to do with our trust in God for our daily needs? Paul makes this clear later in Romans chapter 8 when he says: *'He who did not spare his own Son, but gave him up for us all – how will he not also, along with him, graciously give us all things?'* (Rom 8:32).

Every time I struggle with a sense of need I come back to Calvary. After Jesus every other provision is only a footnote! All we ever need is included in Him and through faith in Him we know that release of His provision into our lives day by day.

C: The virtue of victory

In His death Jesus accomplished victory for us over sin, death, the world and the power of Satan, the great enemies that haunt the footsteps of every human being. Satan continually tries to bring us into defeat and weakness through these means, so we need to be clear of our victory in Him so that we can overcome Satan in his attacks upon our lives.

He has won for us victory over sin. He overcame sin when He overcame death. Death is the result of sin working in us.

> *Therefore, just as sin entered the world through one man, and death through sin, and in this way death came to all men, because all have sinned.*
> *For if the many died by the trespass of the one man, how much more did God's grace and the gift that came by the grace of the one man, Jesus Christ, overflow to the many!* (Rom 5:12, 15)

The two great weapons of Satan – guilt and fear – are thus rendered useless in the life of the Christian who stands on the finished work of the Cross.

Jesus has won for us victory over the world. As we will see later, the world in this sense does not mean the beauty of God's creation or all the good things which the Father has provided for His children to enjoy. John reminds us of what the world is when he writes in his epistle: *'For everything in the world – the cravings of sinful man, the lust of his eyes and the boasting of what he has and does – comes not from the Father but from the world.'* (1 Jn 2:16).

In a later section of the book we will see that the world is that satanic system of evil which has permeated God's order and the society of mankind and which leads men and women into darkness and away from God. But because of the finished work of Christ on the Cross in which He overcame the principles and powers of this world-darkness, we can share His victory in the present power of the Holy Spirit. *'Everyone born of God overcomes the world. This is the victory that has overcome the world, even our faith. Who is it that overcomes the world? Only he who believes that Jesus is the Son of God.'* (1 Jn 5:4, 5).

He has won for us victory over Satan!

The Cross was, in fact, the cataclysmic battle between the power of Satan and the power of God. Everything that flows to us out of the Cross does so because Jesus won the victory. That victory was not achieved in some dark and secret corner but in a public arena for all to see. When Jesus cried out 'It is finished!' He was not crying out in weakness or despair, but proclaiming publicly the mighty victory of God. Paul makes it clear that in Jesus, God has overcome all the powers of darkness and that they no longer pose a threat to those who stand in faith in Christ Jesus:

> ... God made you alive with Christ. He forgave us all our sins, having cancelled the written code, with its regulations, that was against us and that stood opposed to us; he took it away, nailing it to the cross. And having disarmed the powers and authorities, he made a public spectacle of them, triumphing over them by the cross.
>
> (Col 2:13–15)

D: The virtue of healing

It is not possible within the brief scope available here to discuss at any length the subject of healing, but I don't think we can consider the Cross of the Lord Jesus without asking ourselves what this has to say about the character of our ministry today. In his book *Power Healing* John Wimber discusses at some length the theme of Healing and Atonement. I agree with his suggestion that healing is not the primary gift of the Atonement. The primary gift of the Atonement is the forgiveness of sins. As Wimber himself makes clear (and he quotes others in support), the universal gift that comes to mankind from the Cross is the gift of salvation in the sense of forgiveness of sins. Healing, like other provisions, comes to us through the Atonement, rather than in it. What this means is that the Cross of Christ is the basis for every other provision the Father can and will give us according to His will, but there are other factors which control whether these will be given in every case. Some of these factors are obvious to us; for example, when we need to exercise more faith or when our lives inhibit the Father from being as generous as He wants to be. Other factors are hidden and remain a mystery to us at this moment. For myself, I don't object at all to this mystery. It doesn't stop me praying in faith or asking the Father for help in every time of need. I fulfil the commission He has given and, when He makes it clear, I act in faith for healing and many other provisions. When it is less clear I stand on Scripture and pray in obedience, knowing that I can trust the Lord but I cannot manipulate Him.

> *The secret things belong to the Lord our God, but the things revealed belong to us and to our children forever, that we may follow all the words of this law.*
>
> (Deut 29:29)

Three major facts convince me that healing of the body is an integral part of the Father's purpose in the work of Calvary. Because of this we can confidently expect God to accomplish this in us, according to His will. We need to be clear in our thinking that there is no such thing as an unhealed believer. Even physical healing in an immediate sense is only temporary to this life. Absolute healing is the promise of the Father to every one who has faith and it will come to us when we discard the old body which is fashioned after the first Adam and receive our new bodies made in the likeness of the Second Adam, the Man from heaven.

First – God has established the principle of healing in the death and resurrection of Jesus.

Take John, for example, and his record of the resurrection of Jesus from the dead, John writes as an evangelist par excellence. Every point that he makes is a point with a purpose. He is not merely writing a biography or a history. His purpose is not merely to inform us of events which occurred; he writes with the passion of an evangelist. He is out to present us with the power of the truth about Jesus. He does not wish to leave us impressed with the eloquence or charismatic attraction of a great leader or guru. For John, Jesus equals all the power of

God. John's purpose in writing is to convert us, to bring us to following Jesus and knowing His power in our lives: *'These are written that you may believe that Jesus is the Christ, the Son of God, and that by believing you may have life in his name.'* (Jn 20:31).

This is why his witness is so important. For him the tomb was empty, Jesus had risen from the dead. The point he makes in chapter 20 verse 9 is very important. The disciples who looked into the tomb, Peter and doubtless John himself, at that moment had not come to realise from Scripture that Jesus should rise from the dead. Their minds were not coloured by presupposition. They walked head first into a miracle!

After them comes Mary who stands outside the tomb in tears. She bends over and sees two angels seated where the body of Jesus had been. As she speaks with the divine messengers another figure appears whom she does not recognise. He asks her why she is crying. Mary thinks that she is speaking to the gardener and it is not until she hears the voice of Jesus saying her name that her eyes are opened to Who it is. The point surely is that Mary did not recognise Jesus because she did not expect to see Him looking as He did. She had last seen His body hanging on the tree, bruised and bloodied. His body was broken and His visage marred and He had been laid in a tomb, wrapped in spices and bandages. He was marked and torn and His physical frame had been savaged by whipping, crucifixion and burial.

But here He was standing in all the strength and wholeness of young manhood. He had died, bruised and broken, a few days ago but now He was raised, healed and whole. We may learn a lesson from the fact that the Father did leave marks on Him which He will bear for all eternity! These were the wound-marks which drove Thomas to his knees in adoration as his unbelief melted into faith. But otherwise the Lord rose triumphant and whole!

When I saw it in this way I knew in my spirit that we were seeing something that was integral with the work of salvation. From that moment on, healing was the manifestation of God's Kingdom. We don't yet see the Kingdom in all its glory but when Jesus reigns in the fullness of His power we will see the fruit of that testimony then. Now we know in part but thank God, when we see it, our hopelessness is turned to expectation and our unbelief is turned to faith.

Second – The Scriptures clearly witness to the inclusion of physical healing as part of the work of Calvary.

In Romans chapter 8 Paul draws a direct line between what happened in the experience of Jesus when He was raised from the dead and what the Father wants to do in the experience of every believer in Jesus: *'If the Spirit of him who raised Jesus from the dead is living in you, he who raised Christ from the dead will also give life to your mortal bodies through His Spirit, who lives in you.'* (Rom 8:11).

Paul is speaking here not only of a future resurrection of the dead. The life he speaks of is something which we can experience now through the indwelling power of the Holy Spirit. It is something which the Father included in Calvary from the very beginning. Jesus died, not only to bear our sins, but to carry our sorrows and take up our infirmities.

This is the power of which Isaiah prophesied:

> *Surely he took up our infirmities*
> *and carried our sorrows,*
> *yet we considered him stricken by God,*
> *smitten by him, and afflicted.*
> *But he was pierced for our transgressions,*
> *he was crushed for our iniquities;*
> *the punishment that brought us peace was upon him,*
> *and by his wounds we are healed.* (Is 53:4, 5)

These very last words are echoed by Peter when he speaks of the sufferings of Christ.

> *He himself bore our sins in his body on the tree, so that we might die to sins and live for righteousness; by his wounds you have been healed.* (1 Pet 2:24)

It is, I feel, very significant that it is Peter who quotes these very words, because earlier in his own life he had personal experience of this saving power of God within his own family circle. Jesus healed his mother-in-law from a fever. Matthew tells of that event in his Gospel and in the very same context he quotes the words of Isaiah 53:4:

'This was to fulfil what was spoken through the prophet Isaiah:

> *He took up our infirmities*
> *and carried our diseases.'*
>
> (Mt 8:17)

There are many Scriptures, from the Old and New Testaments which bear witness to the healing character of God. John Wimber includes a very helpful survey of these in the back of his book *Power Healing* and I commend it to you. What is clear is that not only is it in the nature of God to heal, but that the Father purposed to include this within the work of the Cross. Jesus died not only to save our souls, but our whole man, spirit, soul and body.

Third – the direct testimony of healing today in the power of the Holy Spirit.

I, like millions of other Christians, was brought up in my Christian life to believe that things like this were special to the early church, that later they died out and that today we are left to accept sickness as part of Christian suffering. We lived with a truncated version of Calvary. We saw the power of Calvary as far as the question of sin was concerned, but we had to be content with half a gospel. So often it led to defeat.

Praise God I have lived to see it another way! In my own team I have people who have tasted the healing power of God in remarkable ways and I have the privilege to preach a full gospel to those who are in any kind of need. In my own life I have known the healing touch of God in spirit, soul and body.

The Scriptures make it clear that God's purpose is not only for the salvation of our souls but for the salvation of the whole man. He has quickened our spirits and made us alive to Himself in Christ through the Holy Spirit. That is the essential heart of what it means to be a Christian believer. This is what distinguishes the Christian gospel as whole message from the partial offer of the faith healer or spiritual healer. We are not only, and we might say not primarily, offering physical healing. Physical healing is an integral part of the Good News, but it is not the Good News by itself!

But the Father does want us to know the saving effect of the Cross in our whole lives. This is why in the New Testament such emphasis is put on the truth that our bodies are the temples of the Holy Spirit. God's purpose is that we should live now in the goodness and power of eternal life.

What I have noticed is that some people seem to express this close affinity between body and spirit much more radically than others. We all know what it is to feel the effects positively and negatively within our bodies if we are out of sorts inside, but it seems that with some people there is almost a direct and immediate link between the two.

Of course, it is for this reason that the integral part of many people's healing is a complete change of lifestyle, eating habits, living habits and so on. The body responds either positively or negatively to the things we do to it. Often our attitude to our body tells the tale with regard to what is going on in our spirits.

Now and not yet

The fact is that the Cross was the decisive encounter in the battle between good and evil. There Satan was finally stripped of his power and his fate was conclusively sealed. Yet there is still a war going on! So it is that the decisive work has been accomplished for our healing but we are not yet fully healed. Every miracle of God's grace is a miracle of promise. It is a type or pointer to what will fully pertain when Jesus comes in His Kingdom glory.

The fact that the battle is won and yet not over does not inhibit us from engaging in spiritual warfare at every level today; rather it stimulates us in it. So it is with the question of healing, for surely that is part of the battle! We should not be inhibited from praying for those who are sick just because we realise that everything is not yet perfect. As Wimber says:

> *Because our sins are forgiven at the cross and our future bodily resurrections are assured through Christ's resurrection, the Holy Spirit can and does break into this age with signs and assurances of the fullness of the kingdom of God yet to come.* (Power Healing p167)

Stand firm in faith

Faith is the principle of discipleship in the present age. God calls us to exercise this faith in responsible obedience in every part of our lives. Sometimes healing is not possible because of failure on our side. We are fallible and our understanding of things is not perfect and often we don't experience what we desire, either because we have come to the wrong conclusions about what we should expect, or we don't believe that God can do it. In his book *Power Healing* John Wimber lists the following as some reasons for our failure:

- *Some people do not have faith in God for healing* (James 5:15)
- *Personal, unconfessed sin creates a barrier to God's grace* (James 5:16)
- *Persistent and widespread disunity, sin and unbelief in bodies of believers and families inhibit healing in individual members of the body* (1 Cor 11:30)
- *Because of incomplete or incorrect diagnosis of what is causing their problems, people do not know how to pray correctly.*
- *Some people assume that God always heals instantly, and when He does not heal immediately they stop praying.* (Power Healing p164)

I would add to that the fact that sometimes we are looking in the wrong direction for our healing. God uses many means by which to fulfil His divine purpose in our lives. This is why it is important for us to hear the word of God for us with regard to the healing process. I am sure that some Christians live with sickness because they persist in looking in the wrong direction for their healing. As I have made clear some people, like myself, never thought of looking to God for a direct touch for healing. Our faith was in the means that were more accessible to our minds and within the normal range of medicine and the like. On the other hand some believers never look anywhere else but to the direct supernatural touch of God for healing and in doing so miss God's opportunity of relief and health through medical or surgical help.

S. D. Gordon lists seven means of healing in his book *The Healing Christ* and it would benefit us all to remember that the Lord is not limited to one way of acting for our good. Gordon also reminds us of the fact that not all healing comes from God and of how important it is for us to exercise the gift of discernment when it comes to these deep areas of life. He says:

> *Supernatural healing should be accepted only where the deity of Christ is distinctly emphasised, and the sacrificial blood he shed for us, as no other did nor could nor can, is made blessedly prominent.* (p175)

The fullness of God's love

Nowhere is unconditional love more fully expressed than in the Cross. John emphasises this when he says:

> *This is love: not that we loved God, but that he loved us and sent his Son as an atoning sacrifice for our sins.*
> (1 Jn 4:10)

We need to be encouraged to come as children to our heavenly Father. He does know what is best for us. We have to come to the throne of grace with confidence, so that we may receive mercy and find grace to help us in our time of need (see Hebrews 4:16). Paul reminds us as well that God has made provision in everything for us in the death of Jesus:

> *He who did not spare his own Son, but gave him up for us all – how will he not also, along with him, graciously give us all things?* (Rom 8:32)

5: The Sufferings of Christ

Suffering is a fact of life. To those outside of Christ it is an enigma, to those who are in Christ it is a necessity! There can be no whole view of discipleship which does not take suffering into its perspective. We are surrounded by it on every hand and we experience it daily in our walk with God.

A: The facts of life?

Suffering is not the same for the believer as for the unbeliever, however. To the person who has not experienced the love of God in Christ for himself, the fact of all the suffering in the world may be the very thing that prevents him from finding God. Why does a God of love allow all these things to happen? How can there be a God of love with such horror and tragedy going on? Questions such as these are wrung from the hearts of well-meaning people who don't know God's love at first hand for themselves. The person who has seen the reality and meaning of the Cross has a very different attitude to the question, although he may also experience the reality of suffering.

Whilst we need to sympathise totally with men and women in their distress and identify with them in their efforts to alleviate suffering, we must not be tempted to begin the discussion at the same level of humanistic thinking. The Cross reveals certain facts to us which inform us at a deeper level of reality altogether. For example, it reminds us above everything of the *awful fact of man's own responsibility* for much of the mess we find ourselves in. The Bible time and again makes a direct link between the world and man's responsibility in it. Man was created as a responsible agent by God and given the government of every created thing. Man's failure to carry out that responsibility is reflected tragically in the distortion and tragedy which we see all around us.

C. S. Lewis once said: 'It is man, not God, who has produced racks, whips, prisons, slavery, guns, bayonets and bombs; it is by human avarice or human stupidity that we have poverty and overwork.' (*The Problem of Pain*). We would have little difficulty in working that thesis out for our own day. Although we express shock and horror at the millions who are threatened with death by hunger and disease in the Third World, it is fairly plain that with a different set of values in operation and a change of will and heart on all sides the problem would be reduced to the point of insignificance.

The Cross, above all, *shows us the magnitude of our sin*. The Scriptures teach us that it was because of sin that Jesus died, but the manner of His death shows us just what sin is like. Jesus has been universally acknowledged as a great and innocent man. At the very least men have seen in Him a symbol of purity and goodness. And yet men took Him and cruelly extinguished His life in one of the most cruel ways ever devised. That is what sin does – it corrupts and distorts, it destroys and opposes anything intrinsically good. Sin is at the root of all suffering in our world today, because it is a world that no longer manifests the harmony, balance and beauty in which God created it.

At a deeper level still, the Cross *is a battle for control*. The world lies under the control of Satan. He has become the 'god of this world' ever since man relinquished his stewardship of Creation. Man's sin gave Satan the opportunity he had been waiting for to take over and pervert the goodness of God's own Creation. It was almost like his evil revenge for the judgement that had been passed on him when he was thrown out of heaven. But the Cross was the reversal of that power, and now Christ is King and His Kingdom rules over all!

The Cross declares, of course, that God *is not indifferent to suffering*. It is no accident that at the heart of the Christian proclamation stands the greatest example of innocent suffering the world has ever known. But it is more than an example of innocent suffering – it is God taking suffering into His very heart! The prophet Isaiah caught the pathos of that when he said: '*Surely he took up our infirmities and carried our sorrows,* ' (Is 53:4).

B: These momentary troubles

The New Testament never makes light of suffering; it accepts it as a fact of life! The Christian walks in the way of the Cross, and this means not only speaking about it but experiencing it: *'It has been granted to you on behalf of Christ not only to believe on him, but also to suffer for him'* (Phil 1:29). The history of the Church started with two great waves: first, the wave of power as the signs and wonders of the Holy Spirit swept through the world; then the wave of persecution which followed in the wake of the first wave. We tend to overlook the fact that the tremendous success of the missionary movement of which the Acts of the Apostles speaks was matched only by the ferocity of the opposition which it encountered.

The Christians went out preaching the Cross, but it was a real part of the declaration that they also *experienced* the Cross. Peter underlines this fact when he writes: *'To this you were called, because Christ suffered for you, leaving you an example, that you should follow in his steps'* (1 Pet 2:21).

(a) **The reality of suffering.** Some words of S. D. Gordon in his book *The Healing Christ* highlight the truth about suffering in the life of the believer. This is from his chapter, 'God's School of Suffering':

> *Experience is the best teacher and charges the biggest fee. It insists on being paid, day by day, as you go along. You don't pay simply with gold and engraved paper and checks. No, you pay with blood and sweat. You pay with your own life given slowly, sometimes painfully, under tense pressure.*

No man or woman has ever achieved anything for God without knowing the truth of these words. The trouble is that we only see the outside of people's lives. We see the fruit of their ministry, we see the effectiveness, we see their success, but we rarely see their suffering. Suffering is rarely seen like that. It is done in secret, in the secret of the home or in the secret of the heart. The greatest and most intense suffering is a highly private affair.

I know that the Church started in suffering and much of it was very public. We will experience that as well. Before many days the apostles were put in prison. Before long Stephen was stoned to death and the Church in Jerusalem came under intense pressure. It is clear that many persecutions and physical afflictions befell the early Christians as they spread out with the gospel. And that has been the case ever since. No generation has been without its martyrs somewhere in the world. The blood of the saints is the seed of the Church.

But read Paul and listen to the anguish of his heart at times. Sometimes he is suffering intensely from the pain of misrepresentation or misunderstanding. At other times his spirit is ploughed by the disappointment of a Demas or John Mark who has chosen a different path from himself. It is difficult to know what was hardest for Paul to bear – the physical pain of the beatings and scourgings or the spiritual pain and hurt of wounds caused by malicious gossip or jealousy among the brethren.

Suffering for Christ, in any event, is a fact of life for all those who take their discipleship seriously. The last part of chapter 11 of Hebrews shows us to what extent that fact is sometimes true in the lives of those who are faithful to God: *'Some faced jeers and flogging, while still others were chained and put in prison. They were stoned; they were sawn in two; they were put to death by the sword. They went about in sheepskins and goatskins, destitute, persecuted and ill-treated – the world was not worthy of them'* (Heb 11:36–38).

It will be clear already that suffering is not directly equivalent to sickness or illness. I have no doubt that illness is sometimes part of suffering, but the two are not co-extensive. Sickness may be part of suffering for a Christian, but that sickness being healed does not mean the suffering is removed, because the suffering may involve elements much wider than the sickness.

(b) The occasions of suffering. *'If you suffer as a Christian, do not be ashamed, but praise God that you bear that name,'* (1 Pet 4:16). Chapter 4 of 1 Peter speaks a great deal about this question of suffering as a Christian. It encourages us to rejoice in our trials because through them we are participating in the *suffering of Christ* (verse 13) and it exhorts those who suffer *according to God's will* (verse 19) to commit themselves to their faithful Creator and continue to do good.

It is clear, therefore, that there is suffering which *is* according to the will of God; it is equally clear that, on occasions, we suffer things that are not God's will. For example, when Paul wrote to the Corinthians he had to remind them that some were suffering sickness which was not according to the will of God. This was because they were playing fast and loose with the truth of the Lord's table and bringing disgrace on the holy things of God and on themselves. The result of this was that some of them were ill and some had even died as a result of their sickness (see 1 Cor 11:27–32).

This leads us to remind ourselves that God will use illness and suffering, if need be, as a means of discipline within our lives. This does not mean that all illness is discipline or due to sin, as we shall see, but it does cause us to acknowledge the right of our heavenly Father to deal with our waywardness in whatever way seems best to Him to achieve His best ends in our lives:

> '*My son, do not make light of the Lord's discipline,*
> *and do not lose heart when he rebukes you,*
> *because the Lord disciplines those he loves,*
> *and he punishes every one he accepts as a son.*'
>
> (Heb 12:5, 6)

There are a number of circumstances and reasons which give rise to the fact of suffering in our experience. The school of suffering has many classrooms and it seems as though we may well need to pass through them all before we can say that we have graduated from this all-important school of life.

Suffering sometimes arises from the *cost and rigours of serving the Lord*. We need to be clear about this. God has promised all that we need to fulfil His will, but there is a cost that needs to be borne to make this service effective. The experience of Paul makes this clear inasmuch as he suffered many hardships and his body often bore the marks of his ministry. It could be argued that Epaphroditus, Timothy and

Trophimus, who are all noted as having suffered illness, were bearing in their bodies the marks of Christ. Maybe, of course, they were like some of us – not as careful as they should have been in the stewardship of their bodies, or maybe they suffered from the common Christian worker's syndrome of having over-taxed themselves to the point of physical and spiritual protest. The need for this balance is, itself, part of the pressure which can give rise to trial in a personal and spiritual sense.

Suffering sometimes arises as a result of *overt persecution and opposition*. One cannot read 2 Corinthians chapter 11 without being moved by the sheer tenacity of the apostle Paul as he battled on against overwhelming odds to take the gospel throughout the world in obedience to Christ. He describes in vivid terms the imprisonments, the floggings, beatings, stonings, shipwrecks, dangers, bandits, exhaustion, hunger, thirst and exposure he faced as well as the inward spiritual pressure from the many churches under his care. Then, to crown it all, he has to endure his 'thorn in the flesh' which he describes as 'a messenger from Satan'. This thorn has been the subject of more debate than almost any other feature of Paul's experience. It is fashionable today to regard it as a person rather than a physical ailment. It is not a discussion worth pursuing at this moment, but for myself, I prefer to stay with the traditional understanding that it was some physical ailment or affliction. When we take a firm position that a servant of God such as Paul could never have been chronically afflicted like this in a physical way, we are on dangerous ground. It is more important, surely, to see that Paul knew how to obtain the victory over this as over every other element of suffering he ever experienced: '*Therefore I will boast all the more gladly about my weaknesses, so that Christ's power may rest on me. That is why, for Christ's sake, I delight in weaknesses, in insults, in hardships, in persecutions, in difficulties. For when I am weak, then I am strong*' (2 Cor 12:9, 10).

Suffering comes as a **test to our faith**. Both James and Peter agree that this is an important feature of our spiritual life: '*Now for a little while you may have had to suffer grief in all kinds of* *trials. These have come so that your faith – of greater worth than gold, which perishes even though refined by fire – may be proved genuine and may result in praise, glory and honour when Jesus Christ is revealed,'* (1 Pet 1:6, 7). It is my experience that this is true, not only in the general sense of the testing of what I believe, but in the particular tests of faith. Whenever I have been called forward into a step of faith I have usually found that somewhere in it there has been a measure of testing. It is through the most trying difficulties that we become most conscious of God, and it is when we are delivered from the greatest trials that our faith is most strengthened and upbuilt.

Suffering is used to **perfect us in service**. Hebrews 2:10 is a scripture which has puzzled many people. It speaks of the life and ministry of the Lord Jesus: *'In bringing many sons to glory, it was fitting that God, for whom and through whom everything exists, should make the author of their salvation perfect through suffering.'* How is it possible, they ask, that the Lord Jesus, who was always sinless and perfect, could be made any more perfect through suffering? Of course, the answer lies in what you think being made perfect involves. There is no question: Jesus did not need to be made more perfect in a moral sense: He was sinless and good in every way. But He did suffer; not only on the Cross, but throughout His life. He suffered the malice and mistrust of men around Him; He suffered the misunderstanding of His own kith and kin. Long before He hung on the tree, inward and personal suffering was no stranger to Him. Through this He became *perfectly equipped* to be the Saviour of men. He entered into their sufferings, He knew their hearts and shared their sorrows, so He was made perfect as the author of salvation.

In the same way we are made perfect. Unlike Jesus, we will never be morally perfect until we get to glory. But *we are perfected* for our work of ministry and service to others. God uses suffering as a way to bring us to that point of moral and spiritual victory where we can stand in the strength of Christ and away from dependence on the things of the flesh: *'Therefore, since Christ suffered in his body, arm yourselves also with the same attitude, because he who has suffered in his body is done with sin. As a result he does not live the rest of his earthly life for evil human desires, but rather for the will of God'* (1 Pet 4:1, 2).

Suffering is a **deep means of ministry to others**. Paul underlines this when he speaks to the Corinthians. It is not the suffering by itself which is effective, but suffering coupled with the comfort and help received from God. When this is felt by other people, they receive the depth and reality which the process of suffering has brought and they also receive the overflow of the comfort which God has given: *'We can comfort those in any trouble with the comfort we ourselves have received from God. For just as the sufferings of Christ flow over into our lives, so also through Christ our comfort overflows'* (2 Cor 1:4, 5).

Suffering without the comfort of God can lead to terrible bitterness of spirit. This is why we need to be careful in our dealings with people. If all we give them is the suffering which we have endured, all they will get will be a spirit full of suffering. But if they perceive in us the process of suffering and the victory of God's comfort and healing, then they will be encouraged in their own situation and built up in their faith.

(c) **The afflictions of Christ.** The full impact of this theme can be felt in some words which Paul uses when he describes his own outlook to the Colossians. He says: *'I fill up in my flesh what is still lacking in regard to Christ's afflictions, for the sake of his body'* (Col 1:24). Is Paul saying that there was something incomplete about the sacrifice of Jesus with regard to the forgiveness of sins? Does it need something still to happen in Paul and perhaps in every other Christian who follows him to atone for sin? I think not. To suggest such a thing would be a direct contradiction of what Paul himself teaches elsewhere and, indeed, to what he teaches in this very letter – namely, that by the death of Christ God has made available full forgiveness from sin and freedom from spiritual bondage for all who believe in Him.

What does Paul mean then? First, we may recall the incident on the Damascus road through which Paul became a Christian. The ascended Christ, who appeared to him then, identifies

Himself to Paul (then Saul) as *'Jesus, whom you are persecuting'* (Acts 9:5). Now it is clear that Paul never persecuted Jesus personally, so what these words signify is that when Paul, as Saul of Tarsus, was persecuting the believers he was, in fact, in them persecuting Jesus. So every time Paul himself now experienced persecution, it was as though Jesus was being persecuted in him.

Second – we can remember how Paul described his own ministry in 2 Corinthians chapter 4, where he said that the treasure of the gospel was held in jars of clay (verse 7). He goes on in that passage to describe the hindrances and constrictions which he experienced day by day. It is almost as though the love of Christ needs to be incarnated into the lives of His servants so that others might have a live object lesson of God's love for them: *'We always carry around in our body the death of Jesus, so that the life of Jesus may also be revealed in our body.'* (2 Cor 4:10).

I remember once hearing a well-known American preacher who told of an incident in his own life. On one occasion another famous preacher was leading some meetings in this man's home town. He had wanted to hear him preach for years, but to his disappointment he found that his diary was full over the period when the preacher would be there. This man asked his son to go in his place to the meeting. Afterwards, the father asked the boy what he thought of the famous preacher. The son thought for a moment and then told his father all that was good about him. Then he stopped and after a time said, 'There was only one thing wrong: he hasn't suffered enough!'

People need not only to see the fruit of our ministry, they need to be able to discern the process of perfection. It is this process of suffering and its effect in our lives that is so valuable for others. It keeps us from pride and it enables them to see how deeply God needs to work in a person's life before fruitfulness of any measure is possible: *'The God of all grace, who called you to his eternal glory in Christ, after you have suffered a little while, will himself restore you and make you strong, firm and steadfast. To him be the power for ever and ever. Amen.'* (1 Pet 5:10).

Chapter 3

Sword of the Spirit

1: The Power of the Word

As the rain and the snow
come down from heaven,
and do not return to it
without watering the earth
and making it bud and flourish,
so that it yields seed for the sower
and bread for the eater,
so is my word that goes out from my mouth:
It will not return to me empty,
but will accomplish what I desire
and achieve the purpose for which I sent it.

(Is 55:10, 11)

The Word of God is the most powerful force in the world. We will see later that it is a vital agent in our own discipleship. God works in our lives with tremendous power to challenge us, cleanse us and heal us through the power of His Word.

This power of God's Word in our lives only reflects what is true on a much wider canvas. Whenever God speaks, things happen. The words of Isaiah demonstrate for us the power of God's prophetic word. He had spoken concerning the life and experience of his people, the nation of Israel. They were in exile because of their disobedience to God, but now God was

99

bringing them back in restoration. He had promised it, and what He had said He would do. His Word never fails!

Throughout the Scriptures we can see the power of God's Word at work. Right from the beginning of time to its end it is through His Word that God works out His purposes in the lives and experience of men.

A: God's Word in creation

Eight times in the first chapter of the Book of Genesis we hear of God speaking. The recurring refrain is 'And God said'. It is followed by creative action, and when that is completed it is sealed with the words, 'and it was so'. The Psalmist makes the same point when he says:

> *By the word of the Lord were the heavens made...*
> *For he spoke and it came to be;*
> *he commanded, and it stood firm.* (Ps 33:6, 9)

This is not a matter of speculation for the writers of Scripture. Neither is it an attempt to describe what precise action is involved in this creation by the Word of God. The Bible is not concerned to present us with scientific niceties but with the fact of divine revelation and power. The writer to the Hebrews further underlines this point when he says: '*By faith we understand that the universe was formed at God's command*' (Heb 11:3). The writer takes us one step further. He identifies this work of creation and its continuance with the Lord Jesus Christ: '*In these last days he has spoken to us by his Son, whom he appointed heir to all things, **and through whom he made the universe. The Son is the radiance of God's glory and the exact representation of his being, sustaining all things by his powerful word***' (Heb 1:2, 3).

True Christian faith does not view God as Creator who brought everything into being and then left it to its own devices. No, faith sees God continually involved in the upholding of all Creation by the power of His Word. This is why we can believe God to continue to do new things, even within the personal details of our daily lives. When God speaks something always happens.

For example, when God, in His grace, heals somebody through faith, He is not breaking any laws of nature. What He is doing rather is being faithful to *His law of nature!* His law of nature is that by which He created the world – namely, by the power of His own Word. When God speaks into a situation to bring healing, salvation or whatever, He is being totally consistent with the laws by which He created everything in the first place.

B: God's Word in new creation

This point is further illustrated when we consider the work of salvation. God's plan of salvation works on the very same principle of the power of His Word. Just as He brought all things into being through His Word, so He brings salvation to those who believe, through His Word. In fact, Jesus is the Word! It is in Him and through Him that the Father has accomplished the great work of salvation. This is how John begins his Gospel: *'In the beginning was the Word, and the Word was with God, and the Word was God. ... He was with God in the beginning...'* (Jn 1:1, 2, 14). When Jesus spoke and acted He spoke and acted in the creative power of God. More than that, of course, He was the Word of God. This means that when we look and listen to Jesus we are seeing and hearing what the Father wants us to know about Himself: *'Anyone who has seen me has seen the Father'* (Jn 14:9).

It is the power of God's Word which creates faith in our hearts to trust in Jesus. Apart from the reality of this Word in our lives we would never turn to God in faith. Paul makes this clear when he writes to the Romans: *'Faith comes from hearing the message, and the message is heard through the word of Christ'* (Rom 10:17). This is the amazing truth. When God spoke in creation He created something out of nothing through the power of His Word. That is the force of what the Old Testament has to say. The very language which it uses tells us that this is what is intended. It was not just that God took something and refashioned it. What He did was to make something completely new out of nothing!

It's the same with our lives. God does something completely new in us through His Word in Jesus. He gives us a new heart and a new life through faith in Christ. The Psalmist recognised this power of God to do something radically new in human experience when he prayed:

> Create in me a pure heart, O God,
> and renew a steadfast spirit within me. (Ps 51:10)

C: God's Word in our lives

The Word of God is the only agent in the whole of Creation that can penetrate right to the very heart of a man. It has power to reach parts that nothing else on earth can reach. Just as God's Word penetrated the chaos and brought forth the order of Creation, so God's Word can search the deepest reaches of my life and speak to the deepest spiritual realities of my experience:

> The word of God is living and active. Sharper than any double-edged sword, it penetrates even to dividing soul and spirit, joints and marrow; it judges the thoughts and attitudes of the heart. Nothing in all creation is hidden from God's sight. Everything is uncovered and laid bare before the eyes of him to whom we must give account.
> (Heb 4:12, 13)

The sheer power of this Word is illustrated in this verse very clearly. Nothing else can divide a man's soul and his spirit. Until the Word of God penetrates our lives, our spirit is hidden and submerged under the power of the soul. Man without the Word of God lives a bipartite existence – that is, he lives to feed his body and satisfy the desires of his soul. His life is at the level of the physical and emotional, but he is not alive to God at the level of his spirit. God's Word is a quickening Word which comes in with power. It searches the heart. It judges the attitudes and thoughts, but above all it divides soul and spirit.

Until we heard the Word of God within our own hearts we

were, as Paul describes in Ephesians, dead in our transgressions and sins. It was God's voice that quickened us to faith and our need of Christ and it was God's Word that brought faith to life in us so that we follow Him.

D: Symbols of the Word

Throughout the Scriptures there are a number of very significant metaphors used to describe the power of God's Word. These pictures describe for us the different actions of the Word of God within our own experience. For example, the Word of God is described as:

Light – '*Your word is a lamp to my feet and light for my path*' (Ps 119:105). God's Word brings illumination and revelation. We know that Satan's business is to keep us, and all men, in the dark as far as God's truth is concerned. But God's Word has the power of truth. It is a Word of revelation and illumination. It reveals to us the truth about Jesus. This is the truth which Jesus Himself said would set men free (see Jn 8:32). It is a Word that brings guidance and direction into our lives: '*Whoever follows me*,' said Jesus, '*will never walk in darkness, but will have the light of life*' (Jn 8:12).

Water – Water brings cleansing. And this is exactly the power of the Word of God in our experience. If we live open to the Word and allow it to challenge us, we will be changed through its power, into the holy people that God wants us to be: '*Christ loved the church and gave himself up for her to make her holy, cleansing her by the washing with water through the word*' (Eph 5:26).

Seed – When Jesus told the Parable of the Sower He used this analogy of the Word of God. The seed was the Word (Lk 8:11) and its purpose was to bring growth and fruitfulness into the lives of those who heard and received it. This Word found many different responses in the hearts of those to whom it came, but in the lives of those who took it to themselves, it was a powerful force for good: '*The seed on good soil stands for those with a noble and good heart, who hear the word, retain it, and by persevering produce a crop*' (Lk 8:15).

Fire and hammer – These two powerful images of the Word of God come from the experience of Jeremiah the prophet. The Word he bore from God was a very strong Word. It needed to be because it was addressed to a people who were hard of heart and who were living in disobedience to God. So the Word of God came to them like a fire and a hammer: *"Is not my word like fire,' declares the Lord, "and like a hammer that breaks a rock in pieces?"'* (Jer 23:29). When He needs to, this is exactly how God speaks to us. He does not come all the time like a small still voice; sometimes, because of our wilful disobedience or hardness of hearts, He comes like a hammer and fire. The fire purges and the hammer breaks. I certainly know for myself that this is precisely what needs to happen to me. I need to be broken and cleansed, broken and cleansed!

Honey – But the Father doesn't leave us broken. He breaks us for our healing. Two or three times in the Psalms we are presented with a beautiful picture of the Word of God. It is a picture of honey:

> *They are sweeter than honey,*
> *than honey from the comb.* (Ps 19:10)

Honey is for healing. It is a soothing balm which brings sweetness into bitterness and healing into pain. The Word of God is health to us, healing to our spirits and to our lives. The man who lives in the strength and power of God's Word will find wholesomeness of spirit and the sweetness of God's joy within his life:

> *How sweet are your words to my taste,*
> *sweeter than honey to my mouth.* (Ps 119:103)

From all this we can see the power of the Word of God. God's Word has intrinsic power – that is, it carries its power within itself. This is because it is the voice of God. It is like the breath of God. When it comes forth it is from the very heart of God Himself, so it carries the power of God and the purpose of God.

2: In Many and Various Ways

Now we need to be clear about what we mean when we speak about the Word of God. It is quite clear that God has spoken and God does speak to us in many ways. Many Christian believers become concerned about any talk of the Word of God apart from the revelation of Scripture. This is a right and proper concern because there can be no doubt that many have substituted the clarity and centrality of the Scriptures with a subjective approach to hearing God's Word by other means, such as prophecy, dreams, visions and so on, almost to the extent of ignoring the Bible.

On the other hand, it is clear from within the Scriptures themselves that God chooses many different ways in which to communicate His Word, and what we need to be clear about is the relationship between the two.

What is the relationship between the Word of God and the Scriptures?

Before we proceed, let's take a look at some of the ways in which God has spoken. This will help us to understand the question and give us, I believe, some direction towards the answer.

A: His Word in creation

We have already noticed that it was by His Word that God brought the universe into being. This created order itself manifests something of the nature of God. That which has been created by the Word of God becomes, in some measure, a channel of the Word of God. The Psalmist puts it like this:

> *The heavens declare the glory of God;*
> * the skies proclaim the work of his hands.*
> *Day after day they pour forth speech;*
> * night after night they display knowledge.*
> *There is no speech or language*
> * where their voice is not heard.*
> *Their voice goes out into all the earth,*
> * their words to the ends of the world.*   (Ps 19:1–4)

Paul appeals to this very fact when he argues in Romans chapter 1 that mankind is without excuse before the justice of God: *'For since the creation of the world God's invisible qualities – His eternal power and divine nature – have been clearly seen, being understood from what has been made, so that men are without excuse'* (Rom 1:20).

B: His Word through prophecy

Throughout the centuries God spoke to His people time and again through the channel of the prophet. Sometimes this Word was addressed to individuals, at other times to a whole nation. Sometimes it was addressed to the people of God in particular, at other times to people outside the Covenant. But in all cases the prophetic Word was direct and challenging and called for responsive action on the part of those who heard it. There is no doubt that the prophet spoke as the oracle of God. The most common refrain with regard to the prophetic word is, 'Thus says the Lord', or 'The word of the Lord came to…' These phrases indicate how clearly the link between the words of the prophet and the Word of God was seen to be. Peter speaks of this when he says: *'Above all, you must understand that no prophecy of Scripture came about by the prophet's own interpretation. For prophecy never had its origin in the will of man, but men spoke from God as they were carried along by the Holy Spirit'* (2 Pet 1:20, 21).

C: His Word in Jesus

We have already been reminded that Jesus was *the* Word: *'The Word became flesh and made his dwelling among us'* (Jn 1:14). Never had there been, and never will there be, a clearer Word from God's own heart than that which has been declared in Jesus. This is God's definitive Word – not only a Word about us or the world or circumstances, but about Himself; not only a Word of direction, warning, chastisement, encouragement or even partial revelation; in His Son God has declared all that He wants to say to us. It is *the* Word of divine revelation. *'In the past God spoke to our forefathers through the prophets at many times and in various ways, but in these last days he has spoken to us by his Son'* (Heb 1:1, 2).

D: His Word through Preaching

God will never be done with the preaching of His Word. This has nothing to do with the taste of the age in which we live. Our responsibility is to find any means which are proper to proclaim the Word which God has given us in Jesus and which He gives us through the Holy Spirit. The reason for this is that God has ordained that it is through the proclamation of His Word that men and women will be saved. A discussion group can never take the place of such declaration. God chose *'through the foolishness of what was preached to save those who believe'* (1 Cor 1:21).

Paul again makes this point when he writes to the Romans: *'How can they hear without someone preaching to them? And how can they preach unless they are sent? As it is written, "How beautiful are the feet of those who bring good news!"'* (Rom 10:14, 15).

E: His Word through the Holy Spirit

Of course, every means by which God speaks is through the Holy Spirit. But I am using this term to describe the sort of direct means of communication of which we find examples time and again in both the Old and New Testaments. There are too many examples to list, but one thinks of the experience of such men as Moses (see Acts 7:30–34) or Gideon (see Judges 6:1ff), Samuel (see 1 Sam 3:11–14) and so on.

The Acts of the Apostles is full of instances where God speaks directly to His servants through audible words, dreams, prophecy, signs and wonders and the like. We need only think of the experience of Saul of Tarsus on the road to Damascus (Acts 9:4–6), of Philip and the Ethiopian eunuch (Acts 8:26, 29), of Peter and his vision of the sheet filled with animals (Acts 10:9ff), or of God's direct words of encouragement to Paul which caused him to continue his ministry at Corinth for a year and a half (Acts 18:9, 10). These instances in Acts reflect the outpouring of the Holy Spirit at Pentecost. Although the Holy Spirit had acted in the lives and ministry of significant individuals before this, there had never been such a universal outpouring of the Spirit of God.

Similar experiences of the work of the Holy Spirit can be recounted today, as believers and groups of believers receive the Word of God by means of these various gifts of the Holy Spirit.

F: His Word in Scripture

I believe all Scripture to be the Word of God. It is not sufficient to say, as some modern confessions of faith say, that we believe in the Word of God as *contained* in Scripture. On the surface that may seem a reasonable statement of belief, but in fact it is a compromise. Phrases like this imply that I may, if I am so minded, decide for myself exactly *which* words within the Scriptures are acceptable as God's Word. The Scriptures are then at the mercy of my subjective judgement and I am free to leave out of my reckoning anything in the Bible that I judge not to be the Word of God. I believe that this liberal approach to the Bible has led to a failure of confidence in the Scriptures and, in practice, to a complete ignorance of the Bible on the part of many churchgoers.

The Scriptures speak with many moods and voices and testify to all the other means of God speaking which we have seen. They play a very distinctive part in the life and development of the Christian believer, for *'All Scripture is God-breathed and is useful for teaching, rebuking, correcting and training in righteousness, so that the man of God amy be thoroughly equipped for every good work'* (2 Tim 3:16, 17). The Scriptures are also God's record of how and what He has already spoken, to stimulate us in faith and encourage us in hope: *'For everything that was written in the past was written to teach us, so that through endurance and the encouragement of the Scriptures we might have hope'* (Rom 15:4).

It is important for us to see the link between the fact that the Holy Spirit *has* spoken in Scripture and the fact that he *still needs to speak* to us through Scripture. It is this *twofold* work of the Spirit of God which guarantees that what God has given will be for us, today, the Word of God. It is not by a process of critical analysis that we will decide this, but by an openness to the work of the Holy Spirit. In the words of the old hymn-writer William Cowper:

> *The Spirit breaths upon the Word,*
> *And brings new truths to light.*
> *Precepts and promises afford*
> *A sanctifying sight.*

G: The Word of God and Scripture

How then are we to understand this relationship between the Word of God and Scripture? It is quite clear that the idea of the Word of God is greater than (that is, is more extensive than) Scripture. God speaks in ways other than through the Scriptures and yet the Scriptures are, in totality, the Word of God.

Let me try and illustrate it in this way. Suppose we draw a circle and call that the Word of God. This circle represents the Word of God as it comes to us in many and different forms. God speaks many words to us by means of dreams, visions, circumstances, events, impressions, words and messages which are outside the realm of the Scriptures. Take, for example, the experience of a person before they become a Christian. In such an instance God has often spoken to people by some means or another to awaken them to Himself and their need of Him. The purpose of God speaking in this way is to bring the person eventually to hear His fuller word for them in Jesus.

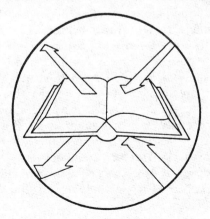

We can recognise that God speaks in many ways, represented by this circle, but all these ways lead us to the Scriptures. Our openness to the Word of God through the Scriptures makes us even more aware of the fact that God can and does speak in other direct ways – for example, by the operation of the gifts of the Holy Spirit. As we open ourselves up to this possibility of hearing God in every situation in our lives, so we begin to experience more and more the variety of how God speaks to us. The effect of this is to take us once more back to Scripture. The reason for this is that there is a uniqueness about God's Word in Scripture which sets it apart from other words. This is not only determined by the *content* of the Scriptures, which of course focuses in on Jesus, but is determined by the *nature* of the Word. It has a permanency about it which words through other means might not or do not have. There is a *given-ness* about the Scripture which makes it stand as a standard and guide in the centre, by which all other words can be judged.

We need to be clear about this fact: no word of message received by any means other than Scripture can add to or detract from the revelation which God has deposited in the Bible. A word of prophecy, for example, can never add to God's revelation in Scripture of Himself or His purpose. It may bring an immediate relevance to the Scripture or it may bring direct guidance as to how we might fulfil Scripture, but it will not be foundational for doctrine or belief in the way Scripture is foundational. This, I believe, is one of the great dangers of our own day. In some quarters we have moved away from the position of recognising prophecy and the like as spiritual helps in direction and action and have received these words as the foundation of our belief and teaching. So in certain areas it becomes enough that we feel God has told us so, or that our experience has taught us so. But we need to recognise that our hearing and our experience are exceedingly susceptible to the inroads of Satan, the father of lies. The question needs always to be asked as to whether what I am doing and what I am believing finds any credible witness from the Word of God in Scripture.

H: The function of the Scriptures

In the light of all this we can see what an important part the Scriptures play in our life of discipleship in the following areas:

(i) **Focus:** The Bible brings the central Word that God has for all our lives into sharp relief. As we read the Scriptures we can see that they are oriented in two main directions. A great section of the Bible – namely the Old Testament – spends its time looking forward to something that has not yet been fulfilled. The New Testament, on the other hand, speaks in the light of something that has been fulfilled. This, of course, is God's revelation of Himself in Jesus, who is Himself described as the Word (see John chapter 1). In His controversy with some who opposed Him, Jesus Himself drew attention to the fact of this focus of the Scriptures: '*You diligently study the Scriptures because you think that by them you possess eternal life. These are the Scriptures that testify about me*' (Jn 5:39).

(ii) **Character:** The Scriptures reveal to us in an unfolding way something of the character of the God who speaks. Although human authors clearly had a hand in the writing of Scriptures, it is not the work of human authors that one is left with after reading them. As the Holy Spirit speaks dynamically through the Scriptures, what we gain is an impression of *the* Author. Through the record of His dealing with men in all sorts of situations we begin to have an insight into the heart of God. The Scriptures also provide us with the opportunity to share other men's responses to God. Some of the most profound parts of Scripture have to do with this. They reveal to us the inner feelings of men and women as they came to realise for themselves *who* this God was that was communicating with them. All these things provide a powerful incentive for us to go on to explore God for ourselves through our prayer, worship and study of His Word.

(iii) **Definition:** Through the unfolding of Biblical revelation we are given examples, teachings, fundamental doctrines and insights which bring definition to the Word so that we can apply it to our daily lives. It is sometimes pointed out that we cannot expect the Bible to answer every problem or address every situation of our contemporary experience because of the time lapse and the tremendous changes there have been with the development of our scientific society. I would make two general responses to such an observation.

Firstly – *whilst* it is true that the Bible does not tackle every practical situation of our lives, the Scriptures, and for a Christian believer, the New Testament in particular, lay down such practical *principles* for living that these can be applied in almost any situation or context.

Secondly – if we read it more carefully and took it more seriously within our lives, we would be amazed at how relevant the Bible is to daily life. More and more I am surprised at the implications of something I read, when I take time to meditate on the Word and let the Holy Spirit open me up to the meaning of it, in depth, for my life today.

(iv) Clarity: One thing we can be sure of is that when we handle the Scriptures we are, in fact, handling the Word of God. The Scriptures are not subject to the whims and fancies of our moods. There is an objectivity about the Word of God through the Scriptures that our personal experience may lack.

(v) Discernment: When Paul spoke to Timothy he described the Scriptures as being able to make a person wise to salvation. The Scriptures can make us wise to many things. Indeed, they can become a *source of wisdom* for us, not just because they teach us principles of wisdom but because *they are wisdom!* Through the work of the Holy Spirit's inspiration, the Scriptures have dynamic power. They become for us, in the power of the Spirit, what they say.

We need this wisdom when it comes to discerning all the other words we receive from God. We will become wise in discernment if we live in the Scriptures, which are wisdom! This is why it is very difficult to provide a set of rules for the discernment of spiritual gifts, because such discernment is given to those who live by the gates of wisdom.

3: Living in the Word

> *Do not merely listen to the word, and so deceive your-*
> *selves. Do what it says. Anyone who listens to the word*
> *but does not do what it says is like a man who looks at his*
> *face in a mirror and, after looking at himself, goes away*
> *and immediately forgets what he looks like. But the man*
> *who looks intently into the perfect law that gives freedom,*
> *and continues to do this, not forgetting what he has heard,*
> *but doing it – he will be blessed in what he does.*
>
> (James 1:22–25)

Obedience to the Word of God is the key to growth and fruitfulness. God speaks to us so that we might respond to what He says and walk in His perfect will. In 1966 my wife and I went to the Keswick Convention which is held each year in Cumbria. We were taken by two other friends on holiday. But on the Friday night of that week our lives were completely changed. I was in business at the time, but over a number of years previously had been feeling very strongly that God was calling me to full-time ministry. However, although He had spoken in a number of distinct ways, I had not obeyed the Word. That night at Keswick a well-known preacher, George Duncan, was speaking. He took as his text James 4:17 – '*Whoever knows what is right to do and fails to do it, for him it is sin*' (RSV). The effect of that Scripture on us was dramatic. We knew that we had been living with God's Word in our lives for some time. Now we had to obey that Word and put in into practice.

Hearing God's Word and doing it, is the most important principle in the life of faith. God speaks so that we might obey, and when we follow His Word we find great reward. This Scripture from James which I have quoted, contains some important basic principles for us to follow if we want to hear and obey the Word of God in our lives. In verse 23 James uses the analogy of a mirror. If we hear the Word but don't do it, we are like people who look into a mirror and immediately go away and forget what we have seen. In verse 25 he extends his analogy. The Word of God, which James beautifully describes as 'the perfect law that gives freedom', becomes the mirror. But it is not our own reflection that we are seeing, it is the reflection of God's Word, which will transform us in the power of the Holy Spirit.

Notice the *three basic principles* which are presented to us in this Scripture. They are contained within three simple phrases which occur in the text:

A: 'Looks intently'

This phrase speaks of our attitude towards the Word which God has spoken to us, indicating that the person is taking this Word very seriously and paying great attention to exactly what he has received.

The phrase speaks of: An attitude of determination. It is a matter of our will whether we are going to respond to the Word of God or not. Indeed, if we are going to hear God's Word for our lives in the first place, then space needs to be made within the schedule of our lives to hear Him. Satan wants nothing more than for us to imagine that we don't have time to listen to our Father. But God does want to speak to every one of us. We need to show that sort of will and purpose which is determined to hear God's Word before anything else.

An attitude of faith. The people who hear most from God are those who expect to hear from God. If we expect nothing in our Christian lives we will be in the happy position of having our ambitions totally fulfilled, because we will get nothing; but we will be in the unhappy position of becoming spiritually bankrupt and dry.

An attitude of sincerity. This means that we are going to take seriously what we hear and put it into practice within our experience. Obedience is the key to fruitfulness for the man or woman of the Spirit.

There are two single principles we need to observe if we are to 'look intently' into the Word of God.

(a) **Make room for God to speak.** I don't mean that we should be taking time only for Bible reading, but reading the Scriptures is of vital importance if we are to grow in our knowledge of the truth and our appreciation of God. In fact, we should take more time to be open to the Scriptures. I commend to you an important book on the subject of how to wait with the Scriptures and hear the Word of God for your own life. It is called *The Practice of Biblical Meditation* by Campbell McAlpine. I know that you will find this book, written by a man who has put every part of his own teaching into practice, a great help in your approach to this subject of hearing and obeying the Word of God.

Sadly, many Christians imagine that once they have read their daily portion along with their study notes they have fulfilled the conditions to hearing God. Of course the Lord is gracious and He often speaks to believers in this way, but imagine how much more clearly we would hear Him if we took a little more time and prepared our hearts to listen for His voice.

Making room for God involves a *preparation of spirit*. I find quietness and praise the two effective helps in this area. I have so many demands on my life that I just need to take a breathing space with the Lord to remind my spirit that it doesn't need to be hassled and in bondage to them. Praise drives back the powers of the flesh and Satan to leave me in a free zone within my spirit to hear the Word of God.

Making room for God involves a *preparation of mind*. Personally, I like to have 'something' on my mind. I find that I need a little stimulation or direction. I am not good at coming to things blank. So I usually have something I am thinking and praying about. Perhaps a theme from Scripture or a particular passage. For those who have no discipline, and find it hard to be systematic in their listening to the Scripture, perhaps some guide would be useful. There are now several publications of The Bible which divide the Scriptures up for a year's reading. Each day includes a portion of New Testament Scripture. You may find this too much, but at least you could take guidance from one part and use it as a guide-line for your mind.

Making time involves a *preparation of life*. At a very basic level this means organising yourself so that there is time. I hear many people saying that they have no time. Many people feel overstretched as it is, what with the demands of work or of children. I have every sympathy for how they feel because I often feel over the limit with the demands of my own life. But isn't this the opportunity to put one promise of God's Word into immediate effect to see if it works?

> *They that wait upon the Lord shall renew their strength;*
> *they shall mount up with wings as eagles;*
> *they shall run and not be weary;*
> *and they shall walk and not faint.* (Is 40:31 NKJ)

I find that it works! Many times I have been tempted to leave out a time of waiting on the Lord because of the kind of pressures I have spoken about. But on every occasion, when I have turned to the Lord I have found that that time has fed in more strength and help than I could every have imagined. It has become the foundation and bulwark of life.

(b) **Take what God says seriously.** As we continue to wait on the Lord, we will gain experience at discerning what we hear. It takes time to sort out the trivia from what is really important, but as we learn to meditate on the Scriptures our minds become more disciplined and we can discern much more clearly what comes from the Spirit of God and what finds its source in our own ideas or feelings. The following points are important:

First, you may find it helpful to take notes of what you are hearing from God. This means that you won't forget so easily what He says, and it enables further meditation. It also helps you to expand on a thought or word the next day or later, when the Lord has more to say to you on the subject.

Second, it is important to hold precious what God says to you. Too many of us receive some word from God and lose the power and good of it by too readily spreading it around amongst other people to whom it will not mean the same thing. It is important that we let the Word of God settle into our own lives before we share it with others – unless, of course it is something pertinent to another person.

Third, it is important to test every word we hear. I find that the best way to do this is to live with the word before the throne of God. This means that through a continued exercise of meditating on Scripture and praying in the Spirit, first impressions will be confirmed, altered or evaporated.

Fourth, explore the consequences of this word for your own life. I often think that a word from God acts like a stone which is thrown into a pond. It makes a splash at first, but the really interesting thing is to watch where the ripples go.

This is one of the ways I find direction. I receive a word from the Lord about a specific issue and by meditating and considering the outcome of that word as I apply it in my mind and to my life, I can see what its implications are. It often becomes clear by this process what the steps are that I need to take, to see the fulfilment of this word in my life. This has helped me through many decisions at a practical and spiritual level.

B: 'Continues to do it'

As I have already said, obedience is the secret of growth. We need to do the Word for it to become effective within our lives. An undone word is an unfulfilled word. How do we continue to do the word?

(a) **By confessing the Word.** God gives us His Word as a real alternative to living under the impulse of our feelings or under the negative domination of circumstances or under the power of our flesh or Satan. Every day that we live we are subjected to many words of different kinds. Our emotions speak volumes to us, mostly full of fear or self-pity. Circumstances and difficulties speak to us and threaten to overwhelm us with their sound. Temptation and desire shout at us and try to divert us from the paths of goodness and wholesomeness. Other people speak into our lives and often it is destructive and damaging. What we need is another word, a word that we can echo, a word that will speak against all these negative and destructive forces of unbelief. This word is the Word of God. As we have already seen, it is full of power and goodness. In our life of faith we are continually faced with a choice of whether to confess these negative thoughts, emotions, circumstances and so on, or whether to take the Word that God has given us and make that our confession of faith. This is where I believe the Scriptures are so important. They are packed full of words of faith. They present us with a completely different picture of ourselves in Christ Jesus from the image our feelings about ourselves might create. They bring us the promise of help and strength through the power of the Holy Spirit and, above all, they give us the words with which to clothe our own confession. Even when we find it hard to express faith, we can take the words of Scripture and make them our confession.

The result of confessing the Word can be very powerful for our lives. It leads to a renewal of our mind, a cleansing of our heart and a disciplining of our tongue, and it brings faith to the forefront of our experience.

(b) By studying the Word. *'Do your best to present yourself to God as one approved, a workman who does not need to be ashamed and who correctly handles the word of truth'* (2 Tim 2:15). A great deal of ignorance at the spiritual level is caused by ignorance of Scripture. Anyone who seriously wants to hear and understand God speaking into their lives needs to start at the level of Scripture. Scripture is our clearest point of revelation. It comes to us at many different levels, through the testimony and example of characters in the Bible and through the direct teaching of the Scriptures to our own heart. It presents us with an entrance into the heart of God. Through His dealings with men in the past we gain an insight into His character and through His revelation in Jesus we come to know the depth of His mercy and love.

When it comes to witnessing to our faith there is no short cut to coming to know the Scriptures, so that we might be able *'to give the reason for the hope that you have'* (see 1 Pet 3:15). In this day of reading of multitudes of books and listening to tapes, there is still no substitute for getting acquainted with the Scriptures.

(c) By applying the Word. Many Christians today are

looking for direct and personal revelation from God on many of the problems in their lives when in fact they need to recognise that a great deal of the direction they require has already been given within the Scriptures. The application of these revealed truths to their lives would make a *dynamic* difference to how they live!

But even the words that are given to us through other means need application. Learning to apply the truths of God leads to the ability to hear clearly from God with discernment, because as we apply the Word of God to our lives we soon learn what is real and what is not.

Surely God's Word would have tremendous power in our lives if we approached it with the intention of bringing it right to the level of our own experience and applying what it said.

(d) By sharing the Word. We cannot share the Word of God with other people without first taking it seriously ourselves. I know that an important element in my own life is the fact that every day I am called to declare the Word of God for other people. This rebounds into my own heart and life and causes me first to receive this Word for myself. There are many words from God that we could share with each other: words of testimony, words of promise, words of encouragement, words of comfort, words of warning, words of love and fellowship. The list is endless.

This is a real part of *doing* the Word. And the fact is that if we *do* the Word for other people, the Word will be *done* in us.

But God wants us to grow in His Word. In fact, Jesus Himself laid it down as a basic principle of discipleship: *'If you continue in my word, you are truly my disciples'* (Jn 8:31, RSV).

C: 'Be Blessed'

Tremendous blessing always results from living in the Word of God. The Psalmist found this to be the case:

> *Blessed is the man (whose)*
> *delight is in the law of the Lord,*
>   *and on his law he meditates day and night.*

He is like a tree planted by streams of water,
*   which yields its fruit in season*
*   and whose leaf does not wither.*
Whatever he does prospers.   (Ps 1:2–3)

The reason for this is that as we share in God's Word we begin to share in everything that the Word is in itself. For example, as we receive and obey the Word of God we will begin to live within the purposes of God, because this is what the Word of God achieves. According to Isaiah 55:10, 11, it never returns to Him empty, but achieves what He desires! So God's Word in us will achieve God's purposes for us, if we obey it and live by it.

In the same way we will share in the power of God. If this Word is becoming effective through me, then I will share in the power of that Word. Also, we will participate in the promise of the Word of God. God's Word is full of hope, and brings us salvation. It is full of promise. If that Word becomes the foundation of our life we will begin to live by faith and not in sin. This is the purpose of the mirror of which James speaks. Instead of reflecting ourselves with all our weaknesses and sin, as we look intently into the perfect law we gain the freedom which that law brings. Hallelujah!

4: Hearing the Word of God

Since the very beginning of my Christian life I have believed that God is able to speak into a person's heart and life. At certain times this had been more clear to me than at others, depending on how closely I am walking in obedience to the Word of God in the Scriptures. If my life is full of rubbish and other voices are having a hearing in my inner man, then I am unlikely to be able to hear the voice of God with the same clarity. Mind you, I have met people whose lives were far away from God when they first heard Him speaking to them. That is what led to their conversion and change of life.

But here I am speaking more about the daily walk of the believer. It is the Father's purpose that we should be open to hear His voice. He has many things to say to us and the more we listen, the more detailed will be what we hear. This is how it works. At first we hear God speaking to us about major issues. He speaks to us for salvation. No man or woman has been saved yet without hearing the Word of God. It was that Word that brought faith to them and quickened their conscience towards Christ. Then we may hear the voice of God in the area of big decisions. Usually this is because we know that we cannot face these by ourselves and so we make particular room to listen for God's direction at these times. The means by which we hear God speaking to us vary immensely. Some people take time to recognise that the hunches of their spirit are the work of God. Nevertheless, I believe that the safest and most productive place to hear God is through the testimony of the Scriptures. This is why we need to take more time to reflect on what we are reading and pay attention to the passages of Scripture to which we are led at special times of waiting on God.

But the more we practice listening for God in our daily lives, the more able we will become in discerning His voice. As we take time to wait before the Father, not only do we get to know more about Him, but we get to know more about ourselves. We get to read the influences on our spirit. We get to know how we react or respond inwardly when we are hearing God as opposed to hearing anything or anyone else.

This inward scanning of our hearts and minds is all-important to our hearing the Father, because gradually we build up an understanding of what goes on inside us when we are hearing God. This is why it is very difficult for one person to describe to another precisely why they know it is the Lord speaking to them. They know for themselves. They have come to recognise the signs. There are levers within their hearts and minds which are tripped and which are the witness of this Word within their hearts.

It is just the same with Scripture. We may read a particular passage or verse many times before it becomes the Word of God for us in a special way. This is not a failure on the part of Scripture, which always has tremendous potential power. No, it is that our hearts and minds have been worked on by the Holy Spirit. He has spoken this particular Word for this particular situation, and it has become vital and real to us as the Word of God for the moment.

The fact is that the more we give room to the voice of the Father within our experience, the more likely we are to recognise His voice. And the more we seek Him for every step of our life, the more we will begin to discern His hand even in the minute and seemingly less important steps we have to take. It is a great experience to know that God will speak into your heart and mind through every situation if you let Him, so that life becomes a kind of dual intercourse. We operate on the outside, speaking with people and entering into situations whilst at the same time being open in another dimension to the voice of the Father. It is almost like the front and the back of a conversation. At the front I am interacting with people, while up at the back of my mind I am looking upward to hear and see what the Lord wants to say. It is very difficult to put into words, and to those who have never experimented in this area of listening to God it may seem strange or even dangerous. But I can recall many instances when I have depended utterly on the fact that the Father would speak to me. Many times I have been directed to make very important decisions or to speak in a particular way or to handle a situation in a certain way by the nudgings of the Holy Spirit within my mind and heart. The trouble for some people, I believe, is that they are looking for something that isn't there. They imagine that when we speak about hearing the voice of God that we must always have a special vision or an actual voice speaking within us, which is clear and unmistakable. It is rarely like this. God's voice within us comes through channels that are mostly already built into our system, so to speak. For example, the Father will speak through our mind and the processes of our thought. He will at other times use the impulses of our heart. He will direct us by feelings of dis-ease or deep peace. At other times He will use the hunches we get within our spirit. Of course, there are moments when He breaks through in a very clear, supernatural way because the situation demands it or because it is something He does not want us to miss. But normally the Father is expecting us to cooperate in this communication of His Word. It is a two-way exercise.

This is why I stress the need to start with your own life. Take the Scriptures and meditate on them. Let them speak to you. Let them cleanse your life. Submit every part of your heart and life to God. Let Him deal with you and remove those things from within your life which will prevent you from living in full fellowship with Him. Obey the Word you read and hear, because this obedience is the secret of cooperating with the Father. If we don't cooperate with Him at the level of getting ourselves sorted out, we will not be able to cooperate with Him at any other level of revelation.

Start here. Listen to the Word as the Holy Spirit illuminates Scripture for you. Apply it and let it speak within your life. Learn to know yourself before the Lord in this way. Then start to open your whole life out to Him. Learn not to go out without committing your action to Him. Develop a Father-consciousness in all your actions. *Expect* to hear from God about everything you are involved in. Don't act as though God was just interested in the 'spiritual' things. Open your heart and mind in the way I have described in every situation of your life. You will begin to recognise the leading of God in many, many situations and your life will be open to His leading and guiding.

A: Personal illustrations

Let me show you from some of the experiences of my own life
how vital it is that we hear the Word of God today. I am sure
that God speaks to different people in an innumerable variety
of ways. But these will serve to show that it is the Father's
purpose to speak into our lives and His will that we should
obey what we hear.

(a) **The preaching of the Word.** I became a Christian
through hearing the Word of God being preached. I cannot
recall the content of the message and, in fact, I didn't actually
take it all in. I was only twelve years of age and some of the
preacher's language and style went completely over my head.
But that night, August 20th 1954, the Holy Spirit did something new in me. I remember being impressed by the obvious
commitment and sincerity of the man. But more than that, I
clearly remember being overcome by a real sense of needing
God.

When it came to the end and the preacher asked those who
would like to find Christ to stay behind, I found myself
staying in the seat where I was. What I do remember ever so
clearly is the Scripture he used to lead me to Christ. That was
the Holy Spirit bringing me a very special and personal word
from God. It was as though that Scripture was emblazoned on
my mind and heart, and that night I obeyed it. The Scripture
was Romans 10:9: *'That if you confess with your mouth,
"Jesus is Lord", and believe in your heart that God raised him
from the dead, you will be saved.'* I did just that! The preacher
led me through that confession as I put my own name into
that Scripture. The Holy Spirit made that word come alive all
right. I received such an assurance that I had become a son of
God. I have never doubted that experience, although at times
I have failed to live true to it. But for me it was, and is, very
real. I was saved and I knew it!

There is a certainty and assurance when we receive the
Word of God for ourselves. It gives us a deep and real certainty of spirit. This is what we need if we are to go on and
follow Jesus in the path of full discipleship.

(b) **The teaching of Scripture.** One of the things I learned very early in my Christian life was to pay attention to what the Scriptures have to say for daily living. If we live in the Scriptures the Holy Spirit will show us very clearly what we need for our lives. In fact, ninety-five percent of all the direction we will ever need had already been laid down in the Scriptures. I am finding it more and more fruitful to come to the Bible with a spirit of expectation, knowing that it is a treasury of vital truth which the Holy Spirit will quicken to my heart so that I can apply it with His help, to my life.

This is what led me to be baptised as an adult believer. I read the words of Romans 6:1–4 and it suddenly became clear to me what the real significance of baptism was. No person taught me. In fact, it happened one day at school. The penny dropped and I announced to my best friend that I was going to be baptised. Amazingly he had been reading the very same passage and a few weeks later we had the great joy of being baptised together.

(c) A vision in the Holy Spirit. In the latter part of 1978 my wife Hilda and myself were waiting on God to hear His direction for an important new phase of our lives. We were leaving our pastorate and following what we believed to be the direction of God. We felt that He had told us to move to London and begin a new ministry, travelling and teaching and preaching the Word wherever He would send us.

The trouble was, we had absolutely no connections in London except some friends who themselves were engaged in this kind of ministry. We decided to go and visit them and, at the same time, visit our denominational headquarters to speak with the officials of our own Church. During this period we stayed for two nights in the home of a Christian friend in Wimbledon. The two days proved absolutely fruitless and, at the end of the second day, we returned to our friend's home exhausted and a bit disappointed.

I just felt like relaxing and taking it easy before we returned north the next morning. To my horror, however, when we got to the house we discovered that there was a prayer and praise meeting in progress. We went in and sat down in an obscure seat so that we would not get too involved in the proceedings.

Suddenly, in the middle of the prayer and praise meeting a woman rose to her feet and gave a word from the Lord. It was in the form of two pictures and, according to her, it was addressed to someone who was seeking God's will for their life at that moment. The first picture was of a large country house. This lady saw herself standing on the veranda looking out over the gardens. The gardens were very beautiful and laid out very neatly with paths and lawns and flower beds. At the end of these gardens was a copse of trees and in the trees was a building. But when she looked closely at the building she saw that is was a folly. It was only there for decoration and was of no practical use.

The second picture was quite different. This time she had an impression of standing in the middle of a very dense wood. Around her on every side were large trees with branches which went up high and inter-locked at the top. Underneath was thick undergrowth. She was standing in a clearing in the middle of this wood but she could see no way out. There seemed to be no path through the trees. However, she had a terrific sensation of peace and warmth, because the sun was shining down through the top branches right to where she was.

She gave her interpretation of these pictures. The person or persons for whom they were meant, she felt, were faced with an important decision. But the pictures were a warning not to take the well-ordered path, because the end of that would be folly. Instead, they had to trust God's love and presence, because He would open a path through the tangle and they would know the warmth and peace of His love.

Hilda and I looked at each other in amazement. We knew at that moment that we had received what we had come to London to hear, but it was from the lips of a person who, at that moment, was completely unknown to us and who certainly knew nothing of us or our circumstances. That word has become foundational for our whole lives and has been used by God to direct us in many subsequent moments when we have been tempted to take the well-ordered and seemingly safe course.

(d) **The promise of Scripture.** On many occasions we have received a direct word from Scripture in the form of a promise of faith or a confirmation of faith. The power of these words is terrific. It is as though the Holy Spirit lifts the words off the page and transforms them into a neon sign which speaks directly into the situation. These promises of Scripture don't come as a result of scratching around the Bible for a suitable word. There is a directness, and a given-ness about them which brings them home with great vitality and freshness.

I have found that they operate in *two major zones* of my experience. Often they are related to *need* and *events*. That is, God speaks through Scripture to give practical guidance or confirmation in relation to the circumstances of our lives.

The other area in which I have been greatly helped by these promises of Scripture is that of *my own inner life* and the battle which takes place there, particularly in relation to my ministry. Often I have to withstand fierce attacks from the enemy. At these times the Father has spoken to me directly through the Scriptures. For example, one time when I was under great personal pressure I received a great deal of encouragement from this source. I was withstanding attacks from other people as well as a profound inward battle. A dear brother came to me with a word from God which he had received for me a few days earlier. It was the words of Isaiah 54:17: '*No weapon forged against you will prevail, and you will refute every tongue that accuses you. This the heritage of the servants of the Lord, and this is their vindication from me.*'

(e) **The inner witness of the Spirit.** Over the years I have come to depend a great deal on this inner witness of the Spirit. I spoke earlier about hunches. It sounds a bit vague, but I have come to know what God wants me to do in certain situations through reading how I am in the realm of the spirit. This is particularly true with regard to timing. Often I will live with something for weeks and then suddenly into my spirit will come a great sense of urgency about it. I have learned that God has times and seasons, and it behoves us to read them well. During these times things move much more rapidly and with greater ease than at other times. We can miss it if we don't learn to read our spirit. It is within my spirit that I receive these certainties which God gives, by inner conviction, that something is right before the Lord. I would not move a step in the realm of faith without this inner witness of the spirit.

There are other areas where we need to learn to depend on this leading of God's Word. For example, when we minister into other people's lives, either publicly or personally, it is vital that we are following the promptings of God's Spirit.

B: Common features

When God speaks into our lives in these immediate ways there are certain characteristics which, I believe, are almost universal. In other words we can expect these features to accompany a word that is from God. They are part of the reason we can recognise these words as God's words for our lives. Such words are:

Immediate. This means that the word comes to us in a direct and personal way which is very powerful and arresting. In my experience there has never been much difficulty in recognising such a word as being a word from God. It is like 'an arrow to a sure place' and in the circumstances is very difficult to avoid or ignore.

Relevant. This means that such a word will be very relevant to the situation we are facing within our lives. A word from God is normally marked by its application and timeliness. It is true that God will sometimes speak a word to us well in advance of an event or situation we have not yet experienced. I have illustrated this from my own life. But that word became a formative force within my life and built in an expectation in my spirit, which was used by God over the years to move me forward.

Effective. God's word always produces an effect. Sometimes it has quite a dramatic and immediate effect; at other times it is quiet and seed-planting. But if we receive it and apply it, it will bear fruit. Sometimes this effect can be physical or emotional. I have known this sensation many times within me when I know that I have heard from the Lord. Sometimes I feel excited, at other times I feel a sense of awe and heaviness, because I know what this word will mean in terms of action, cost, change or the like.

Fitting. A word from God never stands alone! Not only is it fitting in the sense of being relevant to the situation. It is fitting in the sense of being consistent with other witnesses in your life. Whenever I think I am hearing from the Lord in a particular way I look for ratification of the word in other areas. I don't go round trying to make things fit the word – that is a dangerous exercise. I find, rather, that there are already many things into which the word fits. These may be the witness of other types of word, or the witness of other people involved, or the witness of other circumstances. Anyway, usually I am able to see how this word *fits*, and on that ground I can be confident that I am hearing clearly.

5: Studying the Word

Some Christians never seem to progress beyond treating the Bible like some divine promise box. Maybe you've seen the sort of thing I mean. It is a small box with texts from the Scriptures written on pieces of paper which are tightly rolled and packed into the box. To get a promise you take a pair of tweezers and lift one of the pieces of paper out of the box. It's great fun and can often prove a blessing, but it could hardly be described as a systematic approach to the Scriptures! Some of us treat our Bibles in just the same way. We open them at random and pray that the Holy Spirit will direct us to the word for the moment. Now, of course, as I have already illustrated, the Holy Spirit can do just this when the occasion is right. In these instances we usually ignore the question of context and original meaning and take the word as it comes with all its immediacy and relevance to our hearts.

But for a consistent understanding of the Scriptures there needs to be more to it than this. We need to learn to live in the Scriptures on a daily basis and gain an understanding of their coherence and meaning. This is why Paul writes to Timothy: *'Do your best to present yourself to God as one approved, a workman who does not need to be ashamed and who correctly handles the word of truth'* (2 Tim 2:15).

A: Tools for the job

We live in a day when we have at our disposal some magnificent tools to help us in our study of the Scriptures. We don't need to be Greek or Hebrew scholars to make good use of the dependable translations of the Bible we have to hand. I always use more than one translation for my study and meditation of Scripture, because I find it can be so rewarding to consider different inflections of the truth by these means.

For example, I use the New International Version these days as my main reading, studying and preaching the Bible. But I like a paraphrase alongside to give a fluent and popular understanding of the Word. For myself, I still use J. B. Phillips' translation for this purpose, although many people now use The Living Bible or something like it. I also like another 'standard' translation to enable me to understand more clearly any difficulties or to provide a better insight into the meaning of a text. I would still use the Revised Standard Version or the Authorised Version for this purpose.

As well as these translations of Scripture we have many aids to our better understanding of Scripture. The Lion series of books provides a magnificent introduction for people with no formal training into areas of background, history, interpretation and so on. They are highly readable and I enjoy an hour browsing through one of their introductions, reminding myself of facts and truths which I once studied at greater depth during my formal theological education. Many of these books provide Christians with an overview of the Scriptures which help them to see their way much more clearly through the text.

But time given and an open heart to understand the Word of God, are still the main ingredients of successful study of the Scriptures. The Holy Spirit is on stand-by to assist any person who will come with the right attitude to the Scriptures. He will be their teacher and will guide them in all truth: *'The Spirit searches all things, even the deep things of God ... We have not received the spirit of the world but the Spirit who is from God, that we may understand what God has freely given us'* (1 Cor 2:10, 12).

B: Why study the Bible?

There are a number of important reasons why we need to make the study of the Scriptures a prime objective in our lives.

(a) **Revelation.** Nowhere do we have as full a revelation of God as in the Scriptures. Here He reveals truth about Himself and His purposes for His people that we will find nowhere else. Above all we will understand God's revelation in Jesus through the testimony of Scriptures: *'You diligently study the Scriptures because you think that by them you possess eternal life. These are the Scriptures that testify about me'* (Jn 5:39).

(b) **Discipleship and growth.** Paul spoke of the need for us to understand the Scriptures when he wrote to Timothy: *'All Scripture is God-breathed and is useful for teaching, rebuking,* *correcting and training in righteousness, so that the man of God may be thoroughly equipped for every good work'* (2 Tim 3:16). We have already noticed the power of the Word of God. Through the Scriptures the Holy Spirit brings us that conviction which leads us to repentance. Through the Scriptures He reveals to us the holiness of God and the stature of Christ. Through the Scriptures He leads us into all truth so that we can know how to stand firm in 'the faith once delivered to the saints'.

The Scriptures are to the Holy Spirit what the scalpel is to the surgeon. In His hand they are wielded with great skill and power to bring about the healing which God wants to accomplish in our lives.

(c) **Faith and encouragement.** Paul underlines this when he writes: *'For everything that was written in the past was written to teach us, so that through endurance and the encouragement of the Scriptures we might have hope'* (Rom 15:4). We know that faith comes from hearing (Rom 10:17). Through our study of the Scriptures we will hear many things from God which will stimulate our faith and lift up our hearts. We will be given the material with which to proclaim faith and through our encounter with the great men of faith in the Bible we will have our faith challenged and corrected under the guidance of the Holy Spirit.

(d) **Witness and evangelism.** Peter exhorts us: *'Always be prepared to give an answer to everyone who asks you to give the reason for the hope that you have'* (1 Pet 3:15). A great deal of the blame for the failure of evangelism in our churches can be laid at the door of the failure of confidence in the Scriptures. Over the past two or three generations Satan has wreaked havoc in the Church under the impact of liberal teaching and preaching. This has destroyed the confidence of many people in the Scriptures. The more recent movement of Holy Spirit renewal has reversed this trend among many thousands of Christians because the Bible has become, once again, a living and vital book.

This is why we are seeing a renewed interest in evangelism. First, many Christians are becoming aware of their need to fulfil the commands of the Lord through Scripture and be involved in witnessing. Second, people are becoming more confident in the fundamentals of the faith because they are open to the teaching of the Scriptures.

(e) **Spiritual warfare.** In Ephesians 6:17 we are enjoined to take *'the sword of the Spirit, which is the word of God'*. Now, as we have already seen, the Word of God is a greater reality than the contents of Scripture. But I believe that in a very practical way the Scripture provides for us a direct weapon in our warfare in the Spirit. For one thing, the Scriptures direct us how to operate within this warfare. By example and teaching we will learn how to confront the evil one and how to gain the victory. It is the Scriptures that teach us that faith is the ground of our victory (see 1 Jn 5:4). It is the Scriptures that demonstrate for us the power of the name of Jesus (see Acts 4:10–12). It is the Scriptures that teach us to resist the devil, and he will flee from us (see Jas 4:7). You can see what a tremendously important part the Scriptures have to play in spiritual warfare.

C: Why study the Old Testament?

I am amazed how many Christians still ask me this question, even in a day when half the songs they sing are taken directly from the words of the Old Testament!

David Baker once wrote a book called *Two Testaments: One Bible* (published by the Inter-Varsity Press). I like the title because it reminds us of the *necessary* connection between the two parts of our Bible. We are in danger of getting a lop-sided view of things if we read only one part of the Bible.

I commend to you as well a book by the late F. F. Bruce, my old professor at Manchester, called *This is That*, which demonstrates how the most important themes of the Old Testament are taken up in the New. He speaks of the Rule of God, the salvation of God, the Victory of God, the Son of David, the People of God, the Servant Messiah, the Shepherd King and so on, and shows the connection between the insights of the Old and New Testaments in these important areas.

Another important fact to consider is that the New Testament assumes an understanding of certain truths without ever expounding them fully. Take, for example, the great themes of holiness and glory. Without the Old Testament we would never have a clear idea of what is meant by such terms. With the Old Testament we can see what is meant by speaking of God as a holy God and what we mean when we talk of the glory of the Lord.

The Old Testament relates faith to life in a very real way. The Holy Spirit has written it 'warts and all'. We are left with no illusions regarding the humanity of these men of God, but at the same time we see God choosing them and using them with great power. This is a source of great inspiration and encouragement to all who want to walk by faith, as, of course, Hebrews chapter 11 teaches us to do.

For another thing, from the Old Testament we can gain some understanding of the process of revelation. It soon becomes quite clear that some things are time-conditioned whilst others bear the hallmark of eternal truth. I don't think you need a degree in Old Testament theology to perceive this – particulary when, as believers, we see the Old Testament in the light of Jesus. We can begin to see the wisdom of God in how He gradually brought mankind back from the brink of annihilation through His covenant people to the grand plan of redemption in Jesus; where salvation is not for the Jews only, but for all who come to Him in faith.

These are just a few of the important connections between the Old and New Testaments. Of course, the New Testament will take primary place in the life of discipleship and completes for us the revelation of the Old Testament, but it would be a foolish person who lived in ignorance of all that the Father has said and done for us through the revelation of Old Testament Scripture.

D: Six basic steps

As you start, let me give you six very simple steps which will help you find your way into the Scriptures. Exactly where you start is up to you. Some people start right at the beginning and go through to the very end, namely from Genesis to Revelation. For young Christians I usually advise starting somewhere that will be more immediately relevant – say John's Gospel or some other part of the New Testament.

(i) **Observe.** Look and listen to what the Scripture is actually saying. This means that we need to read with some care. It helps to read more slowly than we think we should and to read more than once. It helps to take time to think about what we are reading and to ask ourselves whether we really have got a grasp of what it is about.

(ii) **Interpret.** In other words ask the question, 'Do I know what this means?' There may be reasons why I don't understand and these will become clear if we take time to ask the question. Sometimes when I am listening to my son Jonathan reading his Scripture portion, I stop him and ask if he understands what he is reading. Frequently he tells me that he doesn't. So I get him to go over the reading and ask him the question again. When we do this we discover the reasons why he doesn't know what it means. Sometimes the reasons are very straightforward. For example, there may be words or ideas he does not know or understand. Maybe there is some spiritual truth he doesn't grasp because he has never *experienced* its meaning. Truth experienced is truth understood. It may be that there is some technical reason, such as background or a custom. Well, this is an opportunity to go and find help from one of the resources that are available, such as I have mentioned.

(iii) **Summarise.** I find it very useful to summarise the main points I am learning from a passage or to underline what I see to be the main sections or headings. It is helpful to try and put into your own words what you think the Scripture is saying. So a pen, marker and pad are helpful aids to consistent Bible study.

(iv) **Evaluate.** This can cover a lot of questions. For example, we can ask what type of literature it is we are reading. Is it a letter to someone, is it teaching, is it prophetic literature, is it poetry? and so on. Sometimes this will help us to understand the meaning and whether or not the teaching is relevant to us at this moment.

We can ask what kind of teaching this is we are reading. Is it a universal truth – that is, does it apply to all people in all places and times or is it related only to the time when it was written? This sort of question helps us towards an answer as to whether this applies today or whether it was part of God's particular revelation for the people to whom it was first written.

(v) Apply. Whenever we read the Scriptures we should ask ourselves how this might apply to our own life. This is particularly true of teaching on how we should live, or to what we have become in Christ Jesus and so on. Whenever the Holy Spirit shows us truth that relates to our own life we need to be eager to apply it. So the Word of God will become effective in us and we will benefit from the fruit of it in our lives.

(vi) Compare. It has long been understood that the best interpreter of Scripture is Scripture itself. And so it is good to take time to compare one part of Scripture with another. This is where a concordance or cross-reference Bible is so useful. We can follow an idea or thought through the Scriptures. By doing this our understanding will be enhanced and our interpretation of Scripture will be controlled. A great sense of spiritual satisfaction can be obtained from this sort of exercise.

These six basic principles are only a beginning but they will provide a frame of reference for those who are starting on what is surely the most productive use of time and minds available to Christian believers.

Chapter 4

Effective Faith

1: The Gift of Faith

'Without faith it is impossible to please God!'

(Heb 11:6).

Faith is the greatest power in the universe because it is the means by which the power of God is released into human experience. Without faith *it is impossible to please God!* That is what the Word says and that is what it means. None of us has the means within ourselves to meet God's demands or to fulfil the work of the kingdom. We need a supernatural gift and that gift is the gift of faith.

All this talk about my putting my faith in Jesus to become a Christian falls so far short of how the Bible witnesses to faith. We talk a lot about faith today, but I am sure that we work with far too limited a view of what faith is. We imagine that faith is prayer being answered. That faith is what we exercise in moments of need so that God's power and provision can be released into the situation. Of course that is true, but is that all there is to it?

Jesus said, *'When the Son of Man comes, will he find faith on the earth?'* (Lk 18:8). I think He will find a lot of people living in hope. He will find us with a lot of prayers still needing to be answered, but whether He will find a people who have grasped the magnificence and largeness of faith is open to question.

It is clear when you look at the New Testament that the question of faith is vital to the whole question of discipleship. Faith is the power by which we come into new life in Jesus and it is also the power through which we exercise this new life of God in us. Christian experience is of faith from beginning to end, so it is clearly necessary for us to understand what we mean when we speak about faith.

A: A five-finger exercise of faith

We could answer the question 'What is faith?' in several ways, but from the point of view of the Bible we can see that faith has a number of very important elements which are inter-related and which really need to stand undivided if we are to appreciate the breadth of this great theme. It could be said that without any one of these 'faith strands' we have not fully expressed what faith is, nor can faith be fully operative within our lives if any one of them is missing.

Faith is like a hand with five fingers. If you write 'Faith' across the palm, the fingers gather in to give that firm grip which is faith in action.

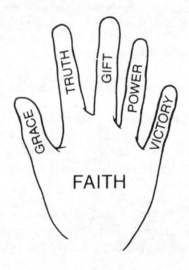

(a) **Faith is grace.** When Paul writes to the Ephesians he makes this great truth clear: *'For it is by grace you have been saved, through faith – and this not from yourselves, it is the gift of God – not by works, so that no-one can boast'* (Eph 2:8, 9). You see, faith is the very basis of our relationship with the Father. We are not saved through our own strength or righteousness but by the grace of God, which is made real in our lives through faith. Faith is the means by which God's grace becomes real within our hearts and lives.

Not one of us is born again by any effort of our own. Not one of us even had the strength to put our trust in God. As we were by nature, even our very minds were hostile to God and found it impossible to submit to God's Word: *'The sinful mind is hostile to God, It does not submit to God's law, nor can it do so. Those controlled by the sinful nature cannot please God'* (Rom 8:7, 8). Sometimes it is said to me, 'Well, surely we put our faith in Jesus when we turn to Him for salvation?' Sometimes an analogy is drawn between putting one's faith in Jesus and putting one's faith, say, in a lift in a department store or in an airplane for a flight. But I want to suggest there is all the difference in the world between the two! My faith in a lift or airplane is based on nothing but rational thinking and hope. I have seen them working many times and I am willing to take the chance that they will not fail this time!

No! Faith in God is a divine gift, and it works like this. Faith is given in response to the Word of God which enters my life under the active power of the Holy Spirit. I have been walking along in one direction in life when suddenly God speaks His word into my situation. It may be through preaching or through a particular circumstance, but in one way or another God speaks to me. The result of this is that I stop, I turn to hear this voice that is speaking to me. (This turning is part of the process of repentance.) When I turn away from my old direction of life and listen instead to the Word of God, then the Holy Spirit brings something to me that I never had before – the gift of faith. This is how Paul in Romans 10:17: *'Consequently, faith comes from hearing the message, and the message is heard through the word of Christ.'*

I believe it is of fundamental importance that we understand this aspect of faith. Faith is grace made real in my life. This is the very foundation of faith as an active principle of my life from now on, because faith always looks to God, and when I know this is where I have looked from the very first moment of my new birth, then my confidence rests in God from the very start.

(b) Faith is truth. *'I felt I had to write and urge you to contend for the faith that was once for all entrusted to the saints'* (Jude 3). On a number of occasions the word 'faith' occurs in the New Testament with the definite article in front of it. This tells us that there is something definite about this faith. There is content to it. Paul uses the same way of speaking when he addresses the Corinthians: *'Be on your guard; stand firm in the faith; be men of courage; be strong'* (1 Cor 16:13). It is not only important *that* we believe, it is important *what* we believe. There is a body of truth which encompasses God's revelation to us in Jesus. This is the *truth* which is the ground of our faith. Faith does not rest on a good idea or some emotional experience we have. It rests on the declared work and Word of God in Jesus.

We urgently need to develop a revelational ground for our Christian lives today, rather than a merely emotional one. Many people base their discipleship on the ground of emotion. How they feel and what they feel like doing is what seems to matter. But it is easy to have faith if you are feeling good or if everything is going dandy. But real men of faith have got past the emotion. They base their lives on the revealed truth of God.

(c) Faith is a gift. Faith is listed among the gifts of the Holy Spirit in 1 Cor 12:9: *'... to another faith by the same Spirit, to another gifts of healing by that one Spirit.'* This is faith for specific occasions and need. Just as we are not born into the Kingdom of God in our own strength and merit, neither can we minister in the power of the Kingdom apart from the gifts of grace. Indeed, the word we translate as 'gifts' (1 Cor 12:4) is closely allied to the word we translate 'grace'. The Greek word is *charismata* – literally the things of grace (*charis*). This gift of faith, like the other spiritual gifts, opens up to a capability and potential that do not belong to our old human nature. It is this faith that looks at the impossible 'and cries it shall be done' (Wesley).

This sort of faith is almost an insult to our flesh and human minds because it relies in child-like dependency on God. It demands that we lay aside our own efforts and plans to work things out our way and throw ourselves afresh on the grace of our heavenly Father to give us the grace we need in time of need.

(d) Faith is power. Faith is vital, dynamic and effective. Whenever we hear of faith in the Scriptures something powerful is happening. God is there showing His power and breaking into the darkness of Satan's kingdom. Look at the Gospels again and see how many times Jesus speaks of faith. Look at the results of it: people healed from all sorts of diseases, people set free from the bondage of Satan, miracles worked in supernatural power. It's just the same in the Acts of the Apostles, we see the very same power at work. People healed and set free through the power of faith, others filled with faith by the Holy Spirit in the most amazing circumstances: *'By faith in the name of Jesus, this man whom you now see and know was made strong. It is Jesus' name and the faith that comes through him that has given complete healing to him, as you can all see'* (Acts 3:16).

Jesus said more about faith and its power than almost anything else. He didn't leave a blueprint for the Church, nor a teaching programme on evangelism, but He gave us some mighty powerful promises of faith:

> *'If two of you on earth agree about anything you ask for, it will be done for you by my Father in heaven'*
>
> (Mt 18:18).

> *'If you believe, you will receive whatever you ask for in prayer'* (Mt 21:22).

'Have faith in God ... whatever you ask for in prayer, believe that you have received it, and it will be yours'
(Mk 11:22, 23).

'You may ask for anything in my name, and I will do it'
(Jn 14:14).

Faith is not a dead doctrine or dull religion. When I look around and see the way Satan has duped the Church it grieves my heart. Men and women are trying to run the Kingdom of God on the principles of the flesh. No wonder it is such an effort! No wonder there is such bankruptcy in financial and spiritual terms because human effort and human reason have been allowed to displace the power and the wisdom of God.

(e) **Faith is victory.** *'That is the victory that has overcome the world, even our faith.'* This is how John in his First Epistle (5:4) expresses it. Men of faith have always been those who have known the secret of the overthrow of the world's system. They have known how to withstand the enemies of God's Kingdom. Of course, faith and obedience are closely linked. Faith enables us to believe God's Word and obedience enables us to fulfil it. In our next chapter we will see the close and indivisible connection between faith and the Word of God. One grows out of the other and together they form an amazing platform of spiritual strength.

It is this strength that has enabled men of faith to undertake seemingly impossible things and to stand against insurmountable odds. Like Abraham, for example:

He is our father in the sight of God, in whom he believed – the God who gives life to the dead and calls things that are not as though they were.

Against all hope, Abraham in hope believed and so became the father of many nations, just as it had been said to him, 'So shall your offspring be'. Without weakening in his faith, he faced the fact that his body was as good as dead ... Yet he did not waver through unbelief regarding the promise of God, but was strengthened in his faith and gave glory to God. (Romans 4:17–20)

To be a Christian believer means to be born in faith and born into faith. The atmosphere the believer breathes is very different from that of the unbeliever. We are in the world right enough, but as Jesus said, we are not of it. And nowhere are we more 'not of it' than with regard to faith. It is this principle and power of life that separates us from the rest of men, and the challenge of Jesus is that we should be true to our birthright and live by faith. These five elements we have discussed help us to understand the breadth and depth of what we are called to and release us from those petty views of faith which view it as little more than a personal convenience given to us by God for our own advantage.

2: Faith and the Word of God

So is my word that goes out from my mouth:
It will not return to me empty,
but will accomplish what I desire
and achieve the purpose for which I sent it.

(Is 55:11)

Faith and the Word of God go hand in hand. Faith is not just a good idea put into practice; real faith depends on a word from God. The exciting fact which faith confesses is the fact that God is a communicating God. He has something to say to every situation and if we will take time to listen we will hear what He is saying to us. Time and again the Scriptures illustrate this great truth for us.

Abraham received the Word of God into his heart. It created faith and it called for faith. That's what God's Word does. We cannot live in real faith until we hear the Word of God for the situation. And once we have heard the Word of God it demands faith to stand in it.

This, for me, is where the difference in praying about something and standing in faith really lies. Praying about something infers a more general approach, in which your mind may or may not be clear about the issue. Standing in faith is an attitude that is taken in the light of a word from God. All the facts may not be clear, and certainly the way in which the faith is going to be fulfilled is unlikely to be obvious at that moment. But faith knows! It has an inner understanding of the issue and a conviction of spirit that makes it certain of the outcome: *'Now faith is being sure of what we hope for and certain of what we do not see'* (Heb 11:1).

The difference between faith and a good idea is the Word of God. This is an area where people can make mistakes, and often they do make mistakes because they let their human desires and ambitions take control and lay claim to divine revelation, when in fact they have no such thing.

Anyway, we need to recognise that from the human level there is an element of risk attached to the life of faith. I like John Wimber's comment that he liked to spell 'faith' with the letters, 'r-i-s-k'.

A: How God speaks

It is difficult for some people to accept the fact that God wants to communicate with them personally. They can't quite see how it will happen. That is usually because they are expecting the wrong thing. I don't imagine it is often that the archangel Michael drops in personally with a telegram, but I am sure that God speaks in many different ways to those who will listen for Him.

Personally I never go far away from my Bible when I am waiting in faith over a specific issue. Time and again the Lord had opened the Word through the Scriptures in a new and challenging way. There is something very special about the way the Holy Spirit uses Scriptures in situations of faith. I believe this is why we need to learn the Scriptures. It needs to become our meat and drink. It is terrific to receive guidance and words through all the other means the Spirit has at His disposal, such as dreams, prophecies, visions, words of knowledge and so on. But there is something very tangible about the Scriptures. They do not evaporate before your eyes or change with keeping. They are *there*, and once the Holy Spirit has underlined them for you, you can keep going back and notice they haven't changed. They are not subject to your memory of the experience and they are more susceptible to the test of interpretation and true understanding. Let me encourage you to get into your Bible! In the exercise of faith the Scriptures carry with them a tremendous sense of givenness. It feels as though they were written just for that moment. They have an immediate relevance to the situation and the words carry within themselves an immediate impact.

Let us see just how important the Word of God is to the life of faith.

(a) **God's Word creates faith in us.** '*The word is near you; it is in your mouth and in your heart, that is, the word of faith we are proclaiming*' (Rom 10:8). Without this Word from God there can be no faith. We saw this in the last chapter. Unless God speaks to us and we receive His Word into our lives, true faith cannot be born in us. It is a divine gift of grace to all who respond in repentance to the Word of God. The same principle holds true from that moment on in our Christian walk. There can be no life of faith apart from the Word of faith. It is the Word that creates faith. For new birth or for any enterprise of faith it is God's Word to our hearts that puts there what could never be there by human nature. This thing is 'not born of the flesh nor of the will of man, but of God'.

(b) God's Word prepares us for faith. A basic essential for faith is spelled out by John in his Epistle: *'Dear friends, if our hearts do not condemn us, we have confidence before God and receive from him anything we ask'* (1 Jn 3:21, 22). How can we come in confidence before our heavenly Father to ask Him for anything if our lives are in such a state that we feel unworthy to come into His presence? One of the greatest hindrances to a life of faith is life itself. But the Word of God is powerful – it searches the thoughts and attitudes of the heart. If we are living with our lives exposed to the daily cleansing of God's Word, then the effect will be that all that is not godly and true will be exposed and judged. This is a real cost of faith for many people. There is that in all of us that wants to live with something or other of our old sin. And Satan knows this. That is why he plays on these weaknesses so much. But they are the very things that need to be dealt with if we are to have confidence before God. As long as there is something wrong in my life I cannot come into the Father's presence with any real measure of spiritual confidence. This is where we need to have the courage to live under the searchlight of God's Word:

> *The word of God is living and active. Sharper than any double-edged sword, it penetrates even to dividing soul and spirit, joints and marrow; it judges the thoughts and attitudes of the heart. Nothing in all creation is hidden from God's sight. Everything is uncovered and laid bare before the eyes of him to whom we must give account.*
>
> (Heb 4:12, 13)

(c) God's Word enables us in faith. The tremendous thing about the Word of God is that *it provides us with an active alternative* to all the negative thoughts and attitudes of our old nature. Our minds are so important to the life of faith. We are susceptible to all the impressions of our five senses. Satan tries to bring us into bondage to what is tangible and obvious. He wants us to live our lives at the level of what we see immediately before our eyes. God's purpose is that we should be renewed in the attitudes of our minds: *'Do not conform any longer to the pattern of this world, but be transformed by the renewing of your mind. Then you will be able to test and approve what God's will is – his good, pleasing and perfect will'* (Rom 12:2).

In a later chapter we will explore what it means to stand in the living power of the Word of God. For the moment let us notice this provision of God's living Word as an alternative to all the other 'words' which infest our minds and imaginations.

(d) God's Word directs us in faith. There is a lovely scripture in the prophecy of Isaiah which I often lean on. It is the picture of a people coming back in repentance to a loving God. They have felt His hand of discipline upon their lives, but now He is wooing them and calling them home. Included in the prophecy there is a lovely promise: *'Whether you turn to the right or to the left, your ears will hear a voice behind you saying, "This is the way, walk in it"'* (Is 30:21). How often I have praised God for that promise! I know it was given to a people two and a half thousand years ago, but thank God His Word never changes. His promise is still the same, that to those who will listen to Him and pay attention to what He has to say there is this promise of divine direction:

> *He has preserved our lives
>   and kept our feet from slipping.*   (Ps 66:9)

It is not only in preservation that this word of direction works, although that is most important. How often I have known God's deliverance, like the Psalmist, from 'the snare of the fowler' because of something specific the Lord has given me through Scripture or some other means.

(e) God's Word confirms faith in us. I remember an incident some time ago when I worked alongside Colin Urquhart.

We were in the process of buying Roffey Place and still needed £300,000 to complete the deal. There were only four days left. I was in my upstairs study on a Monday evening waiting on God. I had received a letter that day via our solicitors from the party who were selling the place to us. They knew our situation and, from their point of view, our crazy approach to it! Their letter reminded us that four days from then we had to complete or else! It also confided to our solicitor that they, the vendors, did not have the same faith in the power of prayer as we seemed to be having.

I looked at the letter and got mad! I took it to my study and started to show it to the Lord. (I had forgotten that He had probably read it before I had seen it!) I felt a tremendous indignation on behalf of the name of the Lord. Just then Hilda my wife came running upstairs with a scripture that God had just shown to her in a powerful way. It was from the prophecy of Isaiah.

Now, if I tell you that I did a post-graduate degree on nothing else but the text of Isaiah it may surprise you to know that I felt I had never seen this scripture before in my life! I had read Isaiah many times but for some reason could not recall having noted this verse before. It read:

> 'Before she goes into labour, she gives birth;
> before the pains come upon her, she delivers a son.
> Who has ever heard of such a thing?
> Who has seen such things? ...
> Do I bring to the moment of birth
> and not give delivery?' says the Lord.
> 'Do I close up the womb
> when I bring to delivery?' says your God.   (Is 66:7–9)

The effect of that word was electric. I could have danced around the house – in fact I think I did! From the human point of view nothing had changed. Imagine dancing round the house when what we wanted was £300,000! Yet that is the effect of the Word of God. I felt I had something much more precious than money and besides, of course, the Lord followed up His promise with the goods. Within twenty-four hours a cheque arrived for the exact amount.

B: A word of warning

There is something that cannot be copied about a life of faith. It is this Word of faith. Men of real faith are par excellence men of the Word of God. They know how to listen for it. They know how to receive it and, above all, they know how to obey it. Many people make a mistake here. They confuse faith with its mechanism. God has told me to do things in so many different ways. There is not one way of fulfilling the Word of faith. But the root lies in the Word. This is what we need. We need to be hearers and doers of the Word of God.

3: Sowing and Reaping

I was preaching in a local church one Sunday night when I had a remarkable experience. Just before I preached they took the offering and I saw a picture in my mind at that moment. Instead of stewards going round taking the offering I saw all the people get up out of their seats and bring their offering to the front to present to the Lord. But instead of having money in their hands they each carried a plastic container. These containers were in all shapes and sizes. Some people had large open plastic bowls whilst others only had small plastic cups. In between was every conceivable size and shape. In these containers the people were bringing their offerings to the Lord. Each one came and emptied their container at the front in the presence of God. Then a strange thing happened! As each person emptied their container and turned away to go back to their seat it was as though a divine hand came and prevented them.

This hand took their empty containers from them and filled them with something until they were brimming over. I couldn't see what was being put in the containers but I knew that it was meant to signify the blessing of God. The faces of the people were a picture! Those who had brought big bowls could hardly stagger back to their places, and it took them all their time to contain the blessing in their bowl, for it seemed to be flowing all over the place. There was surprise and joy all over their faces. The faces of the ones who had come with small cups said it all! You could see just what they were thinking. They were wishing that they had brought far bigger containers in the first place!

The picture reminded me immediately of the words of Jesus in Luke 6:38: *'Give, and it will be given to you. A good measure, pressed down, shaken together and running over, will be poured into your lap. For with the measure you use, it will be measured to you.'* Some people seem to have the impression that faith is all about 'getting' from God. Of course, it is that, for the New Testament is full of the promises of God which encourage us to believe that He will give us all we need to fulfil His will. Jesus spoke many times about being able to ask the Father so that we might be able to receive the good things He has in store for us (see Lk 11:9ff). We are encouraged to come and ask the Father for those things we need. He is a good Father who knows how to give good gifts to His children. But that is not all there is to it!

James makes it clear in his letter that God is very interested in our motives. It is not a matter of asking the Father so that we can be self-indulgent or just fulfil our own desires: '*You do not have, because you do not ask God. When you ask, you do not receive, because you ask with the wrong motives, that you may spend what you get on your pleasures*' (Jas 4:2, 3)

A: Sowing for God

Faith operates on God's principle of sowing and reaping. Paul spells this out for us in 2 Cor 9:6: '*Remember this: Whoever sows sparingly will also reap sparingly, and whoever sows generously will also reap generously.*' Those people in my picture got such a surprise when God gave *them* something back! So much so that those who only gave a little were wishing that they had doubled or trebled their giving. If only they had known the principle of sowing and reaping!

Now maybe you will object that some of the folks did not have that much to give in the first place. Perhaps they couldn't afford to give a big offering. This is missing the point. God doesn't look at the *amount* of money that we give. He looks at the heart with which we give it. This is the next point that Paul makes: '*Each man should give what he had decided in his heart to give, not reluctantly or under compulsion, for God loves a cheerful giver*' (2 Cor 9:7). When Jesus saw the widow giving her two mites He looked right into her heart. To Him that was far greater treasure than all the offerings of the scribes and Pharisees put together.

This is God's principle of spiritual success. If you sow for God you will reap for God. If you sow to God you will reap from God. If you sow a mean spirit you will reap a mean spirit. If you sow poverty of spirit you will reap poverty of spirit. God desires us to be successful in spiritual terms.

There is a great deal of controversy today about the 'prosperity gospel'. I am quite aware that the truth can be and has been abused by some. But this fact does not change the truth of Scripture that it is God's purpose to bless those who will sow for Him. Whenever I see a brother whose ministry is blessed in terms of souls and growth I always ask myself the question, 'Where has this man sown for God?'

B: The principle of creation and new creation

God has built this very principle into the natural order of things. No farmer in his right mind would sit and look at the seed in his barn. It would profit him nothing to gloat over what little he had. What he must do is get out his plough and break up the fallow ground. After he has sown his seed he can look forward to a rich harvest.

This is how God has always worked. It is the very heart-principle of Calvary. Jesus knew this when he said: *'The hour has come for the Son of Man to be glorified. I tell you the truth, unless a grain of wheat falls to the ground and dies it remains only a single seed. But it if dies, it produces many seeds'* (Jn 12:23, 24).

C: God's multiplication tables

God has promised a hundred-fold to those who sow for him. This is a principle that seems to have been forgotten in our churches to a great extent. The way to spiritual success and financial viability in the kingdom of God is not to be found by endless, weary appeals to the flesh. It is no good trying to squeeze more money out of people who have lost heart and have no vision for the future. God's way is the way of growth: *'And everyone who has left houses or brothers or sisters or father or mother or children or fields for my sake will receive a hundred times as much and will inherit eternal life'* (Mt 19:29). Men of faith sow for God. If God says sow money, they sow money. If God says sow time, they sow time. If God says sow energy, they sow energy. If God says sow life itself, they sow life. For they believe the promise of the Father that He will return them a hundred-fold!

This is not a mathematical formula. Men of faith don't just give their time and money away to get more back. Their concern is with the Kingdom. They want to be rich for the Kingdom! There are no paupers in God's Kingdom: *'Seek first his kingdom and his righteousness, and all these things will be given to you as well'* (Mt 6:33). The way we act, you would think that Jesus had never said such words! Satan has got us into a position of apologising for God's great promises. The apostle Paul never once apologised for taking money or resources from those who supported him because he returned to them the greatest possible promise: *'My God will meet all your needs according to his glorious riches in Christ Jesus'* (Phil 4:19).

D: No waste with God

I often think of Jim Elliott. He was a missionary in Ecuador who, with four others, was martyred as he tried to reach the Auca Indians for Christ. To outside observers it seemed such a waste. But Jim Elliott knew better than that. Sometime before he died he wrote these words in his diary: 'He is no fool who gives what he cannot keep to gain what he cannot lose.'

When I get to heaven I want to shake Jim's hand because God spoke to me through those words one night, and they changed the whole direction of my life. They enabled me to get to grips with God's priorities and I gave my life to serve the Lord in my full-time ministry. I have often wondered how many other young men have been arrested by the very same words. What a harvest has been reaped through the sowing of one life! To say nothing of the fact that the tribe that killed him became Christians through the testimony of those deaths. God never wastes His seeds and He promises the best return possible on everything that is sown for Him: *'Whoever wants to save his life will lose it, but whoever loses his life for me will find it'* (Mt 16:25).

E: Apply it to life

I have learned to apply this principle to the most basic aspects of daily life. All I can say is that over the twelve years or so my wife and myself have lived according to this principle of sowing and reaping, God has never let us down. In fact, not only have we been provided for in every way but we have been able to be the source of blessing for many other people.

I am often asked, 'Well, what about the poor and needy in Africa and places like that?' It just so happens that I go often to Africa to minister and I believe that God means us to be *part of the answer and not part of the problem*. How can a poverty-ridden church with hardly enough to meet its own bills become a blessing to those who need their help? God means us to exercise our faith on behalf of other people as well. Over the years I have had the privilege of being able to minister materially and spiritually to areas of need where, if it were not for my faith in this principle, I would never be able to do a thing. If we taught our people to give away of themselves and their means according to this principle of faith, we would see God's resources released around this world in the most amazing ways.

As it is, Satan is robbing the resources of heaven. Through self-interest, self-pity and greed he has paralysed the saints of God. The Church ought to be the greatest powerhouse on earth for releasing the resources of faith. Instead it has chosen to follow the way of the world, with its investment funds and worldly financial attitudes. No wonder God can't bless it, because He can only bless those who walk in the way of faith.

I make a practice now of regarding any money I have in my pocket as 'seed' money for God. Just recently I had £100 in my pocket. I had been putting it aside bit by bit to pay a bill at the end of the week. On the Monday I met a brother and the Spirit showed me that he was in real need. So I emptied my pocket and gave him what I had. The joy on his face was enough reward, but later that day I was given thirty pounds. I felt good because that was well on the way to recouping the amount for the bill.

The next morning a couple came to see me and as I spoke with them God told me to give them the thirty pounds. It transpired that they had nothing. Nor had I, but later that day I received fifty pounds. The same thing happened the next day, and so I was left with nothing again. But that afternoon within the space of a few minutes we received £400 from two different sources. The bills were paid, the needs of others were met, and God was glorified. Praise God!

F: Go with God

I want to encourage you to live by the principles of sowing and reaping. God will surprise you! He often returns the blessing in ways that are quite different from the seed that is sown, but He never pays short!

Jesus said that it was more blessed to give than to receive, and He was so right. It is blessed to receive to be able to give. Paul put it like this: *'You will be made rich in every way so that you can be generous on every occasion, and ... your generosity will result in thanksgiving to God'* (2 Cor 9:11). I believe that there is nothing so encouraging as seed faith: seeing it grow and flourish; seeing the surprise and joy that it brings to the lives of those who benefit from the principle; and above all growing in faith to the glory of God, for *'without faith it is impossible to please God'* (Heb 11:6).

4: Faith Under Pressure

> 'This is victory that has overcome the world, even our faith'   (1 Jn 5:4)

A: Your God is too small

This was the title of a book written by J. B. Phillips. It was an attack on modern theology, which diminishes our ideas of God. That is exactly what Satan wants to do, because he knows that if we live with a diminished view of God then our faith will never rise to the need. The writer to the Hebrews lays down the fundamental condition for faith: *'anyone who comes to him must believe that he exists and that he rewards those who earnestly seek him'* (Heb 11:6). Actually that NIV translation does less than justice to the import of the Scripture. The Authorised Version is much more near the point when it says: *'he that cometh to God must believe **that he is** and that he is a rewarder of them that diligently seek him.'*

Millions of people believe in the *existence* of God. The devils also believe and tremble. But it is not a question of the existence of God. I might believe that God exists but not that He engages Himself in the daily and practical affairs of mankind. I might have a view of the existence of God that keeps Him outside of my private universe. No, faith rests on the *'is-ness'* of God. This is the God who reveals Himself to Abraham in the heart of his pagan culture. This is the God who speaks to Moses and reveals His character to him. This is the God who delivers His people with a mighty hand and leads them out of bondage. He is the God who deals with the very same people when they sin against Him and who restores them in love and mercy again. He is the God who delivers Daniel from the den of lions and sends His messenger to be with those in the fiery furnace. He is the God of Elijah, who stood for the is-ness of his God against the immobility of the Baalim on Mount Carmel.

The whole Bible breathes the is-ness of God. His ear is not deaf nor is His arm shortened that He cannot save. In fact, this is what *makes* Him God. The idols are nothing – they are incapable of saving anyone, they need to be shaped from wood and stones and carried on the backs of men. That's how Isaiah the prophet saw it. Go and read Exodus chapter 15 and you'll see a powerful testimony to the God of the Bible:

> *Who is like you*
> *majestic in holiness,*
> *awesome in glory,*
> *working wonders?* (Ex 15:11)

This is the God of whom Darius the Mede wrote his eulogy after he had seen His power in saving Daniel:

> *He is the living God,*
> *and he endures for ever;*
> *his kingdom will not be destroyed,*
> *his dominion will never end.*
> *He rescues and he saves;*
> *he performs signs and wonders*
> *in the heavens and on the earth.* (Dan 6:26, 27)

God is the greatest fact of faith! For me this is tremendous. Time and again when I am facing critical decisions or praying about great needs I think of God. To me it is *the* most exciting fact that God is alive and active. Just think of it! We have been put in touch with the God who made the universe! To me faith is *a great experiment of God*. If God is not there, then faith will fail. Oh, I know that you can make some things look like faith. You can engineer situations and make arrangements seem like provision. But eventually the bubble will burst. Eventually the truth will be out because the day will come when the situation far exceeds any power of arrangement. One day God will ask you to do something that is far beyond your human capacity or power, and then you will be left only with God! Then you will see the size of your God!

This is the test of any doctrine or theology. Is it sufficient? Will it meet *any* need? Is the God whom it confesses big enough for any eventuality or does it fail at the point of its greatest test? As far as I am concerned this is what Christian faith is. It is putting God to the test. I don't mean that in an irreverent way or in any sense of doubt. I mean it in the way the Bible often speaks of it. God invites His people to put Him to the test: *'"Test me in this," says the Lord Almighty, "and see if I will not throw open the floodgates of heaven and pour out so much blessing that you will not have room enough for it."'* (Mal 3:10).

Many Christian people are in bondage today because they are living with a wrong conception of God. Some even think it presumptuous to come and ask God for anything. They seem to think that it is in some way irreverent. That is what Satan does. By one means or another his plan is to close us up to a God whose arms are open wide to bless us.

It is no accident today that we are surrounded by doubt in the theological realm. When I did my theological training some of the most important issues were the ones which were most disputed. Did Jesus really rise physically from the dead? Satan has a prime interest in denying that, because he knows better than we do that the answer is vitally connected to this question of faith. Paul makes this clear in Ephesians chapter 1 when he draws a direct line between the power of God in raising Jesus from the dead and the power that is available to us as believers today: *'... this incomparably great power for us who believe. That power is like the working of his mighty strength, which he exerted in Christ when he raised him from the dead and seated him at his right hand in the heavenly realms'* (Eph 1:19, 20). This is the power that is available to our faith – the same mighty power which God used when he raised Jesus from the dead!

B: You are too small

If Satan fails in his attack on our view of God, he turns invariably to our view of ourselves. And, of course, here he has material evidence on which to base his attack. We all know our own weaknesses only too well. What Satan does is to start with what we know to be the weakness of our flesh and nature and blow it out of all proportion until we have no vestige of faith left in ourselves at all.

I often think of that *Peanuts* cartoon where Snoopy is having one of his morose philosophical sessions. He lies flat along the top of his kennel with his nose down over the end. The balloon over his head says it all: 'Yesterday I was a dog, today I am a dog, tomorrow I will be a dog. I see little room for advancement.'

We need to enter into what we are in Jesus, to see that God has a different view of us through the saving power of His Son. The Bible says: *'If anyone is in Christ, he is a new creation; the old has gone, the new has come!'* (2 Cor 5:17). Hallelujah! I love that song we sometimes sing:

> *I am a new creation*
> *No more in condemnation,*
> *Here in the grace of God I stand.*
> *My heart is overflowing,*
> *My love just keeps on growing.*
> *Here in the grace of God I stand.*

That kind of affirmation takes me beyond the weakness and sin of my old nature and places me firmly 'in Christ Jesus'. Many people live with such a low self-image that they find faith impossible.

When we are standing in faith for any particular issue there are certain factors we look for as a matter of course. For example, after a period of revelation when we have heard God's word and direction and we begin to stand on that word of faith, we know that the next move of Satan will be to try and throw doubt on that word. And he does it in the most devious ways. What he does is mix a little rationalism with faith. Some well-meaning brother or sister, who has not shared in the experience of the word at a personal level, may come along and begin to ask questions about the venture, very reasonable questions. So reasonable, in fact, that you begin to wonder whether you heard right or not. This is how doubt begins. James warns us about the danger of this kind of doubt to faith: *'he who doubts is like a wave of the sea, blown and tossed by the wind. That man should not think he will receive anything from the Lord; he is a double-minded man, unstable in all he does.'* (Jas 1:6–8).

Satan will use whatever he can to discourage us and turn us away from faith; feelings of weakness, of unworthiness, of darkness and depression; feelings of despair on those days when we seem to get overwhelmed with a sense of hopelessness; feelings of death, even. There are grounds, at the rational level, for all of these things and the devil will help us to read the headlines of our hearts in capital letters so that these things seem to be total reality. But they are *not total reality!* The total reality is God! It is what God has done for us in Jesus. It is what God does and will do for us in the power of His Holy Spirit. That is not an escape route from reality. It is not to try and pretend the difficulties are not there. Faith is not illusion. We are not Christian Scientists. We are not denying the reality of pain nor the truth about the situation. The question that faith poses is this – *is there a higher truth than that which seems obvious at this moment?* And faith cries, 'Yes there is! That truth is God!'

Habakkuk knew that truth. His faith was not in faith. He was not blind to the *facts* of the situations. But beyond all that he trusted in God:

> *Though the fig-tree does not bud*
> *and there are no grapes on the vines,*
> *though the olive crop fails*
> *and the fields produce no food,*
> *though there are no sheep in the pen*
> *and no cattle in the stalls*
> *yet I will rejoice in the Lord,*
> *I will be joyful in God my Saviour.*   (Hab 3:17, 18)

The Bible says we've got to make a decision. We've either got to live at the level of life as it is or at the level of God. If Abraham had 'faced the facts', where would that have left him? He looked beyond and listened to the promise of God: *'And so from this one man, and he as good as dead, came descendants as numerous as the stars in the sky and as countless as the sand on the seashore'* (Heb 11:12). And what about Moses with Pharaoh? The dice seemed pretty heavily loaded against him. Or Joshua at the walls of Jericho, with his marching and trumpets? Or Gideon with Midian, or Elijah with Baal? Or Elisha at Dothan, surrounded by the enemies of God? But Elisha knew something on one else knew. He knew that those who were with him were greater than those who were against him: *'Then the Lord opened the servant's eyes, and he looked and saw the hills full of horses and chariots of fire all round Elisha'* (2 Kings 6:17).

Faith is always a matter of making a choice. We have to choose between the testimony of God or the testimony of men. We have to choose to accept things as they are or seem to be, or stand in faith with God, who says that nothing is impossible for Him. Faith looks to God. Faith sees the power of God. Faith rests on the Word of God. Faith claims the promise of God. Faith operates in the power of God. Faith is from God from first to last. It is born in His heart and He plants it in our hearts. That is why faith is our victory because *'the one who is in you is **greater** than the one who is in the world'* (1 Jn 4:4). Hallelujah!

5: Seven Steps to Effective Faith

'Have faith in God' (Mk 11:22).

I have discovered seven basic steps in the life of faith. I know it is dangerous to make these seem to be a law, because we all need to find our own way with God. God deals with us differently according to the situation and He has, at times, called on His servants to do unique things in faith. Nevertheless, in my experience I have found certain factors to be more of less constant and I believe that it is open to every Christian believer to experiment more in faith. These steps grow out of much of what has already been said, but it helps to lay them out clearly so that we can see them and begin to put them into practice.

A: Building our relationship with the Father

When Jesus taught His disciples to pray, He told them to pray to their Father in heaven (Mt 6:9). That, for me, is about the most winsome fact of Christian faith. Nowhere else do we meet God as our Father but in His Son and through the inner witness of the Holy Spirit: *'The Spirit himself testifies with our spirit that we are God's children'* (Rom 8:16). It is this relationship that needs fostering. Truth in our heavenly Father is the basis of faith. Anything that breaks this relationship breaks faith. John is right when he says: *'Dear friends, if our hearts do not condemn us, we have confidence before God and receive from him anything we ask'* (1 Jn 3:21, 22). That is why at the heart of faith there needs to be an open relationship between the Father and the child. We are coming to ask of Him momentous things. We need to be able to look Him in the eye and know that there is confidence between us. This is why those other words of John are just as important: *'If we claim to be without sin, we deceive ourselves and the truth is not in us. If we confess our sins, he is faithful and just and will forgive us our sins and purify us from all unrighteousness'* (1 Jn 1:8, 9).

Faith works best on a clean sheet, and so we need to keep our account up to date on a daily basis with the Father in heaven. Faith is confession; not just confession of sin but confession of God's Word and of all that God has done for us in Jesus. It is confession of all that God will do for us through faith. But it starts with confession of our own hearts. It's not that the Father doesn't already know. He does, but He wants us to share His knowledge so that there is nothing between us and so that we can share His righteousness. Confession each day keeps the devil away. Satan loves nothing better than to play on our unconfessed sin to breed guilt and doubt. This is the first step towards a healthy faith relationship.

B: Listening for God

I believe that one factor which spoils the work of God in our lives is the fact that we so often run before Him. The ancient people of Israel were never allowed to run before the Lord, He always went ahead of them. Look at the example of them entering through the Jordan. God told them to follow the Ark of the Covenant but to be careful to keep a thousand yards between it and them (Joshua 3).

Faith depends on hearing the Word of God. It is the Word that turns our fretting into faith. Once we have heard God's Word on the matter we can afford to wait for His answer, no matter how long it takes. In these times of waiting it is important to meditate on the Scriptures and to allow God to use your mind. Often He will communicate with you through a vision or a word, so it is important that you are in the place to hear Him.

I am sometimes asked about fasting in faith. The fact is that my team and I fast fairly often, usually as the Lord tells us and not often for a long period. However, it is important to notice that fasting is not what brings the provision. I don't believe we need to fast to claim the Word of God. The Father has promised to give us everything we need according to His riches in glory in Christ Jesus. We do fast, however, while we are listening for the Lord to speak. Sometimes there is an element of spiritual warfare involved in the situation and we fast as part of that. Sometimes we feel led to fast 'to the Lord' – that is, not for a particular purpose, but as an offering to

God. Faith is a very serious business and it is good to give ourselves to the issue with our whole hearts and minds. Fasting provides that opportunity. It removes the distraction of normal activities like eating meals and it focuses the mind and spirit on the issue in hand. In any event, it is important to wait for God's Word and to test it and hold it to ensure that you are standing on faith ground.

C: Build your Ebenezers

After the victory over the Philistines at Mizpah Samuel took a stone and set it up as a pillar. He called it Ebenezer or 'stone of help' because he said *'Thus far has the Lord helped us'* (1 Sam 7:12). There are other examples in the Old Testament where men build pillars of stone as a witness to the help God had given. These served as a testimony for themselves and future generations of the goodness of God.

I have found this to be an essential element of the life of faith. Faith builds on faith. The more you go on in faith, the more testimony you have personally of the saving power of God. This is why real men of faith cannot be shaken in their confidence in God. For them it is not a matter of speculation. They can take you on a tour of their Ebenezers.

Every fresh act of faith brings its own challenge and the devil is very ready to throw doubt on your trust in God. I have found it necessary at times to go and look in faith again at the things God has done before in my life. They are there and they stand as indisputable witnesses of the goodness of God. I know they didn't happen by chance and they certainly didn't come about through my own strength. God did it!

D: Use the gifts of the Holy Spirit

If you read 1 Corinthians 12:7–11 you will discover that God has provided a whole variety of gifts that are useful for the life of faith. There is spiritual understanding and knowledge and gifts of discernment and faith. They are all part of God's provision for the life of faith and they are available to all who seek them.

For myself, I find the gift of tongues particularly appropriate if I am seeking the mind of God on a certain matter. Paul teaches us that 'We do not know what we ought to pray for, but the Spirit himself intercedes for us with groans that words cannot express' (Rom 8:26). I am not suggesting that these groans of the Spirit of which Paul speaks is the gift of tongues; it is surely something more profound concerning the inner working of the Holy Spirit. However, I have found time and again as I use the private gift of tongues that I have become increasingly aware in my spirit of the direction in which God is taking me. Through this, and other gifts in operation, I have been able clearly to discern the will of God in the matter and so pray confidently in faith.

E: Ask in faith

Jesus taught his disciples a very simple principle: 'Ask and it will be given to you; seek and you will find; knock and the door will be opened to you' (Lk 11:9). The prayer of faith is different from the activity of intercession. Intercession has many levels and really involves wrestling within the situation in prayer. Faith is knowing the will of God and simply coming in that knowledge before the Father to confirm the request.

This is a dimension of faith that many people miss. They pray not knowing and therefore unsure whether their prayer will be answered or not. In my experience the most challenging and sometimes most prolonged part of the faith exercise is not the asking in faith but the process of becoming sure in faith. Once you are sure, there is a great peace and certainty in the Spirit, and it does not matter in one sense then how long it takes for the answer to appear. The Scriptures encourage us to come in faith and present our requests before the Father, knowing that he will hear and answer us: 'Therefore I tell you, whatever you ask for in prayer, believe that you have received it, and it will be yours' (Mk 11:24).

F: Gain release from Satan

I am not speaking here of personal deliverance. I mean that it is necessary to claim God's resources for His own use. Satan holds tremendous sway in the areas of finance and power. He tries to withhold what is rightfully God's and to keep the people of God in poverty and need for their work for the kingdom. This is not right and we need to learn to prevail against the devil in praise and prayer and release these things from his hand. This is why we need to learn to let the enemy be aware of our prayers. We are not asking him for anything but we are letting him know that we are not going to allow him to withhold any good thing that belongs to God.

One time when we were meeting together in prayer one of the group had an amazing picture. It was of a bank with a long counter, behind which were a number of bank tellers. Then into the picture came some bank robbers. They wore masks and carried guns and began to demand money from the tellers behind the counter. Now what the tellers didn't know was that the weapons were phoney. They looked real, so the bank clerks were terrified. As the vision continued two other elements became clear. The first was that every bank teller was only one move away from a button which could have sounded the alarm and automatically sealed the vault from the robbers. The second was that along at the end of the counter stood the bank manager, and he was the only person who did not have a button.

The message was clear to us. At that time we were standing in faith for something important and it seemed like there was a hold-up. Satan was trying to attack the very people who should have been standing in faith, and they were failing to realise their power. They were being faced with an apparent attack but they failed to realise that the one who was attacking them did not in fact have real power. All the time they were looking to someone else who did not have the key to the situation. The key was right beside them if only they had the courage to move.

Fear is often a factor that prevents people moving in faith. We need to see that in Jesus we have been given the authority to overcome the enemy and release the resources that are needed in His name. '*And whatever you do, whether in word or deed, do it all in the name of the Lord Jesus, giving thanks to God the Father through him*' (Col 3:17).

G: Go back to the first word

In the period after receiving the assurance of faith we are often vulnerable to attack through seeds of confusion. This can happen in many ways. Sometimes by other people who are not deeply involved in the faith move making alternative suggestions that grow out of honest concern or common sense, with no regard to the revelation of the Holy Spirit. Sometimes circumstances seem to go wrong, and it can be tempting to feel that perhaps you got the word wrong to begin with. Many a good faith venture has been scuppered by such vacillation.

You need to go right back to the first word of assurance. There is usually a simplicity about that sort of witness which later discussion and suggestion lack. God is not a God of confusion but of order. These things take a bit of practice and once you have moved in faith a few times you will be less susceptible to the fear and panic that can easily arise in unfamiliar situations. If you have real problems, then take your difficulty and share it with a person of faith whom you know you can trust. Don't just share your feelings but lay out the pattern of faith as you see it and let them help you by their discernment and experience.

I can testify to the faithfulness of God. If we will live by His Word, we will prove its truth:

> So is my word that goes out from my mouth;
>   It will not return to me empty,
> but will accomplish what I desire
>   and achieve the purpose for which I sent it.
> You will go out in joy
>   and be led forth in peace;
> the mountains and hills
>   will burst into song before you,
> and all the trees of the field will clap their hands ...
> This will be for the Lord's renown,
>   for an everlasting sign,
> which will not be destroyed.   (Is 55:11–13)

Chapter 5

Fruitbearers Incorporated

1: Called to be Fruitful

> *'This is to my Father's glory, that you bear much fruit,*
> *showing yourselves to be my disciples.'* (Jn 15:8)

Fruitfulness is a necessary part of discipleship. In fact, it could
be said that fruitfulness is the goal of discipleship. The outcome of growth in personal holiness and gift ought to be
effectiveness for the sake of the Kingdom of God within our
lives.

Fruitfulness is also productive for our own development.
Someone who is being continually productive will be healthy
and motivated in their onward walk with God. Stagnation
brings frustration and frustration leads back into a lack of
fruitfulness.

The ancient picture of Jeremiah the prophet holds good
today. It is those whose heart and hope are fixed in God who
are fruitful and who know how to survive even under the
most intense pressure of life:

> *Blessed is the man who trusts in the Lord,*
> *   whose confidence is in him.*
> *He will be like a tree planted by the water*
> *   that sends out its roots by the stream.*

It does not fear when heat comes;
    its leaves are always green.
It has no worries in a year of drought
    and never fails to bear fruit.   (Jer 17:7, 8)

Fruitfulness is a major key of the New Testament. The Holy Spirit is given to us to bear within our lives fruit towards God. By our willingness or yieldedness we can enable Him or by our disobedience and stubbornness we can prevent Him. In the parable of the rich fool the Lord Jesus warns us against getting our priorities wrong and becoming rich towards ourselves rather than being rich towards God (see Lk 12:21).

God's purpose for us is that our whole lives – that is, every part of our life – should be rich towards Him, bearing fruit for our benefit and His glory. In Chapter 4 we saw already the areas in which the Father means us to be fruitful:

A fruitful spirit: *'The fruit of the Spirit is love, joy, peace, patience, kindness, goodness, faithfulness, gentleness and self-control'* (Gal 5:22).

A fruitful mind: *'Finally brothers, whatever is true, whatever is noble, whatever is right, whatever is pure, whatever is lovely, whatever is admirable – if anything is excellent or praiseworthy – think about such things'* (Phil 4:8).

Fruitful in deeds: *'Whoever would love life and see good days must keep his tongue from evil and his lips from deceitful speech'* (1 Pet 3:10).

Fruitful in gift: *'Each one should use whatever gift he has received to serve others, faithfully administering God's grace in its various forms'* (1 Pet 4:10).

Fruitful in fellowship: *'Let us consider how we may spur one another on towards love and good deeds. Let us not give up meeting together, as some are in the habit of doing, but let us encourage one another – and all the more as you see the Day approaching'* (Heb 10:24, 25).

These scriptures are only samples of the many passages which speak of the need for fruitfulness in our lives as believers. Jesus said that it was *'by their fruit you shall know them'*. There are, I believe, some extremely important issues at stake here and they lie within areas where many Christians never find the answer. Many of the commonest reasons for lack of fruitfulness lie within areas which relate to our own personal lives and emotions. Unless we get our house in order in these areas the inner battles and fears will always dominate us and overwhelm whatever potential there might be for God.

Over the years as I have looked at my own life and experience and that of many others with whom I have worked I have noticed *four* major areas in which we need to ask searching questions of ourselves. It is my conviction that a great deal of the lack of achievement and fruitfulness in our spiritual lives can be traced to a failure to get to grips with these areas in particular.

A: Clear understanding of the faith

We have noticed already that a disciple is a person who commits himself to live continually in the Word of Jesus. But for that to be real there needs to be an openness to and understanding of spiritual truth. This can only be achieved through application to the Word of God through the Scriptures. Many times I have been appalled at the sheer lack of knowledge of the Scriptures in Christians. It is easy to listen to tapes and read popular books, but failure to go to the source of divine revelation will lead to an inability to discern between truth and error. In the end we will be led by the teacher with the greatest charismatic personality or by what most appeals to our emotions or taste.

This issue of understanding the faith is crucial to a number of aspects of our lives as disciples. For example, Paul reminds us that we do not preach 'ourselves' (2 Cor 4:5). This is true – there needs to come a time when we can go beyond our personal testimony. Peter agrees: *'Always be prepared to give an answer to everyone who asks you to give the reason for the hope you have'* (1 Pet 3:15). If we are to be effective in our evangelism, we need to develop a clear understanding of what we believe and why we believe it. You don't need to take a course in theology to be able to do this. The Holy Spirit has promised to be the teacher and guide of all who seek to know more of the deeper things of God (see 1 Corinthians 2).

The same is true for our daily living. An understanding of the faith into which we have been called delivers us from the petty dominance of our own feelings and emotions. There is a great spiritual strength to be gained from standing in *the* faith. This means that we have got hold of the tremendous truths of Scripture and have made them our very own, so that now we have a foundation for our lives that is more secure and stable than our feelings or circumstances.

B: Integrity in the whole of life

Our lives are like car batteries. They are made up of more than one cell. In a car battery there may be six cells. For that battery to function effectively every cell needs to be in good condition. If one or two cells are damaged the efficiency of the whole battery is affected. It is just the same with our lives. Maturity has to do with the *whole* of life. It is no good putting a lot of emphasis on the 'spiritual' areas without realising that Jesus needs to be Lord of one's whole life.

Spiritual power has to do with confidence. We cannot be confident before God if we know that a certain part of our life is a contradiction to all the rest of it. That is why John says: *'Dear friends, if our hearts do not condemn us, we have confidence before God and receive from him anything we ask, because we obey his commands and do what pleases him'* (1 Jn 3:21, 22).

C: Discipline of time and life

Most people waste a tremendous amount of time and energy simply because they don't exercise a real stewardship in the area of their time and its employment. We don't need to become slaves to any time and method mentality; rather we need to ask questions about the purpose of our lives and the use of our time: *'God did not give us a spirit of timidity, but a spirit of power, of love and of self-discipline.'* (2 Tim 1:7).

The results of this sloppiness are many and varied. Lack of spiritual discipline means that we find ourselves living under the wrong kind of pressure and with no clearly established priorities in our life. Such lack of purpose soon breeds spiritual dissatisfaction and a loss of spiritual vitality.

D: Spiritual goals and their fulfilment

Paul's life was consumed by one great goal. To achieve this he needed to fulfil a great number of lesser steps. But he was a man who knew what he was aiming at in his service for Christ. Paul is one of the great men of God whose lives move between two important poles: what he is coming *from* and where he is going *to*: '*I press on to take hold of that for which Christ Jesus took hold of me*' (Phil 3:12).

Fruitfulness calls for a discipline of life, time and energy. This is a discipline which has been sadly lacking amongst many in the so-called charismatic movement. The attitude is portrayed by some, sadly, that the days in which we are living are so urgent and drawing so fast to a close that it is not worth the effort taking any time to prepare for one's life and service with God. This is, among many believers today, a laziness of spirit which is the complete antitheses to fruitfulness in the Kingdom.

2: Overcoming Myself

The more I have gone forward in ministry the more I have recognised the truth that to be effective means knowing where I stand with myself. It means recognising what affects me, in what areas I need to know the overcoming power of Christ, and above all, where I need to alter my reactions and response from the negative to the positive, to enable me to be free to operate without fear or favour in the zone which God has called me into.

There are, I find, *three* great enemies of this personal freedom which rear their head time and again, even in the lives of people with well-known and important ministries. In fact, these very factors have wrought havoc in the lives and ministry of such people, often bringing them to the brink of failure or personal defeat. It is my view that very few 'normal' Christians are really aware to what extent Satan can attack men in leading ministries at the level of personal fears, jealousies and related pettiness, which in other circumstances would be shrugged off as meaningless.

A: Fear

This is the grand-daddy of them all. It presents itself in a multitude of disguises but at root it is the same. It is interesting to see how strongly the Scriptures speak against fear: *'There is no fear in love. But perfect love drives out fear, because fear is not made perfect in love'* (1 Jn 4:18). We can see immediately that the love being spoken of here has nothing to do with sentimental or romantic love. Indeed, Satan often manages to trap us into fear through these very things when they go wrong in our lives. No, here we are dealing with *agape* love, the strong love of God which rids us of this awful grip of fear.

Fear is the half-brother of insecurity. Indeed, the relationship between deep-seated fear and insecurity is very close. One of the most common factors which robs us of our effectiveness in ministry is comparing ourselves with others and the resulting lack of peace and security we feel about our own ministries. Paul was very aware of this problem when he wrote to the Corinthians. Drawing the wrong kinds of comparisons between ourselves and others leads not to an increase of effectiveness but to debilitation and loss of confidence: '*We do not dare to classify or compare ourselves with some who commend themselves. When they measure themselves by themselves and compare themselves with themselves, they are not wise*' (2 Cor 10:12).

On the other hand there is a kind of comparison which can be stimulating and lead to an even greater effectiveness. This is the kind of comparison which is based on a confident understanding of our own life and ministry in the Lord and which views others with openness and gratitude and seeks to learn lessons and take principles from their experience.

B: Pride

I have already spoken elsewhere about the need for brokenness as the central principle of our lives and ministry. In fact, I become more and more convinced that this is so, because Satan can so easily find an opportunity within a successful life and ministry to pander to the flesh. That which begins in the Spirit can so easily end up in the flesh. The tragedy of a case like this is that most other people see or feel that the anointing of the Lord has gone from the situation except the person at the centre of it. Pride dims spiritual eyesight and hardens the heart. It leads to a loss of spiritual sensitivity so that, not only do we become closed to God, but blind to the needs of other people. In fact, the heart of scriptural humility is not a mean-minded attitude but openness to God and others. This is the hall-mark of real humility and meekness and is the opposite of a proud and haughty spirit.

Notice what stands at the top of the list of God's hates in Proverbs 6:16–18:

> *There are six things the Lord hates,*
> *seven that are detestable to him:*
> *   haughty (proud) eyes,*
> *   a lying tongue,*
> *   hands that shed innocent blood,*

a heart that devises wicked schemes,
feet that are quick to rush into evil,
a false witness who pours out lies
and a man who stirs up dissension among brothers.

We can be as spiritually gifted as possible but all the good of it and the potential of fruitfulness is destroyed by having a wrong spirit and attitude. God only deals with pride in one way – that is, He opposes it. It was the sin which led to the fall of Lucifer from glory and thence to every sin that has infected the human race. Pride is no light thing as far as God is concerned and He opposes it on every hand: *'Clothe yourselves with humility towards one another, because, "God opposes the proud but gives grace to the humble." Humble yourselves, therefore, under God's mighty hand, that he may lift you up in due time'* (1 Pet 5:5, 6).

C: Inconsistency

Inconsistency is undependability. When we change direction with every wind that blows and keep altering our principles and attitudes, so that other people don't know where they stand with us. This breeds a terrible insecurity in others and leads to a breakdown of confidence in our relationships with them. To be effective with and for other people they need to be able to depend on us, even if they don't agree with us! God's purpose for all our lives is maturity and integrity of heart and life. Paul knew what he was aiming for and he knew what he stood on. His future goals were closely related to his past experience between the two.

Integrity, humility and faith are the three greatest needs of effective leadership. We need to be available to people. They need to be able to read our lives and perceive the grounds for our actions and behaviour. People who are really fruitful to the benefit of others are not only those who teach the principles but those who manifest them. By that I mean that others are allowed to read us and see the principles at work within us.

Humility is not a 'Uriah Heep' sort of mentality that is always trying, in an artificial way, to disclaim any gift or effectiveness we might have in our ministry or life. To be effective we need to know our gift and our call and not feel apologetic about either. A humble man is a man who has opened his will to the will of God. He is a person who sees himself in the light of God's call on his life and of his true position in Christ.

So often we confuse the wrong kind of softness with humility. Moses was known as the meekest man who ever lived, but we could hardly describe him as soft! No, the secret was he was completely sold out to the will of God and submitted himself to God's purpose in a total way. This is the secret of true humility, because then we are truly open to whatever God wants to do in our lives and with them. The words of the prophet Hanani to Asa, king of Judah in 2 Chronicles 16:9 are entirely appropriate here: *'The eyes of the Lord range throughout the earth to strengthen those whose hearts are fully committed to him.'*

We reproduce what we are – that is the great principle of fruitfulness! If we are weak in character, we will produce moral weaklings who are no more consistent than ourselves. If we live in fear of others and with unresolved fear as the motivating factor in our lives, we will reproduce that fear in those with whom we associate. A person who is driven or dominated by personal fears cannot afford to have people of real strength and promise working with or for him because these very people become a threat to that person. How can we lead others into faith unless we ourselves are people of faith? We cannot. And yet it is the great need of the day. We need men who will trust God and be unafraid and do exploits in the name of the Lord of Hosts!

All of this is making the important point that *the root of fruitfulness is within ourselves*. This is why we need to be open to God. It is why we need to allow the Holy Spirit to search us and cleanse us from every wrong motive, every personal doubt and fear and from the inconsistency which so often is the hallmark of our human endeavours.

D: A prayer for fruitfulness

> '*Lord* **make** *me that I may become...*
> '*Lord* **show** *me that I may become...*
> '*Lord* **give** *me that I may become...*'

This threefold prayer contains, I believe, very important elements for growth. The first line of the prayer deals with what we have just been discussing – the need for our own personal lives to be sorted out to free us for the demands of life and ministry God wants to make of us.

The second line follows on from that. This has to do with catching God's vision for your life. It's a chicken and egg situation sometimes. Some people never get God's vision for their lives because they never seem to get into that fit-enough state in their own inward life where they can hear or receive God's vision. Their continual lack of spiritual maturity seems to disable them from being led forward into any sense of purpose for their lives.

On the other hand, vision encourages self-discipline. I know that it is my vision for my life with God which maintains the stimulus for me to keep myself right with God. If I did not feel the demand of God's call, I doubt if I could continue to be open and allow God to deal with me and make me fit for the vision.

I believe that if we can see what God wants to do with our lives we can also often see what needs to change in us for that to become a reality. This is a powerful incentive towards change. I know people very well who, if they had not had the stimulus of God's call upon their lives coupled with a real desire to serve God in that way, might never have progressed through some of the personal challenges and difficulties they have had to face.

Not long ago I was ministering in a new fellowship in which there was a fair percentage of new Christians who had some very colourful and worldly backgrounds. The leaders were concerned about their growth and development. My advice was in the form of an analogy. I told them to find the deepest swimming pool there was and throw them in at the deep end. What I meant was that the answer for some of these people was not to focus on their own needs only but to catch sight of a new potential of service in Christ. They would soon find that if they wanted to be fruitful in that sphere they would need lives to match the challenge. It is here that we often soft-pedal with new believers. We think they need to become spiritual paragons before they are launched out into the deep. We should pay more attention to our own lives and failures and wonder how the Lord ever used us!

The third line of the prayer reminds us that we don't need to be gifted in every way before we can be fruitful. Praise God that He can and will make up the deficiencies of our nature so that we can more purposefully pursue His will. James reminds us of that when he writes: *'If any of you lacks wisdom, he should ask God, who gives generously to all without finding fault, and it will be given to him'* (Jas 1:5). We all need to make this prayer because it contains the secret of real fruitfulness. Fruitfulness is *becoming* what I am meant to be in Christ. It is being totally open to the Holy Spirit and allowing Him to deal with those negative areas in the power of the Cross. It is the surrender of our wills and human frailties to the Lord so that He can reshape us into a more perfect vessel ready for the Master's use:

> *In a large house there are articles not only of gold and silver, but also of wood and clay; some are for noble purposes and some for ignoble. If a man cleanses himself from the latter, he will be an instrument for noble purposes, made holy, useful to the Master and prepared to do any good work.* (2 Tim 2:20, 21)

Recently I was greatly challenged by the words of James 1:21: *'Humbly accept the word planted in you.'* We need to *make room* for God's Word and purpose in our lives; we should not shut ourselves off from them but be open and receive them. I believe that the greatest factor for fruitfulness to the benefit of other people is that they can perceive this process going on in my life. They will recognise that I am not perfect but they will see that I am open and available to the Word of God for my life. People can see our *sticking points*. They usually accommodate them on our behalf and say, 'Well, that's old so and so, anyway.' But real fruitfulness will come when that is not necessary and when we become people who are ready to respond to God's Word in our lives and overcome these negative factors we have considered, which so easily dominate us and inhibit our fruitfulness.

3: Setting Goals for My Life

'I press on to take hold of that for which Christ Jesus took hold of me' (Phil 3:12).

Lorne Sanny of the Navigators movement is reported as asking those whom he interviewed four basic questions:

(i)   What are your objectives?
(ii) What are your opportunities?
(iii) What are your resources?
(iv) What is your strategy for applying these resources to your objectives?

Now for some of us these might seem very cut and dried questions. Indeed, I have no doubt that for some they may seem too 'unspiritual'. Yet time and again I have been pushed back in my own experience to fundamental issues like this.

We are just not going to fulfil what God wants us to achieve unless we develop some clear idea of where we are going and how to get there. Rather than diminish the need for the guidance of the Holy Spirit, this seems to me to increase such a need. I know full well that anybody can sit and ask themselves questions like this, but if we want to come up with the right answers – namely, God's answers to the questions – then we need to understand our dependency on the Holy Spirit.

God expects us to cooperate with Him in the planning and accomplishment of our lives. It is not His plan for us to sit about waiting on the archangel Gabriel delivering a telegram to relieve us of the responsibilities of stewardship and responsible thought. God has created us with natural and spiritual faculties to enable us to be involved at this very level of discernment.

Some people seem frightened by the thought of goals – maybe, of course, for the very reason that such clarification would highlight for them the very poverty of their existence. We are not called to be spiritual drifters. We are called to be fulfillers. *What would happen if we applied Sanny's questions to our own lives?*

181

A: Applying the questions

(a) Objectives. Imagine the effect, for example, if we asked this question of every event in our lives. What is the purpose of this action? What is my aim in going to this meeting? What do I want to accomplish in this day? What am I aiming at in this relationship? What will I achieve by this action? So much time and energy is wasted without recall because we never address ourselves and our actions with these searching questions. If we made a practice of asking this sort of question about the main events of our lives, then it would soon become second nature and we would find that fruitfulness would become a daily habit. I am not suggesting we become automatons or that we fall into a kind of bondage to this principle, but any improvement would be a great improvement for most of us who live in a world that is drifting. '*Be very careful then, how you live – not as unwise but as wise, making the most of every opportunity, because the days are evil*' (Eph 5:15, 16). I still like the A.V. translation of that scripture – '*redeeming the time, because the days are evil*'.

One major step for most of us in redeeming the time would be in being able to recognise what we are doing with it or what we have just done with it. This sense of achievement breeds terrific spiritual satisfaction and is one major principle of fruitfulness.

(b) Opportunities. It seems to me that any true call of God will carry with it its own opportunities. A man's gift makes room for itself. I am often confronted by people who presume they have certain gifts and callings but always seem to be in a quandary as to how to fulfil them. We need to ask ourselves whether we are sitting around expecting other people or circumstances to do something for us when we should be doing something for ourselves. Of course, lack of opportunity presenting itself may mean that we have to look carefully at our presuppositions, because it is just possible that we are living in the unreality of copying someone else's vision. As we will see later, goals ought to arise out of calling. In spiritual terms goals need to fit and enable the call which God has placed on my life. It is here, I feel, that so many inexperienced

Christians go wrong. They make their own goals the call! In setting goals they are actually expressing nothing more than their own desire, which for some reason or another they have come to have. But their goals are not capable of being fulfilled because they are not rooted in reality.

(c) **Resources.** This all fits together because God never calls but He equips. Whether in personal, spiritual or material terms, the promise is that what He intends He will do in our lives. It is here that faith is replaced often by unreality or presumption. Sanny is right when he insists that it is here that we cannot afford to be other than realistic. We must not be mystical and over-spiritualise.

(d) **Strategy.** Strategy is very simple. It is the thread that joins our call to its fulfilment, or our goals to their achievement. It brings all the resources into play and directs them towards the fulfilment of the objectives in hand.

Spiritual goals are very important factors if we are to be fruitful for God. We needn't act or imagine that we are making something immutable because we are establishing a goal. That is why, I think, some people are afraid of the idea. They imagine you are then closing the issue up as far as divine revelation is concerned, as though it is all becoming automatic and Spirit-less. But we are not doing that. At best we are refining and clarifying God's will and purpose for our lives. At worst we are building-in standards of measurement and growth which will enable us to see where we are going and where we have been. Goals are like the tape-measure of the soul, which demonstrates our growth or lack of it.

B: Busy-ness versus fruitfulness

This is a very important principle if we are to become more productive. Many people confuse busy-ness with fruitfulness. But in a real sense we can be busy doing nothing. Busy-ness is a dangerous diversion of the soul. It satisfies the soul but it is not productive to the spirit, and lulls us into a false sense of achievement. We think because we have been busy that we must have been busy to a productive end. The real question is: was it relevant to what I should have been doing? In fact busy-ness is, for some people, a blind to reality. Their very busy-ness keeps them from facing deeper realities about themselves and their lives. They can live down a rabbit-hole of busy-ness to help them escape ultimate questions about what they should be doing with their lives.

When I was in business I had to address myself to this question time and again: Will the plan that I have enable me to get the job done? On the other hand, a great deal of Christian work flies by the seat of its pants. There is no clear idea and no clear strategy. The enterprise drifts along and depends on goodwill and blundering. I believe the call of the Holy Spirit today is for us to examine our use of God's precious resources like time and money and energy and gift, and ensure that as far as we can we are being honest in the goals we set to enable fruitfulness to be the outcome in our work for God.

C: Choosing goals

I need to exercise choice out of the variety of possible goals which are before me. Life is made up of objectives of differing nature and function. Not all goals need to be 'total life goals'. Indeed some will be very short-lived. Sometimes I find myself setting a goal for the next five minutes. These short-lived goals can have dynamic significance in a busy life because they ensure that the next item is shifted before it becomes a bondage buried in an unfulfilled past.

The goals we need spiritually can usually be defined as short-term, intermediate goals and long-term or life goals. The latter are those which set the tone of life and its direction over a major period of time, perhaps for the rest of your life. The others are servants of the latter inasmuch as they provide stepping-stones to its fulfilment. For the same reasons they may be to one extent or another more dispensable. In fact a short-term goal has dispensability built into it by its very nature.

So we need to be continually exercising discretion about what goal is being met or served and as to how flexible it can be or needs to be. Spiritual goals provide coherence for our lives. They have a ribbon-like effect which ties everything else together and gathers them up into one whole.

D: How do I set goals for my own life?

This is a question I am often asked. At the outset let me say that I am not given to sitting down for long periods and writing lists of goals or objectives, because for years the practice of seeing clearly what I need to be doing has become inbuilt to my life and thought. So living with spiritual goals has become almost as natural as breathing. I don't concentrate on them too much, because I have come to see that they are to be a tool and not a cause for bondage. However, there are certain basic principles which I find it helpful to be clear about:

(a) **Goals must be consistent with God's call on my life.** I find we are so easily diverted from the main task God wants us to take on board. So many demands make their call on our lives which divert us from the main call of God. The question needs to be asked, 'How am I to fulfil what God wants?' It is absolutely essential if we are to redeem the time that we become more ruthless in this area. I don't believe this appertains only to men and women in 'full-time' ministry. So much time and effort are expended meaninglessly in normal Christian living that we should all be asking this question.

Some people seem reluctant to accept the answer. I remember responding to God's call to the full-time ministry. I felt called to be a minister of the gospel, to be ordained and to serve a church. At the time I was a businessman and for the call to be fulfilled meant a four-year stint at a theological college. Some people today would frown at the time involved, but I recall seeing clearly that if this goal was to be accomplished, then this time would need to be given. It may have seemed a slow way to achieve my aim of being a preacher, but I can honestly say that it was worth it and it paid great dividends in my own life and mind. Some people even then wanted me to reconsider whether this was not a great waste and a slow start, but I feel that history has proved them wrong and I would be the poorer without all the preparation that went into my life through that discipline. If we want to accomplish anything worthwhile for God, we need to be ready to bear the cost of the fulfilment of our goal.

Nowadays I find myself even more intensively involved in the same struggle to make my daily and longer-term goals consistent with God's call upon my life. Every day other diversions are introduced, many of them on seemingly good and godly grounds. But if I were more ruthless to God's call, many of them would go by the board, and I know that I would be more productive in terms of my fruitfulness in ministry.

We need to plan the management of these goals to assist in their fulfilment. For some of us this might mean nothing more than making a mental note of what we are aiming at or *making a list of our goals on a piece of paper*. In a more complex situation it usually calls for some more sophisticated approach. I am very fortunate in having a marvellous personal assistant who helps me with the demands of a very busy life. The principle is the same, however, whatever the degree of involvement. We need to clarify our aims and take the appropriate steps towards their fulfilment. Otherwise the outcome is spiritual confusion and disability, which leads to frustration and dissatisfaction.

(b) **We need to recognise the interaction of different goals.** I operate with different goals in different zones of my life. For example, I have goals which are related more to my ministry and goals which are related more to my times of relaxation. I like to have goals for my days off because this fills them with creative purpose rather than that awful feeling of just being laid back and wasting time.

But we need to recognise the interdependence of such goals. A goal fulfilled as far as a day off is concerned will create tremendous spiritual benefit to the fruitfulness of ministry. If I have been frustrated in my enjoyment with the family on a day off, then it means that when I turn my attention to more serious work I approach it in a spirit of dissatisfaction and disturbance. Conversely, if my goal for rest and relaxation has been achieved, I come back to my more serious ministry with a refreshed spirit and a feeling of enjoyment.

'*The secret things belong to the Lord our God, but the things revealed belong to us and to our children for ever, that we may follow all the words of this law'* (Deut 29:29). This scripture reveals two elements of God's dealings with us – namely, those things that remain hidden from us but which belong to the heart of God, and those things which are revealed to us to that we walk in obedience to the known will of God. These are tow poles between which we need to learn to operate all the time. We are walking in the light of what we know and in the expectation of more yet to be revealed. This has an important bearing on how we go about setting goals for our lives.

To me it means that I need to set goals *for what I know.* These are identifiable factors, both short-term and long-term. I can take into account what I already clearly know to be God's will and the steps needed to accomplish it. It also means that I can set goals *for what I don't know.* This is a dimension of goal-setting that many never enter into. It includes setting goals to enable me to seek God, to wait for His Word; a goal of faith, for example, that by a certain time or through a certain exercise I will move closer to understanding or hearing the Word of God for a particular situation.

4: Redeeming the Time

'Be very careful, then, how you live – not as unwise but as wise, making the most of every opportunity, because the days are evil' (Eph 5:15, 16). Another translation urges us to *'make the best use of the time'*. This seems an awesome challenge to many people who have lived for years with little or no discipline at the heart of their lives. In fact, in my experience it is one of the most crucial lessons for those who want to serve the Lord most fruitfully to have to learn. Time is a precious gift and it is given on a non-repeatable basis. We should approach every day with a sense of awe and purpose. Here is a stretch of road that we will never pass over again. I am not suggesting that we develop a neurotic attitude towards our lives, but we need to become better stewards of the gift of time.

I have found the following areas important to this question of how I use my time.

A: Procrastination

'Procrastination is the thief of time' is how the old saying goes, and it is true. Many of the items which become a bugbear in our lives are those which are put off to another day. The other day has a habit of never arriving and we discover that we have collected a bad debt of unfulfilled business which sabotages our effectiveness. I find this to be particularly true with letters, which I don't like writing.

In fact, this is another area where we need to take control in the power of God – namely, the area of likes and dislikes. Most people operate quite well in areas which they like but a real secret of fruitfulness is to learn to be effective in areas we don't like. We can see the principle of 'do it now', being worked out in the men of faith in Scripture – Moses, for example, who must have been a very busy man. God laid one demand after another on his back. In Numbers chapter 1 Moses is told to conduct a census of all the children of Israel. Now there's a job! What did he do? Notice in verse 1 that he is given the instruction or task on 'the first day of the second month'. Notice the day on which Moses got on with the job according to verse 18: 'they called the whole community together on the first day of the second month'. This is not a matter of running ahead of God, but it is a matter of expediting the Word of God when it is given instead of shelving it for when you feel more like obeying it.

B: Haste and urgency

Someone will object and say to me that 'the servant of the Lord must not make haste'. But there is a great difference between haste and urgency. It is a most dangerous thing to run before the Lord, and this is where my goal in taking time to listen to God is so important. But there is an urgency with God. He works in the divine today: *'Now is the accepted time; behold, now is the day of salvation'* (2 Cor 6:2 A.V.).

C: Obstacles and objectives

There are two main ways of looking at the demands of our lives – either as problems or challenges. Part of growing into maturity is to recognise that challenges will contain problems. The man or woman of God who becomes truly fruitful learns by the help of God what to do about problems. Even Moses sometimes managed to get swamped by the negative. If you read Numbers chapter 11 you will find his reaction to God's promise that He would feed the people. Moses was so overcome by the wailing of the people in their need and by his concern for them that he lost sight of God's power in the situation. What ought to have been a goal of faith, even for all its seeming impossibility, suddenly became an obstacle of faith:

> But Moses said, 'Here I am among six hundred thousand men on foot, and you say, "I will give them meat to eat for a whole month!" Would they have enough if flocks and herds were slaughtered for them? Would they have enough if all the fish in the sea were caught for them?'
>
> The Lord answered Moses, 'Is the Lord's arm too short? You will now see whether or not what I say will come true for you.' (Num 11:21–23)

D: Asking God's help

What I have said above leads directly on to this all-important principle – we are not alone. Setting goals for action or faith is not to presume in the power of the flesh. The man or woman of faith is merely bringing order to enable their action, vision and prayer. But their reliance is on God. And the Lord has promised that He will withhold no good thing from those that love Him.

James exhorts us in his epistle to ask God for the wisdom we need: *'If any of you lacks wisdom, he should ask God who gives generously to all without finding fault'* (Jas 1:5). For 'wisdom' read 'whatever you need'. God wants to add to us those gifts and attributes needed to perform His will, which we don't have by nature. I believe that there is a great reservoir of divine help available to the person who will open his heart and humbly come to the Father for His help. The alternative is that we refuse to recognise our need and try to walk in our own strength and fulfil God's will in the limited power of the flesh. This is the road to disaster and unfruitfulness. The best purposes of God have withered in the hands of many a man who will insist on running within the limits of his own natural talents or rational capacities.

E: Stickability

It is here that we need to emulate the attitude of Jesus with regard to the work of God: *'My food,'* said Jesus, *'is to do the will of him who sent me and to finish his work'* (Jn 4:34). So many people start well but never get to the end. Quite apart from the larger question of their lives' work, there are so many unfinished tasks and calls that clutter up their time. Trying to move forward is like trying to walk through a wood full of undergrowth. Every step is a battle and leaves them exhausted, till in the end there is no strength to go further.

God wants us to go on and to complete what we have been given to do. Even the spectacular career of Solomon was marred because at the end he did not display the tenacity which he showed at the first: *'His wives turned his heart after other gods, and his heart was not fully devoted to the Lord his God, as the heart of David his father had been'* (1 Kings 11:4).

F: Divine direction

I believe that this is the heart-secret of establishing the proper goals in both the long and short terms. It is the knowledge that we can wait before God and He will direct us by His Holy Spirit, so that as we turn to the left and to the right we will hear a voice behind us saying *'This is the way; walk in it'* (see Is 30:21).

But just as many of us have still so much to learn about bringing God's proper order to our lives and work, so we have as much to learn about waiting upon the Lord for His divine direction and say-so. I sometimes wonder how I could see clearly through the welter of calls and demands with any certainty if I did not believe that I can depend on this sort of direct divine guidance.

5: Changing the Polarity

A real part of the secret of fruitfulness lies in learning how to respond to the difficulties and challenges that arise in life. How to handle the negative and respond to the positive is an all-important subject if we are to be effective for God.

To be fruitful we need to learn how to handle life and to make the things that happen to us productive to the glory of God. It is not only the seemingly negative factors that pose a threat to our effectiveness. Sometimes the successful event is the very thing that trips us up. We need to learn how to handle success as well as failure so that Satan does not have an opportunity in our lives through pride.

Pride of place has been a stumbling-block for many people who have become successful in their life for God. Faith then turns to presumption and the pride of life and place becomes the motivation for our work and service. Even our successes need to die at the foot of the Cross of Jesus, so that in a real sense we remain 'nothings' for God's use.

We learn some great lessons from Scripture about how the greatest men of God were able to turn the tables on all sorts of adversity and change the flow in their lives from the negative to the positive. Paul was certainly a great exponent of this gift through the power of the Holy Spirit: *'I have learned to be content whatever the circumstances'* (Phil 4:11). That is the voice of a man who has come to know how to handle life and to bring the right response out of circumstances that would seem thoroughly impossible to a lesser man. Yet this is probably one of the greatest lessons we need to learn if we are to be fruitful for the Lord in our lives and ministries. We will all have our own particular areas of conflict and pressure. Over the years I have found the following some of the most demanding and challenging as far as my own experience has been concerned.

A: Discouragement

In the natural I am a person who, at certain levels, is easily discouraged. Like most men who have tried to serve the Lord, I have found that the greatest times of discouragement are those which follow immediately after some moment of spiritual victory or success. It is almost as though Satan lies in hiding, waiting to trap us and cause us to stumble into a pit of despond.

Elijah was one man who went through this very phase in his ministry. He had no sooner routed the prophets of Baal in the power of God than he fell into the trap of discouragement. It was the report of Queen Jezebel's reaction which got right into his spirit and flattened him from the height of spiritual victory to the depths of personal despair. I know what he felt like, for this man of God had probably expended every part of himself inwardly in his struggle with the Baal prophets. He had seen great victory, but like most of us who have run with God, he was left very vulnerable inside himself at this time, and down he went! 1 Kings chapter 19 portrays the sequence of events and teaches us some of the deepest lessons about this attack of discouragement:

First, discouragement *introduces a false sense of values.* 'Take my life,' cried the prophet; 'I am no better than my ancestors' (verse 4). Elijah, to put it literally, felt like death and all the spunk he had manifested on Mount Carmel had evaporated under a cloud of false values.

Second, discouragement causes us to *run away from our real responsibilities.* Elijah ran away to a cave on Mount Horeb until the Lord found him there and asked him, *'What are you doing here, Elijah?'* (verse 9). You notice then how self-pity began to rule the roost in the experience of Elijah? Self-pity is surely the most destructive force of human nature. It turns us against ourselves and envelopes us in a cloud of darkness through which we are unable to see reality. Self-pity paralyses us to our responsibilities for others and makes us spiritually and often physically immobile.

Third, discouragement leads us to *blame other people for the state of affairs.* This is exactly Elijah's next move: *'I have been very zealous for the Lord God Almighty. The Israelites have rejected your covenant, broken down your altars, and put your prophets to death with the sword'* (verse 10). No doubt there was more than an element of truth in Elijah's complaint, but when it arose out of a heart filled with self-pity, it made absolutely no difference to the situation.

Fourth, discouragement causes us to *blow everything out of perspective*. To Elijah things seemed 7,000 times worse than they really were. He felt that he was the only one left who stood where he stood, but God had a very different point of view: '*Yet I reserve seven thousand in Israel – all whose knees have not bowed down to Baal and all whose mouths have not kissed him*' (verse 18).

David was another man who, at times, suffered severe discouragement. But 1 Samuel 30:6 shows us that he was also a man who knew how to overcome this dreadful attack and open himself to a source of strength and help that was far deeper than any circumstance that could affect him. We are told that David 'encouraged himself in the Lord'. What a tremendous thought. I have found a great need to be able to do that in my own life and ministry.

B: Comparisons

We do not serve the Lord in a vacuum. We are part of the Body of Christ as a whole, and at times very closely related to others who are serving the Lord with their own gifts and in their own way. This ought to be a cause for great rejoicing, that God has in His infinite wisdom chosen a whole variety of people and enabled them in various ministries to serve the Kingdom.

But what should be a cause for rejoicing is in reality often the cause of pain. There are a whole number of reasons for this, many of them springing from deep wells of inadequacy and deficiency in our own hearts. Instead of feeling joyful at others' fruitfulness, we feel threatened. Instead of being able to applaud the work of the Holy Spirit through them, we harbour envy and jealousy in our hearts. Instead of allowing their success to stimulate us to greater effort and commitment, we become paralysed and ineffective in our own work. Instead of being able to speak positively about them we become critical and negative, always looking for the loophole that will allow us to pull down instead of build up.

There are three things we need to learn to do: *One*, recognise as clearly as we can our own calling before the Lord and live within that. It is a most dangerous thing to live inside the calling of another man. *Two*, relax in God's power and always try to be aware that unless God does it in you and through you, no one else will. *Three*, rejoice in the fruitfulness of others. This is not always easy, especially if there are elements that you have an honest disagreement about. But I have found it very helpful to focus on what is positive and leave the other aside, so that I can rejoice with a free heart in what the Lord is achieving in the life and ministry of a fellow believer.

C: Disappointment

Disappointment comes from many sources, often from the failed hopes and aspirations of our own hearts. A sense of failure can prove disastrous to effective ministry. Some time ago my dear friend in Christ, Campbell McAlpine, was a source of real blessing to many in our fellowship when he ministered out of the Book of Exodus. He showed at one point how Moses had to walk back past the place of his own failure (where he had smashed the original tablets of the Law) when he was called to appear before the Lord a second time with two new stone tablets. The first attempt had ended in failure with the anger of Moses and the sin of the people. But Moses had to walk back past his failure to meet with God and start all over again.

Disappointment comes also from the lives of others. Our hopes for them are not fulfilled. Our faith aims never seem any nearer being achieved. The book of Proverbs aptly describes the effect of this sort of disappointment: *'Hope deferred makes the heart sick'* (Prov 13:12).

I try to let my disappointments be a proving ground for faith. For example, if something has not yet been achieved in faith, I let this circumstance challenge my own presuppositions. Were they right or was I wrong? I try to stand back from the intensity of the disappointment in my spirit and let the heat go out of it so that it can become a refining fire for my faith. There is no doubt, anyway, that it does our souls good not always to get what we want, or at least, *when* we want it. I know that I am much better at this now than when I was a younger Christian. I don't think this is only a sign of advancing years. I believe it is part of the maturing process of the Holy Spirit within me, as He has helped me to make disappointment a productive rather than a destructive force within my life.

The apostle Paul knew the real secret of overcoming disappointment when he wrote 2 Corinthians chapter 4:

> *Therefore we do not lose heart. Though outwardly we are wasting away, yet inwardly we are being renewed day by day. For our light and momentary troubles are achieving for us an eternal glory that far outweighs them all. So we* **fix our eyes not on what is seen, but on what is unseen.** *For what is seen is temporary, but what is unseen is eternal.* (verse 16–18)

D: Pressure

We need to face the fact that any real ministry is going to carry with it a commensurate measure of responsibility. Responsibility carries pressure with it – that's the name of the game, so to speak! But if we face pressure in the wrong way it will crush us. The pressure of need or of a particular faith enterprise can prove a tremendous stimulus or heavy burden. For myself, I need a certain measure of pressure to enable me to operate in the right way. The good Lord must know that, for he certainly allows it to happen! James speaks of the effect of pressure rightly felt when he says: *'Consider it pure joy ... whenever you face trials of many kinds'* (Jas 1:2). If we are to be fruitful, particularly on behalf of other people, we will need to develop the gift of recognising right pressure from wrong pressure and the ability to accept what is right and throw off what is wrong.

I have found pressure to be productive when borne in the power of God. As James says, it develops perseverance, which is an absolutely necessary quality in the days in which we live. It develops in me a greater capacity for the work God has given me. Without a proper response to pressure I would never have found that my capacity could be greater than I ever imagined. Pressure also demonstrates the areas of weakness within my life and personality, so that I can become aware of trouble before it starts or take the necessary spiritual steps to affect a change.

The trouble comes when we are carrying wrong pressure. This happens when we have accepted a task or position which we were neither called to nor fitted for. Satan will see to it that our egos will call the tune and instead of being at peace to accept and work within the will of God for our lives, we will become subject to demands and pressures which the Father never intended for us.

Our gifts and capabilities are polished under pressure, and I am sure that some of the best work is achieved when we are responding to the proper nudgings of the Holy Spirit. We know how lazy we are and how long it would take some of us to go anywhere for God, and so He knows how to be a proper Comforter to us, by prodding us forward into the action in the power of God.

E: Disagreement

Somebody once said that conformity in behaviour in an organisation is essential, but conformity in ideas in an organisation is tragic. Now, I suppose you could take that too far in spiritual terms. How can two walk together unless they be agreed? For example, in my sort of ministry there really does need to be a basic agreement of spiritual ideas and approach. However, loyalty does not mean necessarily that you agree on every minute detail with each other. It is not spiritual leadership that demands this kind of conformity but spiritual dictatorship.

Part of every one of us wants everybody else to agree with us all the time. But it is rarely the case that this is so, and if it seems to be, perhaps you'd better enquire whether you are surrounded by true loyalty or by a bunch of yes-men who will be of no use when the time of testing comes.

I have been tempted on more than one occasion and in more than one context to cut myself off from those who disagree with me. That is a natural reaction on the part of someone who holds dearly fought-for convictions. But I have come to the conclusion just as many times that this is not right. For one thing, I need to recognise that I am not the holder of all truth and virtue. For another, I have found creative conflict a very productive element in the development of my own thoughts and ministry. Through the pressure of other people's approaches and ideas, I have had my own modified or confirmed, and if they are confirmed they are all the clearer and all the stronger for the challenge of the seeming conflict. Anyway, surely we should be more mature than to regard this process as conflict?

Of course, I would need to say that there are boundaries beyond which this difference of views is no longer creative. I would find it hard to justify the open-ended comprehensiveness that is widely accepted within much of the Church, simply because in this case I don't find it a discussion between people who share a basic common premise. It is more like inter-planetary warfare with parties coming at each other from different sides of the galaxy!

F: Gossip, slander, misunderstanding

The Book of Proverbs sums up very potently the power of the gossiping tongue and the terrible carnage it can inflict in the life of another person, and at the end of the New Testament James also had occasion to express his feelings strongly on the same subject: *'A perverse man stirs up dissension, and a gossip separates close friends'* (Prov 16:28); *'The words of a gossip are like choice morsels; they go down to a man's inmost parts'* (Prov 18:8). These last words carry within them all the pain and hurt that can be felt and known through the power of a wounding word. Someone who plays fast and loose with their tongue never stops to take stock of the damage, sadly often beyond repair, that is caused by their action. James describes the curse of an untamed tongue in a most emphatic way: *'The tongue also is a fire, a world of evil among the parts of the body. It corrupts the whole person, sets the whole course of his life on fire, and is itself set on fire by hell'* (Jas 3:6).

We need to lean certain lessons about the tongue:

First, there is *no self-defence league in the kingdom of heaven*. There is no good getting on to your high horse and attempting some kind of misguided defence. In the first instance, we need to remember the old Red Indian adage: 'Him speak with forked tongue'. If we respond by lashing out immediately we will be in danger of being bitten twice, because here we are confronting an evil which comes from the very pit of hell. The tragedy is, of course, that it is an evil that has pervaded the entire Body of Christ.

Secondly, we need to know *when to leave the evil alone or when to lift it and confront it with the truth*. There are times when either course of action may be right, but we need the gift of discernment in the Holy Spirit to know the difference. There are times when gossip is based on nothing more than misinformation, and it only takes a small dose of the truth to put it right. I find that in this kind of case there usually results a recognition of the truth and an apology, followed by forgiveness which can clear the air and set things on the right footing again.

Thirdly, we need to know how to *let the hurtful word challenge your own life and action*. The old saying goes: 'There is no smoke without fire', and if there is a fire you should know about it and put it out!

But gossip rarely deeply disturbs and certainly cannot destroy a heart and life at peace with God. If you know where you stand and have that open relationship with the Father that tells you that all is well, then you have nothing to fear: *'The peace of God, which transcends all understanding, will guard your hearts and your minds in Christ Jesus'* (Phil 4:7).

G: Hurts and personal problems

I don't need to go into depth about this here because we have already spoken elsewhere about what needs to happen within ourselves. But hurts can lead to a terrible crushing of the spirit: *'A man's spirit sustains him in sickness, but a crushed spirit who can bear?'* (Prov 18:14). Perhaps mostly due to my own fault I have suffered tremendous hurts to my spirit at times. It is at times like this that the Lord had taught me the art of throwing *everything* on to Him. There is no answer to this deepest need of our spirits. The Father knows our spirit – He created it! He knows how to handle it, how to heal it, how to woo it back to life again. He knows how to put His balm into our hearts without allowing us to indulge in self-pity. His hand is loving, but it is strong. He is indeed our heavenly Father.

There are no words more dear to me in these circumstances than those of 1 Peter 5:7: *'Casting all your care upon him; for he cares for you'* (A.V.). I would go as far as saying that until we have walked this way with God, through the weeping of a broken spirit, we have never really experienced what it means to have a real heavenly Father.

Chapter 6

The Pierced Ear

1: Personal Authority

Whenever one human being relates to another positively they are exercising or receiving authority at a very personal level. For example, when two people commit themselves in a love relationship this authority is being expressed in a very deep way. They are being mutually open to each other, listening, submitting and responding to each other. In fact, at the heart of true love is a willingness to receive the authority of another person in a way that has perhaps never been done before by the individuals concerned.

Human society would cease to operate in any meaningful way if this was not true at almost every level of experience – in business, in social relationships, in government and in the home. Without the recognition of personal authority we could not exist as we do.

This is even more true at the level of the spiritual. The ground on which we relate to each other is the ground of our mutual authority in Christ, and within the Body of Christ – that is, the local Church – there needs to be a clear recognition of the principles of spiritual authority if the fellowship is to operate meaningfully and in harmony. Whenever we witness or minister to another person we are claiming a certain authority within their lives. In fact, without the reality of personal authority we really cannot be effective in our ministry to others.

This question of authority is a very important issue if we are to minster effectively into the lives of other people. If we operate with a wrong idea of authority we can so easily crush people or dominate them in the wrong way. We are given *power* through the gifts of the Holy Spirit in which to fulfil our ministry, whatever it might be. But raw power can be a very destructive force unless it is manifested within a context of maturity and sensitivity. Does authority equal power? Or is there another ground of authority which tempers power so that it is effective and positive?

I believe this is a crucial issue today because of the very moment in history in which we stand. The Church has for centuries lived with traditional ideas of authority, in which this authority has been vested in an office rather than in a particular individual. One would trust that the individual who is elected to the office would have personal spiritual authority, and certainly with those gifts of the Spirit which bring power into a ministry. Sadly, though, this has often not been the case, with the result that, in spiritual terms, the authority is hollow and the power is missing.

On the other hand, we have seen the burgeoning of another type of authority within the Body of Christ. This is charismatic authority, vested very much in the life of an individual or group of individuals who have been given a fair measure of authority in the lives of other believers. I don't mean in any sense to sound a critical note, but it is all too easy for this authority to become as sterile and 'official' as the traditional approach.

For all our sakes, and for the sake of all that is best in both camps, we need to examine the ground of our authority and be sure that we are standing on the ground that God wants us to, so that what we are doing with other people's lives will be fruitful for the kingdom of God and to their benefit.

A: The authority of Jesus

I have always been greatly attracted by the account in Luke 7:1–10 of the exchange between Jesus and the Roman centurion. We are not told whether they ever actually met but the man obviously knew quite a lot about the ministry of Jesus. Above all he recognised that in Jesus he was dealing with a man of authority to whom he was willing to submit his life and circumstances. This was the hallmark of the life and ministry of Jesus. He lived, spoke and ministered with authority. There was something about Him which made a tremendous impact in the lives of other people and to which they responded often willingly and positively, sometimes negatively and in reaction: *'The crowds were amazed at his teaching; because he taught as one who had authority, and not as their teachers of the law'* (Mt 7:28, 29).

Two Greek words characterise the power in which Jesus operated. The first of these, *exousia*, is often translated 'authority'; the second, *dunamis*, is translated 'power'. This authority and power was passed on by Jesus to His disciples, and He passes it on to us through the Holy Spirit. We can see that *exousia* (authority) occurs as far as the disciples of Jesus are concerned within two main contexts: *'Yet to all who received him, to those who believed in his name, he gave the right* (exousia) *to become children of God'* (Jn 1:12). Here the emphasis is on the place we have been given in Christ through faith in His name. We have been brought into the family of God and given the right to become God's children. This is the very basis of redemption and the ground of our assurance as believers: *'I have given you authority to trample on snakes and scorpions and to overcome all the power of the enemy'* (Lk 10:19). Here the emphasis was on the right and ability they and we have been given to operate in a ministry of power in the name of Jesus against all the principalities and powers of wickedness. It is our position in Christ and our relationship with the Father through Him which gives us the authority to be involved in the ministry of God's kingdom.

B: Our authority in Christ

This term *exousia* is never used, however, in contexts which speak of Christian leadership or oversight. These 'power' words seem entirely inappropriate when it comes to describing the spiritual relationship one human being has with another. We exercise ministry on the ground of our authority in Christ, undoubtedly, but we don't exercise it with an attitude of power or superiority. In fact the only context where it is used with any regularity in the sense of someone having authority over someone else's life is when it is used with reference to unbelievers and pagan overlords: *'You know that the rulers of the Gentiles lord it over them, and their high officials exercise authority over them'* (Mt 20:25). The reason for this is, I believe, not too hard to find. Spiritual authority is not a claimed thing. It is something that is worked out in us. *Exousia*, the ground of our authority in Christ, comes from grace. It is the gift of God made real within our hearts. It does not lead to pride of place or status but to assurance: *'The Spirit himself testifies with our spirit that we are God's children'* (Rom 8:16).

This is what the centurion recognised about Jesus – that He was a man *under* authority! This was the true secret of the power which Jesus had in the lives of other men and women. They perceived in Him, although no doubt they were hardly ever able to express it, the authority of the Father. This centurion put into words what many others would have seen and felt. *'I myself am a man under authority, with soldiers under me'* (Lk 7:8). The Lord has been teaching me this deep lesson over the past year or two. I don't have authority just because I am in a certain place or hold a certain position. In fact I have found that the response or reaction of people themselves will tell you whether you have any real spiritual authority or not. We only have real spiritual authority when people come and submit their lives to us – not in the sense that we become their overlord, but because they have seen or felt signs in our lives of the authority of God.

In the sections which follow we will look at the *four main grounds* of our authority in Christ: the authority of life; the authority of a submitted heart; the authority of gift; the authority of commitment.

2: The Authority of Life

True spiritual authority is the authority of a life. It is not only what we say or teach; it is what we are that is important. Wasn't it Bertrand Russell, the celebrated atheist, who said, 'I can't hear what you are saying for what you are'? I don't think it is even a matter that people always agree with us. What they respond to and trust is integrity of life and action: that we live in accordance with our own principles, and that our teaching reflects how we live. This kind of life-authority has a very powerful effect on other people. Conversely, the absence of such integrity has an equally negative effect. People may submit to our authority because we are in a position of authority, but without this integrity of life and action it will be an unwilling submission and not that free and willing response of hearts that leads to real fruitfulness and unity within the Body of Christ.

Spiritual authority is, of necessity, moral authority. By that I mean it is an authority that grows out of life. It finds its source in the life of the person who is holding the authority. What we are speaks far more powerfully and eloquently than what we say. This is one of the most fundamental insights of the New Testament. Those of us who seek to serve the Lord through ministering into the lives of other people need to take very seriously this challenge to our own lives.

A: The pattern of leadership

Time and again in the Scriptures the exhortation is given to follow the example of those who are in leadership or ministry. Paul is probably the most frequent exponent of this exhortation, as when he wrote to the church he founded in Corinth: *'Even though you have ten thousand guardians in Christ, you do not have many fathers, for in Christ Jesus I became your father through the gospel. Therefore I urge you to imitate me'* (1 Cor 4:15, 16). Paul then goes on to inform his readers that he is about to send Timothy to them to remind them of his way of life in Christ Jesus. What an awesome statement! Neither is this the only time that Paul issues such an exhortation. When he wrote to the church in Philippi he said much the same thing: *'Whatever you have learned or received or heard from me,* **or seen in me** *– put it into practice'* (Phil 4:9).

When he wrote to the Thessalonians he could remind them of the power of the testimony of his own life among them. In fact, it seems that this testimony was one of the main reasons for their own strong foundation in faith which had become known through the world: *'You know how we lived among you for your sake. You became imitators of us and of the Lord; in spite of severe suffering, you welcomed the message with the joy given by the Holy Spirit'* (1 Thess 1:5, 6). In the Epistle to the Hebrews the same sort of exhortation is given to the readers: *'Remember your leaders, who spoke the word of God to you. Consider the outcome of their way of life and imitate their faith'* (Heb 13:7). What a lesson to take into our own lives! I find that people can sniff out what is in you and they can soon tell whether what you are giving them is only words or whatever it is the outcome of a life that is itself lived under the authority of God. I doubt if any one of us can read words like these and fail to wonder whether we dare be bold enough to give our converts the same advice.

B: The truth will out

When Paul speaks to Timothy he draws the contrast between those teachers whose lives do not live up to what they say and the example of his own ministry. Their message is hollow because it has no basis within their experience. Their lives do not match their message, with the result that they wreak spiritual havoc among the immature and unwary (see 1 Tim 3:1–9). But the man of God is all of one piece. His message is matched by his life and his life bears witness to his words. This consistency brings great strength to his ministry and sets him in a place apart from spiritual charlatans.

In 2 Timothy 3:10 Paul outlines in one brief sweep those areas of his life and experience in which this integrity can be discerned. His life was like an open book and he could quite plainly appeal to this testimony as the basis of his authority in the lives of his disciples such as Timothy and the others who followed him in ministry: *'You, however, know all about my teaching, my way of life, my purpose, faith, patience, love, endurance, persecutions, sufferings.'* This verse highlights six important aspects of Paul's life which hang together to construct a very cohesive and integrated life of maturity and fruitfulness. This is surely God's purpose for every one of us who seek to serve Him: that our lives will also reflect the same unity of spirit and purpose as Paul's so that others will see in us an authority that is born of God.

(a) **Teaching.** Paul's life was based on truth. It was not truth which he had received second-hand, or only as a package of doctrine unapplied to his life. You could describe the teaching of Paul as *doctrine informed by experience*. What I mean by that is that Paul had received his teaching as from the very hand of God. It was what had made his life what it was. It became Paul's own gospel. Not that it differed from *'the faith once delivered unto the saints'* (Jude 3) but that it had been made personal to Paul because it had been allowed to shape him as a man and had become the very foundation of all his life, attitudes and actions. It is this kind of teaching that we need to know for ourselves. Where the Word of God is becoming formed in us and is reforming us into the likeness of Christ, it will become a Word of great power and authority for the lives of other people.

(b) **Way of life.** The Greek word that Paul uses here is interesting. It literally means 'the way I conduct myself'. When he writes to Timothy elsewhere he encourages the younger man in this area: *'Set an example for the believers in speech, in life, in love, in faith and in purity'* (1 Tim 4:12). This is what used to impress me greatly as a young Christian about some of the older men I knew. There was a dignity about them. There was something about the way they carried themselves and, it seemed to me, that the gospel they preached had actually made a great difference to them as men. I knew then, and I know now, that they were far from perfect. But for all that, I could see that their aspiration was to live according to their gospel. That is a great aim and it has left its mark indelibly on my mind ever since.

(c) **Purpose.** The original Greek word used here could be translated 'chief aim' – that which, in the midst of all other calls, demands and ambitions of life, stands out above everything else. This is what I live for, this is what I aim at, this is what provides the chief motivating force in my life and experience. Paul spells out for us what this meant for him:

> I want to know Christ and the power of his resurrection and the fellowship of sharing in his sufferings, becoming like him in his death, and so, somehow, to attain to the resurrection from the dead. Not that I have already obtained all this, or have already been made perfect, but I press on to take hold of that for which Christ Jesus took hold of me. (Phil 3:10–12)

This is what produces the authority of a committed life, of which I have more to say in section 5.

(d) **Faith.** The exhortation to copy the faith of those who lead us is part of the message of Hebrews 13:7 which we have noted already: '*Consider the outcome of their way of life and imitate their faith.*' Faith is a powerful stimulus to discipleship. There is nothing more challenging or inspiring, I believe, than the demand of faith. But it is more than faith as an active attitude of belief that is required. What is needed is *faithfulness* – that is, a steadfastness and dependability of attitude and commitment to those who are depending on us. When people see and feel in us this constancy of character and dependability of action on their behalf, then it engenders the very same attitudes and actions in them.

(e) **Patience, love, endurance.** These three beautiful words described Paul's attitude of heart. The first word, 'patience', translates a beautiful Greek word, *makrothumia*. It is used a number of times in the New Testament and is usually translated as here. But it is a very special kind of patience. On a number of occasions it is used to describe God's attitude towards us while we were still in a state of unbelief: '*Do you show contempt for the riches of his kindness, tolerance and patience, not realising that God's kindness leads you towards* *repentance?'* (Rom 2:4). Another way of describing this patience is by the older word, 'forbearance'. It expresses a positive attitude of love and kindness which is shown in circumstances or towards people who do not warrant or deserve it.

The second word is *agape* which, as we all know, is the very special word in the New Testament for the love of God. This is the love of Calvary. It is selfless and sacrificial. It lays down its life for those to whom it is directed. It does not depend on the response of the other party. It is not the love with which we are born or gifted in the natural, and the only way we are able to experience and demonstrate this love is in the power of the Holy Spirit: *'Hope does not disappoint us, because God has poured out his love into our hearts by the Holy Spirit, whom he has given us'* (Rom 5:5).

The third word is sometimes translated 'perseverance'. Like *makrothumia* it has the idea of patience at its heart but whereas that carries the thought of *forbearance in kindness*, this word speaks more of *patience or perseverance in expectation*: *'If we hope for what we do not yet have, we wait for it patiently'* (Rom 8:25). It was this sense of expectation which was at the heart of Paul's amazing ability to stand firm in the challenging and severe circumstances: *'Therefore we do not lose heart ... we fix our eyes not on what is seen but on what is unseen. For what is seen is temporary, but what is unseen is eternal'* (2 Cor 4:16, 18).

(f) Persecution and sufferings. Paul was totally realistic about suffering and persecution. He knew that any servant of God involved as he was in front-line action for the kingdom would have his share of them. They are not the same thing, although one may well be involved in the other.

The mark of Christ's sufferings on a man's life lends total credibility to his gospel. I am not saying that we need pursue these things, but I hardly think we will need to chase after them if we are being faithful to God's call. A great danger today has been a tendency on the part of some to follow the big names of faith and to imagine that they achieve great things for God without suffering. I don't believe this is so! If we were able to see behind the scenes of the life of any who had achieved great things for God, we would perceive the reality of this fact: *'To this you were called, because Christ suffered for you, leaving you an example, that you should follow in his steps'* (1 Pet 2:21). This Scripture provides us with a template by which to judge our own hearts and lives. Before we go any further, perhaps it would be a good idea to take it and meditate on it and allow the Holy Spirit to show us where we are with regard to this question of authority of our own lives.

3: The Authority of a Submitted Heart

As we have already seen, what the centurion recognised about Jesus was that Jesus Himself was a man who lived His life under an even higher authority. I believe that we have here the hallmark of all true spiritual authority. But it is not just a question of being 'under' someone's authority or covering, as we like to speak of it today. It is a question of living under the authority of a servant heart. The amazing fact is that Jesus was not only submitted to the Father, but He also submitted Himself to those around Him in as much as He was there to serve them. As we will see, this does not mean that Jesus suspended all His powers of discernment or put Himself at the mercy of those people who were only out to get what they wanted for themselves. Jesus never served selfishness or self-interest. But such was His relationship with and openness to His Father that His heart was always sensitive to *how* and *where* the Father wanted Him to serve: '*Jesus gave them this answer: "I tell you the truth, the Son can do nothing by himself; he can do only what he sees his Father doing, because whatever the Father does the Son also does"*' (Jn 5:19).

In a discourse with His disciples Jesus teaches them the absolute importance of this principle of the servant heart. It all arose, typically, out of the concern of a mother that her two sons should occupy the most important places in the kingdom.

> *Jesus called them together and said, 'You know that the rulers of the Gentiles lord it over them, and their high officials exercise authority over them. Not so with you. Instead, whoever wants to become great among you must be your servant, and whoever wants to be first must be your slave – just as the Son of Man did not come to be served, but to serve, and to give his life as a ransom for many.* (Mt 20:25–28)

A: The meek shall inherit the earth

True brokenness and humility of heart are the hallmarks of real spiritual authority. *Meekness* is the prime key to this understanding of authority. Of course, we must be clear what we mean when we speak about meekness. Moses is known in the Scriptures as the epitome of meekness: *'Now Moses was a very humble* (A.V.: 'meek') *man, more humble than anyone else on the face of the earth'* (Num 12:3). But although Moses has this reputation we know quite clearly from the testimony of Scripture that there was nothing molly-coddlish about him at all. When the chips were down Moses could be tough and resolute in his stand for the things of God and I cannot imagine that he as a person was very easily fooled. No, true meekness comes to a man when his will and heart are totally submitted to the will of God. Moses was such a man. His whole life was devoted to God and to seeing the will of God being fulfilled in the lives of the unruly mob which he had under his hand.

When Paul speaks of the authority of his own ministry in 1 Corinthians chapter 9 he makes it clear that although he could claim every qualification required for apostleship, it was this same servant heart which stood as the foundation of his own ministry: *'Though I am free and belong to no man, I make myself a slave to everyone'* (1 Cor 9:19).

B: The marks of true submission

Submission is one of those words that has been overworked and undervalued in our own age.

(a) Submission is not: Being submissive in spirit does not mean adopting a Uriah Heep-type of attitude in life, as we have already seen, always proclaiming how very humble we are and building a facade of false humility. It does not call for the denial of any proper gift or calling which God has placed on our lives. It is false humility to pretend that we are not what we clearly are!

Being submissive does not mean that we will tolerate error, wrong teaching or wrong attitudes in life or relationships. In fact, having a submissive heart means that we ourselves are first in submission to God's Word of truth, which will bring great wisdom and maturity into our attitudes to life.

Being submissive does not mean that we will never pass

judgement on anything or anybody. It does mean that criticism and negative thinking will not dominate our attitudes and actions. But meekness does not suspend judgement. There is a great tendency to confuse the love of God with human sentimentality. Many people become very sentimental when they have been affected spiritually. They then get into a way of thinking that it is wrong to make a judgement about anything lest the judgement borders on the sin of unwarranted criticism. This attitude has left them exposed to the entrance of error. We are exhorted quite clearly in Scripture to stand by the truth and to test every spirit to see if it be of God.

Being submissive is not the wrong kind of softness or indulgence towards sloppiness, spiritual lethargy, laziness, untidiness or lack of discipline. God's people need to have standards in all they do, and the Scriptures make it plain that we are to be at our best for God: *'Whatever you do work at it with all your heart, as working for the Lord, not for men'* (Col 3:23); *'Do your best to present yourself to God as one approved, a workman who does not need to be ashamed'* (2 Tim 2:15).

(b) Submission is: First and foremost, submission is seeing ourselves properly related to Christ. Let me explain what I mean. The secret of a submitted heart does not lie in the fact that I always feel I am nothing or that I am always crawling across the carpet in self-denigration. No, if we are to be effective in life and ministry we need to have that proper confidence of who we are in Christ and what we are with respect to God's calling on our life. Imagine for a moment that you can see the greatness of the Lord Jesus. It is as though He stretches up far above you in the full stature of His perfect manhood. Now see yourself beside Him. He is not knocking you down but asking you to stand up to the full stature of your new manhood in Him. This is truly what a submitted heart is. It is a heart that has accepted what it is in Christ. It knows that in relation to Him it is as nothing but at the same time, in Him it has become something!

Next, submission is a proper recognition of the gifts and ministries of other people without feeling threatened about your own. We need to learn to submit to one another's ministries. What a tremendous enrichment of heart and spirit would accrue among us if we were open to each other in this way. Of course, this will only happen if we have a measure of confidence in the Lord for ourselves. But where my heart is right with God and I am clear about where I stand with Him in relation to life and work, I am free to accept the calling on someone else's life.

A servant heart also wants to consider and serve the real needs of other people. Too often we are subconsciously conditioned these days to do it if there is something in it for us. I firmly believe that we need to proclaim more clearly and urgently the truth of the heavenly rewards of the believer. If we are working for what we can get or what the immediate benefit will be, we will never be able to express the servant heart of Jesus.

Above all, submission is having a servant heart toward the Word of God. That is what we are called to do – to serve the Lord through serving His Word. How do we serve the Word of God? Chiefly through obeying it and putting it into practice in our lives with the help of the Holy Spirit. The Father is looking for those who have a right heart-attitude towards His Word, because it will be in those lives what he will be able to manifest His fruitfulness. In those lives all the attributes of God which His Word displays to us will become a reality. This is the power of the Word, that for those who serve it, *it becomes what it says!*

C: Clothed with humility

This is how Peter expressed this challenging truth: 'Clothe yourself with humility towards one another, because,

> *"God opposes the proud*
> *but gives grace to the humble"'*   (1 Pet 5:5, 6)

Humility of spirit and a servant heart are the two most productive elements in the Kingdom of God. We save ourselves a lot of the heartache that comes through aggression and pride and we are free to involve ourselves in the lives of others, not only because we are available, but because when they read our spirits they will want to respond to us. Surely that is true authority!

Submission, in this sense, has some wonderful spin-offs in life. First, it liberates us from the awful strain of feeling that we have to prove ourselves in our lives and ministry. When we are open to God and open to man in this way it produces a tremendous sense of peace and self-acceptance in our hearts. The reason for this is that we no longer need to live in fear and we can experience that perfect freedom of spirit which comes through a deep awareness of the love of God.

Second, submission gives us a great capacity to enjoy the gifts and ministry of others. One of the great benefits of knowing where you stand is that you also come to know where other people stand alongside you. This means that, as you employ the gifts God has given you, you are free to enjoy those He has given to others with no sense of shame, envy or pride.

Third, submission means that we are in the situation of being able to take into account the true needs of other people and have a heart to serve them. Because our aim is to be open to the Father, we will develop that sensitivity of spirit which will bring wisdom and discernment into every situation. This means that we are not at the mercy of greed or Satan but that in our service we are responding to the touch of the Father as He guides us through the Holy Spirit from one place to another. So fruitfulness is the outcome of servanthood.

4: The Authority of Gift

> *We have different gifts, according to the grace given us. If a man's gift is prophesying, let him use it in proportion to his faith. If it is serving, let him serve; if it is teaching, let him teach; if it is encouraging, let him encourage; if it is contributing to the needs of others, let him give generously; if it is leadership, let him govern diligently; if it is showing mercy, let him do it cheerfully.* (Rom 12:6–8)

The authority of gift is recognised in the world as the 'authority of competence'. This means that a person's authority rests on his proven and apparent ability to function at a given level and with a given ability. The spiritual equivalent of this is seen in terms of gifting or anointing. This is why, in the Body of Christ, people are given a place of authority sometimes which bears no relation to their social, educational or professional backgrounds. God is no respecter of persons when He distributes His gifts by the Holy Spirit. But a spiritual gift can carry with it a tremendous level of authority into the lives of other people, because in this gift they perceive the anointing of God and they submit their lives to this anointing.

A: The grace of God

It is interesting to notice how often Paul uses the word 'grace' in a very special and specific way. We all know what grace in a general sense is – it is the bestowal by the Father of His mercy and undeserved favour into our lives. Not one of us deserved God's kindness but He has shown it and given it in Jesus. In this sense we are all recipients of the grace of God and it is in this grace we stand. But Paul uses the word 'grace' many times, not only in this general way, but to indicate a vital truth about the ministry to which he was called and the authority he had been given by the Lord. He speaks about *'the* grace'. He was overcome by the fact that God had not only given him grace in salvation but had also given him a grace which was the foundation of his life and service. Many times he appeals to this special grace as the foundation of his ministry and the ground of his authority in the lives of others: *'By the grace*

216

given me I say to every one of you: Do not think of yourself more highly than you ought' (Rom 12:3). Paul was controlled and directed by *the* grace which God had given him. Paul is not here speaking about 'graciousness' in speech or manner. He is speaking of the *authority* of the grace which as been manifested in his life. This grace is Paul's particular call and gifting to the special ministry which was his through the election of the Father.

There are many more instances of this same use of the word in the New Testament through which it becomes clear that Paul had a tremendous grasp of what was involved in his calling by God to His work and service. For him it was the very expression of the heart of God and, as such, carried with it the very hallmark of heaven. It was something he prized and valued and which he was concerned to work out in the most effective way possible. He was constantly encouraging others to polish this gift of God which had been given to them and use it to its greatest potential for the good of others: *'For this reason I remind you to fan into flame the gift of God, which is in you through the laying on of my hands'* (2 Tim 1:6). As far as Paul was concerned this grace which he had received and been called in was the motivating power of his whole life and work. He knew *what that grace was.* He identified the grace within his life. He was saved in grace and called into grace:

*The grace **God gave me to be a minister of Christ Jesus**.*
(Rom 15:15, 16)

*By **the grace** of God I am what I am.*   (1 Cor 15:10)

*For God, who was at work in the ministry of Peter as an apostle to the Jews, was also at work in my ministry as an apostle to the Gentiles. James, Peter and John, those reputed to be pillars, gave me and Barnabas the right hand of fellowship **when they recognised the grace given to me**.*   (Gal 2:8, 9)

I became a servant of this gospel by the gift of God's grace given me through the working of his power. Although I am less than the least of all God's people, **this grace was given to me: to preach to the Gentiles the unsearchable riches of Christ.** (Eph 3:7, 8)

This is a tremendous insight into the grace of God. Not only is it general in terms of salvation, but it is special in the sense of call. It is more than the particular gifts of the Spirit; it is more like the hand of God coming upon someone's life to single them out for a particular work or area of working. The gifting no doubt comes with the grace, but it seems to me that this grace is a deep and powerful reality in the lives of those who know its calling.

B: The gifts of grace

Of course, the word 'gift' in the New Testament is closely related to the word 'grace'. In fact they both share the same root. The word for gift is *charisma*; the word for grace is *charis*. You can see how closely related they are. In fact charisma has an ending which could properly be translated 'the thing of' – that is, what we call spiritual gifts is 'the thing of grace'. In other words it is the expression or result of God's grace being let loose through the Spirit in my experience. So we call it a 'gift' of the Spirit: *'Each one should use whatever gift* (charisma) *he has received to serve others, faithfully administering God's grace* (charis) *in its various forms'* (1 Pet 4:10).

(a) Body gifts. Two things are clear when we examine what the Scriptures have to say about these gifts. First, they are manifested through the lives of specific individuals. That is, they are people-related gifts. From the beginning this was God's way of witnessing to the power and reality of the Gospel: *'This salvation, which was first announced by the Lord, was confirmed to us by those who heard him. God also testified to it by signs, wonders and various miracles,* **and gifts of the Holy Spirit distributed according to his will'** (Heb 2:3, 4).

Secondly, the gifts of the Holy Spirit are gifts *to and for* the Body of Christ. They are to be employed within the Body.

Each gift is inter-connected to gifts operating within other members of the Body. They are generally available to the members of the Body and contribute to the upbuilding and harmony of the Body. It would seem that the 'body gifts' are available to whoever seeks the Lord for the gift, and according to the need at that moment within the Body in general. All of this and more seems obvious from 1 Corinthians chapter 12 and 14: *'Now to each one the manifestation of the Spirit is given for the common good'* (1 Cor 12:7).

(b) Ministry giftings. However, it is clear from what we have already seen and from passages like Ephesians chapter 4 that there were gifts given to some, of a different and more permanent nature. At the end of 1 Corinthians chapter 12 Paul seems to delineate some who hold particular offices or functions within the body and in Ephesians chapter 4 he highlights five well-known giftings: *'But to each one of us grace has been given as Christ apportioned it ... It was he who gave some to be apostles, some to be prophets, some to be evangelists, and some to be pastors and teachers'* (Eph 4:7, 11).

If we consider these gifts in terms of spiritual authority it would probably be right to make a distinction of kind. The fist kind is the gift which operates occasionally and temporarily carries its authority within itself in an immediate and temporary way. But the second carries an authority of gifting which goes beyond any immediate operation of the gift in practice. That is, one who is recognised as an apostle, prophet, teacher, evangelist or pastor bears the authority of that calling within himself even in those moments when he is not operating in any of the specific gifts of the Holy Spirit which may be given for the exercise of his calling.

It seems to me essential that we are clear about this distinction, because many people today seem to be striving and straining to be something God has never called them to be. We confuse *body gifting* with *ministry calling* to the degradation of both. Often we cause ourselves and other people great pain and hassle as a result, and frequently we can suffer so much disappointment that we can become disillusioned.

C: Grace and gift

Every Christian needs to be open to the gifts of the Holy Spirit in their lives and to learn how to operate in the power and authority of these gifts. What I am more concerned with at this moment, however, is the fact that to be effective in ministry we need to be clear about this wider issue of the calling of God upon our lives. Much confusion has arisen in recent years because we have failed to observe the distinction which I have spoken of above. There are at least four major factors which need to be taken into account with regard to a call to ministry.

(a) **A clear sense of God's call.** Perhaps some will think I am extreme in this, but I don't believe we can operate with the power and freedom that is called for in ministry today unless we have a clear call from God to the work. In the Church at large other factors seem to have overridden the need for a burning sense of call like this. Educational qualifications and the like are demanded as a priority before a spiritual setting-apart. I quite realise that a man needs to be equipped to serve and that he needs to meet certain standards of proficiency and ability. But if we looked for a strong enough call of God, we would see individuals with quite remarkable capacities who were teachable and able to achieve great things in the power of God.

On the other hand I believe we have, in many quarters, lost the idea of what a call of God really is. Many Christians seem to confuse a call with their own desire or wish to serve God. Perhaps they have been excited and stimulated by the ministry of some other person. Today I believe we have fallen into the trap of everyone wanting to be an international teacher, prophet or evangelist when, in fact, what God wants is a fully equipped and very effective Body through whom He can express His power and love.

(b) **A heart for the work of God.** This does not mean that we will enjoy every experience we have in our ministry for God. Often the burden of the work lies so heavily upon us that is seems as though it will break us. Sometimes we will experience frustration when we realise how much there is to be done and how little we can give to meet the demand. Nevertheless, to the man whom God calls, these things act as a stimulus to the spirit and to a greater dedication to the task.

A deep sense of spiritual satisfaction comes when we know we are where God wants us to be. Of recent days I have been learning that to be really effective for God in my ministry there has to be that sense of satisfaction. I have a new contentment in my spirit because, for all its difficulties and challenges, I know that what I am doing is what God wants me to do. This has led to a far greater measure of fruitfulness and effectiveness and brings about a freedom in my spirit which gives me the strength to undertake far more work than ever before.

(c) **Exercising the gift.** A man's ministry makes room for itself. God does not call or appoint into inertia. There is an inbuilt dynamic about the call of God through which it will find expression in practical terms. I would go as far as to say that the call of God creates a sort of spiritual ambition in the heart. Not an ambition of the flesh, or self-interest, but a desire that comes from God to be going on in the work and to find the means and outlets for what is inside to be fulfilled in practice. This spiritual drive (not strive!) is integral to a real call of God and it is what leads a person forward to take the steps that are necessary to bring the work to fruition.

(d) **Fruitfulness.** Fruit is the real sign of ministry. God's grace is always effective and it produces fruit in us and in the lives of those to whom we minister.

Some Christians seem to speak in terms of gift with no evidence of fruitfulness. But effectiveness is the real witness of the fact that we are called and gifted by God.

I am sometimes asked about the difference between spiritual gift and natural talent. As far as the work of God is concerned there is none. If we have been born with natural gifts, then for them to be useful in the service of the kingdom they need to come the same way as we have done – namely, by way of the Cross, where all that we are and have is surrendered up to the Lord Jesus Christ. I am sure that God wants to use the gifts we have been born with. But for that to happen they need to be consecrated to Him and every vestige of human pride and achievement taken from them. God can only use what has been made holy.

It is clear that even Paul used what we might regard as natural talent in the service of his ministry. He was not averse to a bit of tent-making to support the work. It is clear that God used his great powers of intellect and training when He used Paul as the means of expounding many of the deepest revelations of the gospel. Without Paul's letters we should be missing a large portion of our understanding of the faith. Nevertheless, Paul did not stand on the authority of these talents when he came declaring the gospel: 'My message and my preaching were not with wise and persuasive words, but with a demonstration of the Spirit's power, so that your faith might not rest on men's wisdom but on God's power' (1 Cor 2:4, 5).

D: Vital questions

All of this leads us to ask some very important questions. The answers to some of these will determine to what extent we are going to be effective in our lives for God. Let me simply list them so that they can be easily recognised.

(a) **Have you a clear sense of call by God?** As far as I am concerned I am sure that my call from God was implicit in the very experience of my conversion as a boy of twelve. From soon after that event I can recall having a sense of excitement and urgency about the work of God. Certainly I can remember some very clear moments when that call has been ratified and clarified. This clear sense of call has kept me stable through moments of extreme challenge and difficulty, and without it I know that I could not have continued in my work for God.

We need to re-establish this sense of call as a priority today. Sadly, in some quarters other considerations are put before this sense of call. Educational qualifications seem more relevant to some people than the hand of God. Of course, men and women need to be fitted for the work they are to do, but I do believe that we have depended on education in secular terms to do something for us that is properly the task of discipleship and ministry training.

(b) **How have you enabled the call of God in your life?** The choices and commitments we make in life have a great deal to say about to what extent God's call will be effective in us. I know many individuals who have ruined or inhibited the call which God has given them by showing a lack of concern, care or wisdom in the decisions they have made in vital areas of their lives. The choice we make in very fundamental areas of life such as our use of time, the partner we choose in life, what we do with the opportunities that have presented themselves to us and so on all have an important bearing on whether or not we will ever come near to fulfilling God's desire for our lives.

(c) **What capacity have you to fulfil what you feel to be God's call?** I know quite well that we always feel inadequate for the job, but the truth is that when we are truly called by God there is that sense deep within us that we can meet the demands of the job. It may mean training or discipline, but underneath it all there needs to be that sense that we have the potential in us to fulfil our calling.

5: The Authority of Commitment

'No-one who puts his hand to the plough and looks back is fit for service in the kingdom of God' (Lk 9:62).

There is, I believe, nothing so profound as the power of a committed life. It was not just His message or His moral goodness which attracted men to Jesus. There was something about Him which told them that He knew where He was going. There was a tremendous feeling of purpose and of direction which characterised all His actions and movements. He did not speak His own words or do only what suited Him. He did not go about doing good for its own sake, but He always said and did that which pleased the Father. His whole life was a fulfilling of the call and purpose of God.

A: My ear you have pierced

In ancient Israel there was a practice which signified the total loyalty of a slave to his master. Slavery was not permitted to perpetuity in Israel. Under the Law a slave could only serve six years and in the seventh year he had to be set free. But it the servant chose to remain in the service of his master, he had to be taken to the doorpost of the house, where his ear was pierced with an awl (see Ex 21:2–6). This was a sign of his commitment for life to his master.

The Psalmist takes up this very picture as he describes the man whose perfect trust is in the Lord and whose desire is to serve the Lord all his days. Of course, the passage speaks prophetically of the Lord Jesus.

> *Sacrifice and offering you did not desire,*
> *but my ears you have pierced;*
> *burnt offerings and sin offerings*
> *you did not require.*
> *Then I said, 'Here I am, I have come –*
> *it is written about me in the scroll.*
> *I desire to do your will, O my God;*
> *your law is within my heart.* (Ps 40:6–9)

B: The cost of commitment

Nowhere is there a more profound and moving picture of commitment to a call than in the words of Isaiah 50:4–7. They are worth reproducing so that we can meditate on them. Of course, they reflect prophetically the experience of the Lord Jesus Himself, the perfect Suffering Servant.

> *The Sovereign Lord has given me an instructed tongue,*
> *to know the word that sustains the weary.*
> *He wakens me morning by morning,*
> *wakens my ear to listen like one being taught.*
> *The Sovereign LORD has opened by ears,*
> *and I have not been rebellious;*
> *I have not drawn back.*
> *I offered my back to those who beat me,*
> *my cheeks to those who pulled out my beard;*
> *I did not hide my face*
> *from mocking and spitting.*
> *Because the Sovereign LORD helps me,*
> *I will not be disgraced.*
> *Therefore* **have I set my face like a flint**
> *and I know I will not be put to shame.*

In an amazing way these words describe in fine detail what it meant for the Lord Jesus to be committed to the call of God upon His life.

One day I was alone in my study when the Lord spoke to me in a very simple yet powerful way. I was given a picture in my mind along with its interpretation in my spirit. The picture was of a field. Along one side of the field I could see a single furrow which had been ploughed. It was straight and fine and went from the bottom of the picture where I was standing right up to the top. At the bottom of the field, near me, was an old horse-drawn plough, the kind that ploughs one furrow at a time. It was standing waiting for the next furrow to be ploughed.

I looked at the picture and wondered what it meant until it seemed that the Lord spoke inside my heart. This is what He said: 'My Son has ploughed this first furrow that you can see. He ploughed it alone. Now the plough is waiting for your hand because I am calling you to plough the next furrow.' As I listened to this inner voice, certain facts about the vision became even more clear. For one thing, I remembered that to plough a furrow as straight and perfect as the one I was seeing called for great concentration and determination. It was essential to keep the eye on some fixed point at the far end of the field, or else the concentration would be lost and the plough-man would be diverted and the furrow would not be straight and true. As I considered this fact it became clear also that to plough like that meant not only fixing the gaze on some distant point of reference but also called for an awareness or everything that was between the start and the finish. The ploughman needed to be clear about the task before him and whether there were any obstacles between him and his goal.

I began to see the implications of all this. I knew what it had meant for the Lord Jesus. He knew the end from the beginning and His whole life and ministry manifested the signs of this commitment. Jesus knew that to plough the furrow the Father had asked of Him meant that He was to pass through the dark night of sorrow and suffering; that it would mean rejection and denial by those who were most dear to Him. Yet He kept on right through to the end – even in the midst of His active and successful earthly ministry, where He could have enjoyed the plaudits of men – and never lost sight of His commitment to the call of God: '*He then began to teach them that the Son of Man must suffer many things and be rejected by the elders, chief priests and teachers of the law, and that he must be killed and after three days rise again*' (Mk 8:31, 32).

I have put these two things – the Scripture and the vision – together because they both underline the same fact. There is a cost of commitment. Jesus made that clear: '*If anyone would come after me, he must deny himself and take up his cross daily and follow me*' (Lk 9:23). It was this fact that hit me so hard when I saw the picture. I knew what the Lord was trying to say to me. There needed to be a single-mindedness, a careless-ness about the opinions of men, a willingness to lay down everything in self-sacrifice if God's will was to be fulfilled in my life and ministry. The further I go in my Christian life the more I become aware of the dimension of cost in following Jesus. I am not speaking about cost in a negative way. After all, the things He is asking us to give up to follow Him and become fruitful are things we can well do without anyway. But the old flesh doesn't know that until we have done it!

C: The power of commitment

But there is also authority in commitment. A man of a committed life will be followed and listened to by others and his commitment earns him the right to lead other people in the ways of God. Commitment like this leaves its mark on the lives of others. Commitment like this brings an authority to life which others feel and recognise. There is a tremendous power about a committed life! The lack of commitment which many of us demonstrate has something to do with a lack of authority other people trust us with. In another chapter of this book I have dealt at length with the question of our goals and aims. May it suffice to say at this moment that when we know where we are going, we will find others who are willing to go with us.

There is something awesome about the power of commitment. But of course we need to be sure that we are committed to the right thing. The human spirit has a yearning for commitment. That is why it is so easy to lead gullible people astray. This is why sects and heresies always find a considerable following because they always insist on a high degree of commitment. In fact, the commitment of some of these movements puts regular Christians to shame. But the commitment of Jesus was to the truth and in the truth, and our commitment must be like His. Satan will try to see to it that our lives become unfruitful because we don't know where we are going or because we commit ourselves to the wrong things.

The American writer Leroy Eims teaches on the theme of leadership in his book, *The Leader You Were Meant To Be*. He makes a very significant point when he says:

A man can destroy his life in one of three ways. The first is to give in to his lazy slothful nature and do nothing ... The second way to destroy your life is to give yourself a goal, work hard, and discover at the end that you gave yourself to the wrong goal ... The third way ... [is to] become a dabbler and never do anything.

This is why what we have discovered already about the power of God's Word is so important for our lives. It is the Word of God which keeps us in the truth. It is God's Word that keeps us in the way. As long as our lives are submitted to and controlled by the pure Word of God, we are far less likely to be led astray by wrong ideas and far more likely to be stimulated to follow God's call for our lives.

D: The fruits of commitment

I believe this sense of commitment which other people can pick up from *our* lives and ministries is of vital significance to the effectiveness of any input we might have into *their* lives. For one thing, *it brings clarity and direction instead of confusion*. Confusion arises when people cannot see clearly where they are going. They don't know what they are doing or what they are following. If we are uncommitted we will never be able to minister anything but more confusion into their lives.

Furthermore, commitment *breeds a sense of purpose*. It is something people can trust. They get the feeling something is being achieved in the life of a committed man, and so they feel that something will be achieved in their lives through him. Spiritual frustration comes about through the continual failure to achieve anything purposefully.

Commitment *engenders loyalty*. When people lose sight of what they are committed to, they also begin to lose sight of how to be committed. This is the root of disloyalty and disharmony. The secret of successful leadership is that people know that their leaders are committed, that they know what it is they are committed to, and that they have the direction to work that commitment through in terms that are practical and applicable to themselves.

Chapter 7

Overcoming the Powers

1: Satan's World System

> *'We know that we are children of God, and that the
> whole world is under the control of the evil one'*
> (1 Jn 5:19).

The fact of spiritual warfare springs from two major sources
as far as the Christian believer is concerned. First, it derives
from the fall of Satan and the fall of man. When Satan rebelled
against God he was cast out of heaven with one third of the
angels. Ever since, he has waged continual warfare against the
purposes of God, in particular within creation and the sphere
of man's influence. When man fell he became completely
susceptible to the power of Satan and his evil forces to such a
degree that mankind in general fails to realise this and lives in
ignorance of the fact that he is actually in spiritual bondage.

Second, spiritual warfare originates at Calvary, for there on
the Cross God's perfect man did battle against all the forces of
spiritual wickedness. Paul speaks of the comprehensive victory that was achieved in the death of Jesus against the powers
of evil: *'And having disarmed the powers and authorities, he
made a public spectacle of them, triumphing over them by the
cross'* (Col 2:15).

We need to see spiritual warfare on the broadest possible
canvas. There has been a tendency in some quarters to define

spiritual warfare almost in terms of personal deliverance or personal salvation. Now there is no doubt that these elements are a real part of spiritual warfare. When a person is born again of the Holy Spirit, this is a major victory which has been accomplished over Satan. A movement has taken place in spiritual terms from one sphere of rule to another, and this is very significant: *'For he has rescued us from the dominion of darkness and brought us into the kingdom of the Son he loves'* (Col 1:13). Likewise, when a person is delivered of evil spirits there is a tremendous victory being achieved within that person's experience. This is making real in personal terms all that Jesus accomplished for us on the Cross of Calvary.

But we need to see spiritual warfare in wider terms than this, because in a very real sense it is what we have been called to as an ongoing part of our spiritual calling in Christ Jesus. In other words, we have been set free ourselves so that we might now engage in this calling to war. Our salvation is like the trumpet of the Lord sounding in our hearts to rise up and wage this war in the name of the Lord our Saviour!

A: World Order of Darkness

When we turn to the New Testament we are presented with a dramatic insight into a world system which is completely opposed to the rule of God. It is controlled by the power of Satan and is based on principles which are totally antipathetic to the ways of the kingdom of God. This satanic kingdom is not a bland system which is inert, passive or neutral. It is dedicated to the overthrow of good and the power of God. It is a system which covers unbelieving mankind like a blanket and which means that men and women are not free to make their own choices or follow their own actions. It is a dark prison over which Satan rules and which is characterised by darkness and blindness to the spiritual reality of God: *'The god of this age has blinded the minds of unbelievers, so that they cannot see the light of the gospel of the glory of Christ'* (2 Cor 4:4).

Two important New Testament words clarify for us the nature of this kingdom of darkness. The first is *aion*, which is usually translated 'age' or 'time'. The emphasis of this word is on the temporal or passing nature of Satan's system. It is not permanent and belongs only to the present state of affairs. Paul uses this term in Galatians 1:4 where he describes the work of Christ: '...*who gave himself for our sins to rescue us from the present evil age according to the will of God our Father.*' It is the same word that Paul uses in Romans 12:2, where he exhorts his readers and ourselves not to conform to '*the pattern of this world*'.

The second term is *kosmos*. This is perhaps even more important than *aion*. The word is used some 185 times in the New Testament and the very fact that it is used so frequently indicates the importance of the subject. Originally *kosmos* meant 'beauty and order', but in the context of spiritual warfare the word has a much more sinister ring about it in the New Testament. Here it has come to mean order all right, but an order of things dedicated against God's order and systematically organised to express all the malevolent power of the evil one.

The term also reminds us of the *location* of this warfare. We are engaged in warfare *right here on earth! Kosmos* is the system of spiritual reality with which we are surrounded and in the midst of which we are called to function. We are vulnerable to this system through our five senses, through relationships with other people who participate in its life and lifestyle, through circumstances and events which reflect the principles and effects of this system in action and through the imposition of its standards and attitudes.

As we will see later, this system of darkness permeates other systems of government, politics, education, society and the like. None of these is impervious to the influence and work of Satan. Indeed his control of these many areas is the means by which he impinges on the life and freedom of the believer as well as continuing his negative direct influence in the Christian's life.

The *characteristics of this world system* are clearly seen from the Scriptures: It is a kingdom of darkness (2 Cor 4:4). It is a kingdom of evil (Gal 1:4). It is a kingdom marked by sin (Mt

18:7), care and anxiety (Mk 4:19), ignorance of God (Jn 1:10), hopelessness (Eph 2:12), corruption (2 Pet 1:4), evil desires and lust (1 Jn 2:16), delusion (2 Jn 7) and evil powers (Eph 6:12). Of course, we can expect nothing else than that this world system should display such awful characteristics, because it does nothing but reflect the character of the one who governs it. Just as the Kingdom of God is a Kingdom of light, love and liberty (because these are the fundamental tenets of God's own nature), so Satan's kingdom reflects his own nature.

B: The prince of the cosmos

This is how Jesus Himself describes the evil one: 'Now the prince of this world will be driven out' (Jn 12:31). We only need scan the pages of the New Testament to catch a glimpse of the devastating nature of the god of this world. The following list provides us with an introduction to some of what the Scriptures have to say about him:

- he is the father of lies (Jn 8:44)
- he is the accuser of believers (Rev 12:10)
- he appears to be an angel of light (2 Cor 11:14)
- he is 'the wicked one' (1 Jn 5:19; Mt 13:38)
- he is a murderer from the beginning (Jn 8:44)
- he is the enemy of the saints (1 Pet 5:8)
- he is the prince of the power of the air (Eph 2:2 A.V.)
- he is the god of this world (2 Cor 4:4)
- he is the originator of evil schemes (Eph 6:11)

We can see from this the tremendous and awful influence that Satan has. His sphere is the earth and the atmosphere immediately around it. The material he works with is the hearts of men. His work is one of deceit and subterfuge and his commitment is the diversion and destruction, if possible, of the work of God.

This evil purpose is directed in *three major directions*. He is out to destroy *God's natural order*. In Genesis chapter 1 we hear of how God spoke and brought order out of chaos. Satan's evil purpose is to bring everything back into chaos; in other words, to reverse God's purpose in creation. He wreaks devastation, earthquake, famine, violence, world-wide wars, rape of the earth and the like to upset the balance God has created in the natural order of things.

He is out to destroy *God's moral order*. Through his work in the hearts of men he blinds them to truth and goodness. Moral values are turned upside down until the very boundaries between good and evil are obliterated. Long ago the prophet Isaiah spoke out against this very trend:

> *Woe to those who call evil good*
> > *and good evil,*
> *who put darkness for light*
> > *and light for darkness,*
> *who put bitter for sweet*
> > *and sweet for bitter.*   (Is 5:20)

He is out to destroy *God's spiritual order*. It is the devil's intention to keep men away from the influence of God's Holy Spirit. As we have already seen, he blinds men to the truth and light of God. Satan's purpose is to deny the spiritual in man so that man operates at the level of soul and body only. He feeds the material and physical and appeals to men and women at the level of the immediate so that they are diverted from the eternal and the spiritual.

C: Two words of warning

First, we must never give the devil the same place in our thinking as the Holy Spirit. I believe many Christians operate with too inflated a view of the evil one. As we have seen he is indeed very powerful and he wields an awesome influence in the lives of unbelieving men and women. But we need to remember that this place was only given to him because mankind surrendered their wills to Satan. Without this surrender of will Satan would have no control in their lives.

We might put it like this: he is powerful but not omnipotent; he is intelligent but not omniscient; he is mobile but not omnipresent; he is organised but not in absolute control.

Never imagine that the devil can be in two places at once! He is a localised created agent in the same way as other angels and beings, and his world-wide influence is, as we shall see, exercised by means of a global network of evil beings and agents who exercise his will. But the Holy Spirit is God and displays all the attributes of God, and so there is no equality in power between the two.

Second, we must never give the devil more significance than he has. He really has no proper name! Many people call him Lucifer, but that is not right. There was a day when he was called Lucifer, the son of the morning. Then he was one of the highest angels in glory. But through his rebellion he fell and led others with him. I believe in that moment he not only lost his place in heaven but he forfeited his true name. Now he is *ha satan* (Hebrew) or *ho diabolos* (Greek). They both mean virtually the same thing. They cannot be described as proper names because they only describe a function. These names mean that he is 'the accuser'.

However, we know the One with the true and proper name:

> '*You are to give him the name Jesus,*' **the angel said to Joseph**, *because he will save his people from their sins.*'
>
> (Mt 1:21)

> '*... that at the name of Jesus every knee should bow, in heaven and on earth and under the earth, and every tongue confess that Jesus Christ is Lord, to the glory of God the Father.*'
>
> (Phil 2:10, 11)

2: Evil Incorporated

A: The powers of this dark world

Nowhere in Scriptures is the shape of this kingdom of darkness more clearly delineated than in Ephesians 6:10–18. In this passage Paul tells us something of the spiritual forces which dominate this kingdom. These are the hierarchy of powers which operate under the command of Satan as he seeks to wield his influence amongst men: *'Our struggle is not against flesh and blood, but against the rulers, against the authorities, against the powers of this dark world and against the spiritual forces of evil in the heavenly realms.'* There are four significant terms used in this passage which give us some insight into the organisation of these forces of evil, although we need to exercise caution in trying to be too strict in our definition of these powers.

(a) **Rulers.** The Authorised Version translates the Greek word *arche* as 'principality'. It occurs a number of times in the New Testament (see Rom 8:38; Eph 1:21; 3:10; Col 1:16; 2:10, 15; Tit 3:1). In Romans 8:38 the New International Version translates the term as 'demons': *'For I am convinced that neither death nor life, neither angels nor demons, neither the present nor the future, nor any powers, neither height nor depth, nor anything else in all creation, will be able to separate us from the love of God that is in Christ Jesus our Lord.'* But the word carries with it a more potent and elevated idea than that which the term 'demons' indicates. The Greek word *arche* bears the thought of 'source, beginning or origin' – though not, of course, in the same way as Jesus is the source of all things. Colossians 1:16 makes it clear that even these principalities find their source in Him. But these rulers are the originators of spiritual evil inasmuch as they exercise authority over many other spiritual powers. We could describe them as the *right-hand men of Satan!* The late F. F. Bruce in his commentary on Colossians has described these rulers as probably representing the highest order of the angelic realm. He does not mean this in a positive sense, but that these principalities are unseen spiritual forces in the kingdom of darkness.

As I have mentioned, Colossians 1:16 makes it clear that even these evil forces once found their origin in the creative work of Christ. Colossians 2:15 makes it just as clear that they will find their final end through Him. He has abolished their power and exposed them publicly through His death on the cross: *'And having disarmed the powers and authorities, he made a public spectacle of them, triumphing over them by the cross.'*

(b) **Authorities.** The Greek word is *exousia*. This word is the same as that used in John 1:12 of the authority given to those who believe in Jesus to become sons of God. This is 'an invested right'. It is authority given to someone to act on behalf of a higher authority such as the case of an ambassador who represents his country in a foreign land. As believers we are given the power or authority to become and live as God's children.

This fact gives us an insight into the nature of these forces of spiritual evil. They work with delegated authority – they are under authority. The authority or power they work with is not their own intrinsic power but that which is given to them by other, higher powers. It is a fact both in Scripture and experience that demons always recognise a higher authority. These spiritual authorities spoken of here are those powers which act as Satan's local enforcement officers.

(c) **Powers of this dark world.** The Greek word is a compound of two words – *kosmos* ('world') and *kratos* ('power'). The world is described in the verse as a world of darkness. Satan is the prince of darkness. He is the source of spiritual darkness in the lives of every person who does not believe in Jesus. These powers of this world darkness are those agencies which Satan employs to control and act upon men in their blindness.

In ancient Greek thought this word was used to signify world-ruling gods or spirit beings who had particular parts of the cosmos under their control. In Jewish teaching as well the word meant evil spirits who acted with authority in the same way. Daniel chapter 10 draws back the veil for us and permits us to catch another glimpse of this tremendous reality. It is easy to interpret a Scripture like this in a rationalistic way and imagine that what is being described is an earthly ruler or potentate. But the context demands some other explanation, I believe. Daniel's interchange at this moment is not on the level of the earthbound or horizontal. He is speaking with an angelic messenger who comes from before the throne of God (see Dan 10:5). This messenger continues his speech to Daniel: *'But the prince of the Persian kingdom resisted me twenty-one days. Then Michael, one of the chief princes, came to help me, because I was detained there with the king of Persia'* (verse 13).

Surely this 'prince of Persia' is none other than a *kosmokrator* – a world spiritual power whose influence spread right across the region of Persia. It is not too difficult to see that if this is the case there, then other spiritual rulers will have authority over great tracts of the earth and will wield their influence through lesser powers under their control. What is glimpsed here in the testimony of Scripture has been borne witness to in the spiritual experience of many people over the years as they have become aware through the exercise of spiritual warfare just what kind of forces they are up against in a particular area or situation.

It is just as clear that the term *kosmokrator* in Ephesians cannot relate to an earthly monarch or dictator, since Paul has just stated in the very same verse that 'our struggle is not against flesh and blood'. We may ask, then, why is it that the Scriptures are not much more specific and detailed about the influence of these world rulers? I believe it is very simple. The Scriptures are not here to advertise the kingdom of Satan and satisfy the natural curiosity of the flesh. They are here to proclaim the coming of God's Kingdom. Also, God is not a God who engenders fear in the hearts of His children. Much spiritual warfare is in secret. Often we come against forces we do not know clearly. But that by no means diminishes the effectiveness of the warfare – it merely ensures that our hearts do not fail us for fear. The main idea behind this category of evil power is that of prevention or bondage or restraint. They keep men from God, they prevent men from seeing the truth and light of God. Their strategy is aimed at inhibiting desire for God and awareness of God.

(d) **Spiritual forces of evil.** Satan himself is described as the wicked or evil one. The Greek word that expresses this evil is *poneria*. It carries with it the idea of malignancy. It is not a clean word. It is almost as though the evil were an infectious thing that corrupts the inward life of those whom it touches.

This description of the powers of darkness in Ephesians chapter 6 highlights for us the comprehensive nature of the opposition. Involved in these four categories are four powerful spiritual antichrist movements that include government, enforcement, restraint and evil opposition. Satan is no passive foe and his forces are not dormant. He and they are highly active. He is portrayed in the New Testament as a cunning and destructive enemy: *'Be self-controlled and alert. Your enemy the devil prowls around like a roaring lion looking for someone to devour'* (1 Pet 5:8).

B: The principles of this world

After what we have learned about the rule of Satan and the activity of his spiritual forces of evil, we will not be surprised to learn as well that there are *basic principles of wickedness* which characterise this world system and which establish the patterns and habits of man's behaviour and actions.

One important Greek word which demonstrates the truth of what we are saying is *stoicheia*. This key word means 'basic principles' and occurs in only a few texts. For example: *'So also, when we were children, we were in slavery under the basic principles of this world'* (Gal 4:3); and again, *'how is it that you are turning back to those weak and miserable principles?'* (Gal 4:9). The same term occurs in the Epistle to the Colossians, where Paul makes it clear that these basic principles stand in opposition to the freedom that has been won for us in Christ: *'See to it that no one takes you captive through hollow and deceptive philosophy, which depends on human tradition and the basic principles of this world rather than on Christ'* (Col 2:8). Paul goes further and emphasises the fact that we have finished with all these things once we have become identified with Christ through His death: *'You died with Christ to the **basic principles of this world***' (Col 2:20). Man is not a free agent. If he is not subject to the Law of God through the Spirit, he comes into bondage to the basic principles of the world. These operate according to 'the law of sin and death' (see Rom 8:2).

We can understand the nature of these basic principles when we read Romans 1:18–25, in which we can clearly see their fundamental characteristics. *This world system is based on six principles of ungodliness.* We can set these six principles out in the following way, which enables us to see clearly their effect on human experience and life. This world system of evil is:

(a) **Based on man rather than God.** *'For although they knew God, they neither glorified him as God nor gave thanks to him'* (Rom 1:21). Satan's great delusion is to lead man into thinking that he is self-sufficient apart from God and that man is *actually* his own master outside of God altogether. The subtlety of the devil's bondage is that he does not appear as man's ruler. He allows man to appear to be his own ruler, and this bondage of the ego of man is Satan's greatest weapon in holding him in his power.

(b) **Based on human reason rather than on knowledge of God.** *'Although they claimed to be wise, they became fools'* (Rom 1:22). This principle almost follows directly on from the first. If man is the master of his fate and the captain of his soul, it follows that what will rule supreme is his own wisdom. The folly of this is that natural man then fails to realise how far short this falls of the wisdom of God. It is this very wisdom which prevents man from accepting God's wisdom in salvation, which to him seems utter foolishness (see 1 Cor 2:14; 3:18, 19).

(c) **Based on 'flesh and 'soul' rather than on 'spirit'.** God created man as a spiritual being in communication with Himself and alive to spiritual realities and values. The result of his disobedience is that he has become subject to the devil and lives, not at the level of the spirit, but at the levels of soul and body, so that what matters is what appeals to him and what is immediate and tangible: *'Therefore God gave them over in the sinful desires of their hearts.'* (Rom 1:24). The results of this judgement on man's sin are demonstrated very clearly on a number of occasions in the Scriptures and the truth of it can be witnessed every day in our own personal experience (see Gal 5:19–21; 1 Jn 2:16; 2 Cor 5:10).

(d) Based on delusion rather than the truth of God. *'They exchanged the truth of God for a lie, and worshipped and served created things rather than the Creator'* (Rom 1:25). The natural connection between these principles is clear to see. It is almost like a descending chain of darkness. The basic fact of man's separation from God leads him into a self-contained existence in which he is utterly susceptible to every inroad of the evil one. Once God's truth is jettisoned, what else is there to live by but a lie?

(e) Based on the fruits of sin rather than righteousness.

> *They have become filled with every kind of wickedness, evil, greed and depravity. They are full of envy, murder, strife, deceit and malice. They are gossips, slanderers, God-haters, insolent, arrogant and boastful; they invent ways of doing evil; they disobey their parents; they are senseless, faithless, heartless, ruthless.*   (Rom 1:29–31)

Such a list as this hardly needs comment. In a world like our own we become daily more aware of the absolute truth of a word like this. Earlier in the chapter Paul uses a turn of phrase that is almost chilling in its relevance to our society today: *'Men committed indecent acts with other men, and received in themselves the due penalty for their perversion'* (Rom 1:27). There never has been a time in history when such a Scripture was so relevant. The spread of AIDS and related diseases today has brought a fear and caution into the hearts of some who previously would never have spoken out on the side of constraint and propriety in sexuality. As never before it is clear that such indulgence bears with it penalties far beyond any sense of shame or guilt and will carry its repercussions into the lives of thousands of innocent people as well.

(f) Based on the pride of life rather than submission to God. The original sin of the woman in the garden was that *although she clearly knew the Word of God* she still disobeyed it. Paul has already argued that man is never left without witness to the things of God. Yet even in the light of the witness of both nature and conscience (as well, of course, as the law and the gospel), he goes ahead and flouts these laws within his life: '*Although they know God's righteous decree that those who do such things deserve death, they not only continue to do these very things but also approve those who practise them*' (Rom 1:32). This is what Paul describes elsewhere (see 1 Cor 2:12) as '*the spirit of the world*'. It is what John describes as 'the pride of life':

> *Do not love the world or anything in the world ... For everything in the world – the cravings of sinful man, the lust of his eyes and the boasting of what he has and does – comes not from the Father but from the world. The world and its desires pass away, but the man who does the will of God lives for ever.* (1 Jn 2:15–17)

3: The Strategy of Evil

We will see later that there are two very significant arenas in which this spiritual warfare occurs continually. These can be described as an arena of the inner self and the arena of battle in heavenly places. Without much need for proof we can all witness to the fact of warfare within our own lives. Paul himself speaks vividly of this in Romans chapter 7. Likewise in Ephesians 2:2 the devil is described as *'the ruler of the kingdom of the air, the spirit who is now at work in those who are disobedient'*. Our approach to warfare in the realm of the spirit must take these two facts seriously.

We need to recognise as well, however, that almost everything we are surrounded with in material and tangible terms in 'this world' participates in open warfare. This is not to take an extreme position or be a scaremonger. It is merely to take the position which the New Testament takes on the subject. Satan is described as the 'prince of this world', which means that he wields amazing control in the most significant areas of human experience. His place is to thwart the will of God on earth at every point he can and to use his power to prevent even believers from acting in the power of the Kingdom of God.

The way he does this is by infiltrating every channel of power that operates among men so that they are kept in bondage to him at every turn. To be effective ourselves in spiritual warfare, we need to recognise the influence of Satan in a number of exceedingly strategic areas. There is no need for us to become fanciful or extreme. Charismatic Christians, in particular, have been too ready to see the demonic in everything and sometimes have made public announcements on various issues which have later proven to be far wide of the mark. I recall the case in the United States which percolated to Britain in which a famous soap manufacturer was publicly proclaimed as being affected by direct demonic influence because of the symbol they had used for years on the packaging of their products. We need to be very wise in the claims or accusations we make. Anyway, our effectiveness in the realm of spiritual warfare does not eventually depend on such pronouncements but on our approach to the throne of God in the name of Jesus. It is often a much less demanding thing for us to denounce the human beings involved than to take the time and effort in spiritual terms to come against these forces at the point where they do need to be defeated – namely, in the realm of the spiritual and invisible warfare of the heavenlies.

There are a number of key areas where, I believe, Satan seeks to gain control and influence in the affairs of men because his influence here ensures his wide control over the thoughts and actions of multitudes.

A: The realm of finance

That much misquoted text from 1 Timothy 6:10 says *'The love of money is the root of all evil'*. Notice how many warnings there are in the New Testament which are addressed to Christian leaders, not to be lovers of money: *'Be shepherds of God's flock that is under your care, serving as overseers – not because you must, but because you are willing, as God wants you to be; not greedy for money, but eager to serve'* (1 Pet 5:2). There are a number of deep principles involved here. First, there is the fact, which we can see on every hand, that money can be the source of tremendous personal and spiritual bondage to many people. The resources which money represents are absolutely necessary for the well-being of human beings and for the fulfilment of God's work on earth. We all need money. Those of us who are in full-time work for the Lord know the tremendous need for resources to be released for God's Kingdom.

By the same token, however, money can be a terrific bondage. Money has never been easier to come by than today. Banks and loan houses are begging to lend us money. For some people the temptation is too great and they find themselves in debt up to their ears. Local councils are now going as far as to appoint special debt counsellors. Ready money like this appeals to the base aspects of our egos and emotions. Equally, the acquisition of wealth has become, for many, such an end in itself that it has taken the place of any spiritual reality in their lives, and money and possessions have become a god for them.

Secondly, there is the question of stewardship. When man is broken off from the ground of his being in God he loses that real sense of being a good steward of the resources which God gives him. When money and its half-brothers become an end in themselves, they lose their proper value and worth and become directed towards ends that are a waste. Think of the millions of dollars and pounds that are spent on horrific so-called systems of defence. Believing Christians really have soft-pedalled this one and have left the field of protest to radical and often atheistic voices. Or think of the prolific squander of resources through supposed mutual help organisations like the European Economic Community. The very name reveals the basis of relationship: economic. No wonder we have such a difficult time demonstrating true unity of will and purpose when the foundation of the relationship is the very rock on which men founder – their greed and love for gain.

Thirdly, from a Christian perspective there is the question of diversion of resources. I firmly believe that Satan's aim is to keep God's own money out of His Hands! It is his purpose to rob God and to divert resources which ought to be directed to the work of God on earth to other more devious and selfish ends. Others no doubt will totally disagree, but this is how I view the vast sums that were recently paid to a bogus Satan worshipper, who is now serving time for his deception. What amazes me is that the unbelievers who were involved in bringing the man to justice and judgement seemed to have more sense than the Christians who were hoodwinked!

B: The area of religion

In a number of places the New Testament is explicit in its warnings about bogus faith and religion. This false religion will appeal to man's own ideas and satisfy the cravings of his own mind and spirit. It will be hallmarked by counterfeit power which will appeal to man's love of the spectacular and to that innate longing for something real that we all possess.

It will also lead men away from the truth of God as revealed in Jesus. The proliferation of cults, sects and heresies in the twentieth century bears witness to the fact that men will more readily believe a complex lie than accept the simple truth of God! When I consider some of the doctrines and practices which men have followed and have even sometimes given their lives for, I have little difficulty in accepting this aspect of devilish influence in the world at large. Indeed there is no other explanation for it.

Another feature of false religion is that time and again it focuses itself around a 'new messiah'. Satan recognises very well man's need for a leader figure. Man was made to worship and there is that about him that needs to worship. So it is significant that the greatest and most consistent attack on the faith of Jesus has been in the form of promoting others to the same rank as Him and in demoting Jesus to the same rank as others. A common claim of many alternative religions and cults is that Jesus was a good man and in the line of divine prophets, but that He was not unique and certainly not 'the way, the truth and the life', by whom only can men come to the Father.

The Scriptures are clear that such movements come from the hand of the evil one and are the signs of spiritual opposition that we need to take seriously:

> *The time will come when men will not put up with sound doctrine. Instead, to suit their own desires, they will gather around them a great number of teachers to say what their itching ears want to hear.* (2 Tim 4:3)

> *The coming of the lawless one will be in accordance with the work of Satan displayed in all kinds of counterfeit miracles, signs and wonders, and in every kind of evil.*
> (2 Thess 2:9, 10)

Sadly, it is not only outside the Church that these signs are to be witnessed. Satan infiltrates the Church by teaching falsehood, imitating the real power of God and by sowing confusion and unbelief. He encourages a religiosity without real power. There is no more powerful a bondage than religious bondage in which people are locked into a system of self-righteous good works without knowing the true power of God in new birth and the Holy Spirit. Paul describes this to Timothy as 'having a form of godliness but denying its power' (2 Tim 3:5).

C: Violence, war and natural disaster
Jesus Himself spoke of the increase of these things which would be manifest more and more as the end draws near:

> 'You will hear of wars and rumours of wars, but see to it that you are not alarmed. Such things must happen, but the end is still to come. Nation will rise against nation, and kingdom against kingdom. There will be famines and earthquakes in various places. All these are the beginning of birth pains.' (Mt 24:6–8)

The great delusion of Satan lies in the fact that in the face of such immense disasters as we see in our world today, men lay the blame at the door of God. This is a ruse of Satan to blind mankind to the love and power of God. Of course, if we live without a proper and deep enough recognition of the Fall and its terrible consequences for man and Creation, these things will seem inexplicable to us. But when we take sin and the power of Satan seriously, as the Scriptures do, then we can lay the blame squarely where it is due – namely at the door of the evil one and his pawn, sinful man.

D: The natural desires and impulses of men and women
John describes how these natural forces of our personalities (which God created originally to bring about harmony, delight, fruitfulness and enjoyment between men and women) have been totally corrupted and have become base and bestial forces which lead men and women to do the most gross and harmful things to each other: 'For everything in the world – the cravings of sinful man, the lust of his eyes and the boasting of what he has and does – comes not from the Father but from the world' (1 Jn 2:16).

We need only look around and within us to see how well Satan has achieved his goal. The 'macho' image, the intense appeal to sexual urge in much advertising, the appeal to the sensual and fleshly through fashion and articles; it is in areas like this that we can see the practical reality of spiritual warfare. Spiritual warfare is not just praying, it is being. It is waged in what we *are* in areas like this as well as what we *do* in our devotional lives.

E: The traditions of men
The amazing need and search for security and meaning expresses itself in all sorts of ways. One of these is an appeal in tradition. Now, I am not against a sense of history or propriety as such, but when you take time to analyze many of the traditions of pomp and ceremony in which we indulge, you see that they are little more than much hot air about very little. Paul describes these things as *'hollow and deceptive philosophy, which depends on human tradition ... rather than on Christ'* (Col 2:8).

Many habits and actions we take for granted have no more real foundation than the fact that they have always been thus. Nowhere has a spirit of tradition become more prevalent than inside the Church. It is for the very same reason that many dear Christian men are affected by movements like the Freemasons. It is not because they have any intention of being overtly involved in an occultish sect or any such thing. What appeals to them is the tradition and the comradeship. No wonder we need to take seriously what the New Testament has to teach about the real fellowship of the Body of Christ as the only alternative to such shallow rubbish! And yet millions are blind to truth today because they are wedded to tradition.

F: The area of education
Nowhere in our day, I believe, has Satan been more active than in education. This is why thousands of Christian believers have felt constrained to withdraw their children from state education and place them within the environment of a Christian school.

The debate of recent years about approaches to sex and religious education in schools has only served to highlight the battle that goes on in this sphere. The overt practice of some education authorities of encouraging the bizarre and following supposedly enlightened principles of teaching have confused and frightened parents far outside the boundaries of Christian belief.

Vast movements of education have affected people for good or ill, not only in the realm of the academic but within the sphere of the family and the rearing of children. Parents have been subjected over the years to the most amazing trivia in the name of enlightenment. Praise God for the work of people like James Dobson and the increasing awareness of Christian parents of the need to be involved in these crucial areas of spiritual warfare.

Those of us who have been active over the years in theological education have clearly seen the devastating effect of liberalism within the Church. Satan has had a field-day in spreading scepticism and unbelief, and their concomitant effects, throughout the ranks of clergy and lay people for generations. This has led to a sterile and anaemic Christianity which has been the root cause of the slide in Church attendance and membership.

G: Politics and nations

Paul exhorts Timothy to encourage the believers to stand in a place of intercession on behalf of those who govern the nations: *'I urge then, first of all that requests, prayers, intercession and thanksgiving be made for everyone – for kings and all those in authority'* (1 Tim 2:1, 2). Satan has a number-one interest in affecting the destiny of nations and of preventing righteousness prevailing by promoting those into power who will enable his evil designs. We are all too aware in our own day of power politics, how the influence of even one man in the seat of authority can steer a nation or group of nations in one direction or another.

In fact, when the New Testament speaks of the last days it talks of evil as being personified in a powerful demagogue who sets himself up against God and the people of God. He is described as the antichrist or 'the lawless one' (see 2 Thess 2:9). Jesus spoke of us as the salt of the earth whose very presence God uses to maintain the necessary spiritual balance to prevent the powers of evil taking absolute control and thwarting the purposes and timing of God.

H: Circumstances and events

Even Paul realised the power of Satan within the events and circumstances of his life. When he writes to the Thessalonians he shows that he never under-estimated the power of the devil to control and influence men and events to thwart the will of God. Paul does not specify the particular reasons, and perhaps it was through the devil's attack in the lives of other people rather than in his own life which prevented his fulfilling his wish. But certainly he says that *'Satan stopped us'* (1 Thess 2:18).

Of course, we may say rightly that we have the authority to come against Satan on such occasions, but unless we take that place of authority, in Christ, we are vulnerable to the attack of the evil one at this point as other men and women certainly are.

4: The Battle Within

Apart from the fact of spiritual warfare in the global terms we have spoken about in the previous section, we need to realise the reality of warfare in the life of every Christian. Peter describes the reality of satanic attack in our lives when he writes: *'Be self-controlled and alert. Your enemy the devil prowls around like a roaring lion looking for someone to devour'* (1 Pet 5:8). This scripture encompasses two important ideas about the battle within our lives. First, the need to be alert to the activity of Satan and to resist him actively in the Spirit. It is possible for the Christian believer to give Satan place in his life through spiritual lethargy or ignorance. This is why Paul warns his readers to be careful not to allow this: *'Do not give the devil a foothold'* (Eph 4:27).

Secondly, we need to realise that we have been given the power to withstand these assaults of Satan in the power of Christ. There is no need for the believer to be passive or defeated under the attack of the evil one. John reminds us powerfully of the fact that the resources of the Holy Spirit are available to everyone of us: *'You, dear children, are from God and have overcome them, because the one who is in you is greater than the one who is in the world'* (1 Jn 4:4).

The devil uses many ways and means to try and find access into our lives but, often his success comes not from his strength but from our weakness. Often Satan is able to find a way into our lives because we fail to understand or to employ just what is available to us in Christ Jesus. In my experience I have noticed certain common causes for the success of satanic attack in the lives of Christians. For example, one chief reason for his success is that many believers are unwilling to receive the direction of the Word of God into their lives and its programme for liberty and holiness through the power of the Holy Spirit. We need to pay attention to what I call the 'moral imperatives' of the Scriptures. By this I mean the many occasions in Scriptures where we are told what to do in the power of the Spirit. Failure to follow these Biblical commands is disobedience and faithlessness and leaves us very exposed to the inroads of evil spirits. Again, a refusal to recognise the need for a disciplined life in the Spirit leaves us vulnerable to deception and spiritual attack. The sad fact of the matter is that Satan is able to find much more room in believer's lives today or than he ought to and much of the blame for this lies at the door of Christians themselves.

We have not the space within the confines of a brief section to examine this subject in any depth, but in recent years some excellent in-depth studies have been published. However, we need to notice two major areas where Satan tries to find an inroad into our lives and where, in many cases, that attempt is all too successful.

A: Battle for the mind

The mind is a veritable battlefield in the experience of many people. Lack of mental discipline leads to chaos in the thought life, an inability to discern truth from error and bondage to an imagination that is able to breed negative ideas, dreams, visions and bogey-men quicker than they can be recognised. This is why Paul writes to the Romans: *'Do not conform any longer to the pattern of this world but be transformed by the renewing of your mind'* (Rom 12:2). Certain steps are needed to close the mind of Satan's influence and to release it to be used by God.

(a) **The mind must be changed.** The natural mind is quite incapable of understanding the things of God. In fact, as Paul teaches in Romans 8:5–7, it is quite hostile to God and will not submit to God's will. By the same token, our natural minds regard spiritual truth as complete foolishness and have been blinded to God's Word by the works of Satan (see 1 Cor 2:14; 4:4). The natural mind is the slave of the old nature and its thoughts and attitudes are expressions of a life which is completely opposed to God's purpose for our lives: *'All of us also lived among them at one time, gratifying the cravings of our sinful nature and following its desires and thoughts'* (Eph 2:3). Faith in Jesus leads to a whole new birth and life, and an essential part of our growth in discipleship is that under the power of the Holy Spirit and the Word of God we undergo a complete change in our thinking.

(b) The mind must be renewed. Our minds and our bodies are the outlets of our spirit. They express in tangible and audible ways what is really in our hearts. In a reverse mode our minds and bodies provide an inlet into our inner man. If we subject our bodies to sin, our spirits will be affected. If we allow our minds to remain in darkness and ignorance, then our spirits will reflect that bondage. Paul highlights the need for this process of renewal to take place when he writes:

> *You were taught, with regard to your former way of life, to put off your self which is being corrupted by its deceitful desires, to be made new **in the attitude of your minds**; and to put on the new self, created to be like God in true righteousness and holiness.* (Eph 4:22–24)

There are a number of simple but powerful exercises we can practice every day, given God's help. They call for commitment and diligence and, sadly, this fact alone is enough to dissuade some of us from ever trying.

First, we can look on our minds like spiritual sieves. I believe that many of us fall into the trap of becoming passive about what passes through our minds. We don't ask active questions about what we are seeing or thinking at any given moment. We just let our eyes wander on whatever comes across their path without realising that an unjudged thought is an untested thought, and it may go on to wreak havoc in deep areas of our life.

Secondly, (this is related directly to the first principle), we can make a deliberate choice about the place of our minds: 'Set your minds on things above, not on earthly things; (Col 3:2). A mind which is firmly fixed on the right things cannot at the same time be taken up with something else. Much of the worry and fear that invades our heart arises from the fact that our minds are set on the difficulties and problems rather than on the One who has promised all His help and strength to meet those very needs.

Thirdly, we can allow God's Word to have its sanctifying

effect in our lives. God's Word, particularly through the Scriptures, has a tremendous power in cleansing our minds and setting them free from every wrong thought and influence: *'For the word of God is living and active. Sharper than any double-edged sword, it penetrates even to dividing soul and spirit, joints and marrow; it judges the thoughts and attitudes of the hearts'* (Heb 4:12).

A real part of the secret of not allowing Satan a foothold in the area of our thought life is the practice we need to develop of immediately refusing any thought that is wrong, negative, hateful or in any way sinful. It is here that the important matter of the surrender of the will comes in. It is a matter of our will whether we make our minds dwell upon God's Word. I think many of us actually live with a kind of fear of our mind, as though it has some independent power. But it only has the power we give it. We can give it negative power by allowing it to remain undisciplined and unrenewed and so at the mercy of Satan and every evil thought. Or we can give it positive power by filling our mind with the Word of God, by confessing God's Word of faith and by concentrating on what comes from God rather than the impulses of our own weak nature.

(c) **The mind needs to be prepared for action.** God has made the mind of the believer to be the vehicle of the Holy Spirit. Instead of being the channel of all sorts of rubbish and the means by which Satan finds an entry into our lives, the Father wants our minds to be prepared for His work: *'Therefore, prepare your minds for action; be self-controlled; set your hope fully on the grace to be given to you when Jesus Christ is revealed'* (1 Pet 1:13).

Our minds take their colour from their context. They are like blotting paper. If we fill them with rubbish they will become rubbish. If they are subjected all the time to shallowness and stupidity, they will become the same. But as believers our eyes have not only been opened to the truth, we have also been made aware of God's beauty, mercy, faithfulness, wonder and every aspect of God's love and grace. This fact means that there is so much that comes from the hand of our heavenly Father on which we can concentrate our mind. If we do this our minds will begin to reflect His mind and we will know and share His thoughts. What power there is in a mind that is set on the things of God! *'Finally, brothers, whatever is true, whatever is noble, whatever is right, whatever is pure, whatever is lovely, whatever is admirable – if anything is excellent or praiseworthy – think about such things'* (Phil 4:8, 9).

B: Overcoming the flesh

The 'flesh' is a most powerful force to be reckoned with in our Christian living. It is that old nature which is opposed to the new life of Christ in all its inclinations and desires. The *New Bible Dictionary* defines the flesh as 'The whole personality of man as organised in the wrong direction, as directed to earthly pursuits rather than the service of God'. That is a good definition, and I am sure that when we read it we all recognise what the statement means, because there is about every one of us that awesome and negative power of our old nature. Flesh, in this sense, does not mean only our physical body, although it includes it, of course. It stands for everything about us which expresses the life and desires of our old self and which displays itself in ways that are quite contrary to God's will for our lives:

> *The acts of the sinful nature [flesh] are obvious: sexual immorality, impurity and debauchery, idolatry and witchcraft; hatred, discord, jealousy, fits of rage, selfish ambition, dissensions, factions, and envy; drunkenness, orgies and the like. I warn you, as I did before, that those who live like this will not inherit the kingdom of God.*
> (Gal 5:19–21)

Before a person is born again it is this power of the flesh which rules him or her. It is through this channel that Satan finds such a hold on our lives. The flesh is a very strong force and responds very readily to all the external appeals which come to it. In Romans chapter 8 Paul demonstrates the power of the flesh. It is the flesh which dominates the mind. Modern man has made the mistake of thinking that the mind is the master of the man and so has concentrated on trying to educate and enlighten the mind. Of course, this is to a large extent the case. But the Scriptures teach us that the mind itself is a slave to something deeper in man and that it takes its colour from what governs the person at this deeper level:

> *Those who live according to the sinful nature [flesh] have their minds set on what that nature desires: but those who live in accordance with the Spirit have their minds set on what the Spirit desires. The mind of sinful man is death, but the mind controlled by the Spirit is life and peace; the sinful mind is hostile to God. It does not submit to God's law, nor can it do so.* **Those controlled by the sinful nature [flesh]** *cannot please God'* (Rom 8:5–8)

Here we readily see the power of the flesh. It is a dominant force within the human personality and time and again it attempts to assert its authority in our lives. Paul himself speaks of the struggle which went on within him:

> *I know that nothing good lives in me, that is, in my sinful nature [flesh]. For I have the desire to do what is good, but I cannot carry it out. For what I do is not the good I want to do; no, the evil I do not want to do – this I keep on doing. Now if I do what I do not want to do, it is no longer I who do it, but the sin living in me that does it.* (Rom 7:18–20)

I imagine we can all readily identify with the struggle which Paul expresses. Not one of us would be so bold as to say that the flesh in us has been completely overcome. Of course, as we will see, our old nature has been put to death in Christ and the process of our sanctification is putting that into effect in our daily lives. But it does not happen overnight and, indeed, will not happen completely until we have discarded these old bodies of ours in the power of the Resurrection. But what is the answer to this warfare? Paul puts it in a few words: 'Who *will rescue me from this body of death? Thanks be to God – through Jesus Christ our Lord!'* (Rom 7:24, 25). This is the truth. We need to adopt a very positive attitude with the help of the Holy Spirit. We need to see ourselves actually where we are in Christ. Paul uses very radical language when he speaks of this: *'I have been crucified with Christ **and I no longer live**, but Christ lives in me. The life I live in the body, I live by faith in the Son of God, who loved me and gave himself for me'* (Gal 2:20).

What are the 'faith steps' we can take in our everyday lives which will give us victory over the flesh? It is clear that just making the statement that our old nature is dead, is not sufficient for us to keep this negative enemy under control. The following six steps will prove helpful in our struggles against the flesh. We don't need to take it lying down. We need to recognise that we have been given both the authority and the power to live as new creations in Christ Jesus. I say this because many people are defeated before they start by attitudes of unworthiness and negative feelings about themselves. Not one of us is worthy for this new life. It is all of grace and God has, as Peter reminds us, given us all that we need for life and godliness through our knowledge of Him (2 Pet 1:3).

(a) Live continously with God's picture of your new self. This is what we are taught in Colossians 3:10: *'put on the new self, which is being renewed in knowledge in the image of its Creator'.* 'How will I do that?' someone will ask. Well, there are very simple helps that we can introduce to ourselves. First, always remain open to the Word of God in the Scriptures. The Scriptures breathe the *hope* of the Holy Spirit. They are a bastion against the despair of the flesh.

Another very simple method is to sing to your spirit. Tell yourself what you are in Christ. Inform your heart and mind:

> *I am a new creation,*
> *No more in condemnation.*
> *Here in the grace of God I stand.*

This is, of course, confessing the Word of God to ourselves, and we can be encouraged as we recall what tremendous power the Word has.

(b) Adopt a proper attitude towards your old life. What I mean by this is that we should be taking the position with regard to our old nature that God does. He has done something absolute about the old nature in the death of Christ. It was to break the power and bondage of the old nature that Jesus died: '*In the same way, count yourselves dead to sin but alive to God in Christ Jesus*' (Rom 6:11). We need to live under a new landlord. The flesh has no legal right to make its demands upon us: '*Therefore, brothers, we have an obligation – but it is not to the sinful nature, to live according to it*' (Rom 8:12).

Time and again we are presented with these 'moral imperatives' of the Holy Spirit in Scriptures. It is quite clear that the man of the Spirit has been given a new authority in Christ which he can exercise against the negative spiritual power of the flesh. Another example of this is Colossians 3:5–8:

> *Put to death, therefore, whatever belongs to your earthly nature: sexual immorality, impurity, lust, evil desires and greed, which is idolatry. Because of these, the wrath of God is coming. You used to walk in these ways, in the life you once lived. But now you must rid yourselves of all such things as these.*

(c) Never under-estimate the power of your baptism into Christ.

> *In him you were also circumcised, in the putting off of the sinful nature, not with a circumcision done by the hands of men but with the circumcision done by Christ, having been buried with him in baptism and raised with him through your faith in the power of God, who raised him from the dead.* (Col 2:11, 12)

Personally, I believe it is very beneficial for Christian believers to experience the reality of baptism by immersion or at least consciously as a believer in Christ. One major reason for this is the tremendous practical effect this has for a life of holiness. To understand clearly what is involved in our baptism can be a tremendously positive factor in our victory over sin and the flesh.

I realise this will be a contentious subject for some, and I don't mean to bring offence. But experience teaches that new converts who are clearly taught the significance of baptism in water and the Holy Spirit, can have a great ground for confidence in their struggles over the flesh. We have been baptised into the death of Christ, which means that just as Jesus died to sin and the flesh, so I am now dead to these things, and just as Jesus was raised in the power of God to a new and eternal life, so I am raised in the power of the Spirit into Resurrection experience.

(d) Positively clothe yourself with alternative attitudes, deeds, speech, desires and so on. Holiness is not an inert and passive attitude. It is an active approach to the life of God. Paul teaches us this in Romans 13:11, 12:

> *And do this, understanding the present time. The hour has come for you to wake up from your slumber, because our salvation is nearer now than when we first believed. The night is nearly over; the day is almost here. So let us put aside the deeds of darkness **and put on the armour of light**.*

God has given us through the Holy Spirit so many alternatives to put on and live in. Christian living becomes an exciting experiment in adopting the new manners and habits of our new lives in Christ. What an encouragement to our spirits when we see ourselves being successful, with God's help, in overcoming habits and attitudes which have dominated us for years. This to me is the most significant aspect of the gospel. Unbelievers are amazed at and convicted by the profound difference they can see in the lives of those who formerly walked and lived in a very different manner of life.

(e) Look on your body as an instrument of God. Many of us have such a low regard for our bodies that Satan has won before he has begun. Sometimes the opposite is the case – we have far too high a view of our bodies for their own sake. I believe that Satan finds great opportunity in the two extremes. If we denigrate our bodies we forget that they are included in God's plan of redemption. If we worship them we forget that really they are God's property now and not ours. Of course, it is true that one day we will discard these old bodies, but until then we are given the responsibility of stewardship because these bodies are the vehicles through which the Holy Spirit wants to express our new life in Christ Jesus. Paul sums up what our attitude to our bodies should be: *'Do you not know that your body is a temple of the Holy Spirit, who is in you, whom you have received from God? You are not your own, you were bought at a price. Therefore honour God with your body'* (1 Cor 6:19, 20).

The outcome of this attitude should be commitment on our part not to render our bodies up to the habits and desires of the old self but to dedicate ourselve entirely to God's purposes for our bodies and lives: *'Do not offer the parts of your body to sin, as instruments of wickedness, but rather offer yourselves to God, as those who have been brought from death to life, and offer the parts of your body as instruments of righteousness'* (Rom 6:13).

(f) Live by the power of the Holy Spirit. I find it interesting that the New Testament has far more to say about the power of the flesh and the need for us to overcome this than about any other aspect of spiritual warfare. This is because it is something that is real to every one of us. We all know only too well the fact of this.

The answer to this problem, as far as the Scriptures are concerned, is equally clear: that is, we are exhorted on many occasions to take into our lives all the resources and power of the Holy Spirit:

> So I say, live by the Spirit, and you will not gratify the desires of the flesh. (Gal 5:16)

It is God who works in you to will and to act according to his good purpose. (Phil 2:13)

The one who is in you is greater than the one who is in the world. (1 Jn 4:4)

His divine power has given us everything we need for life and godliness. (2 Pet 1:3)

The Father has not left us to fight this battle by ourselves or in our own strength. He offers us all the power which He has manifested in Jesus to enable us to become 'more than conquerors in him who loved us'.

C: Resisting the devil

This is not a manual on deliverance, so I am not going to discuss in any depth my approach to this subject. The subject in hand is spiritual warfare and how we engage in it. I believe the Scriptures make it clear that the Spirit-filled believer has the authority and the power to resist every attack of Satan and to be free from the influence of the demonic. I am rather afraid that a certain fearfulness has crept in amongst many Christians who know the reality of demonic workings, almost as though we need to speak in hushed tones and look sideways with a sly glance to see if any demons are watching. We have more authority than that! James tells us, 'resist the devil and he will flee from you'.

I have no doubt that the devil is able to find his way into our lives through disobedience and negligence of the truth. When we are disobedient to the Word of God we are vulnerable to the inroads of Satan. Paul tells us this in Ephesians 4:27 when he says, *'Do not give the devil a foothold'*. Think for a moment of a man who wants to climb a rock face. To onlookers who have no experience of such an enterprise the task may seem impossible. As they look at the sheer rock face it might seem as though there was no possible way the man could get the grips he needed to make the ascent. But he looks at the face with an experienced eye. He can see places of opportunity that would be lost to others. He can spy little handholds and footholds and so he can plan his route up the face from one point to the other until he gets to the top. That's just how the devil scans our lives. He finds opportunity where others would find none. He finds footholds by which he can take a grip on our lives. He progresses through these weak points to gain access into our inner hearts and thoughts and so what started as a foothold soon becomes a stronghold unless it is dealt with in the power of God.

5: Seven Steps to Effective Warfare

We have been left neither defenceless nor powerless in this warfare of the spirit. The means have been made available to every Christian believer to withstand the onslaught of Satan and, more importantly, to take effective measures against him which will not only inhibit his actions, but will bring to other people freedom from his power. These weapons are not hidden, secret resources which are open only to a few specially chosen favourites. They are ours in Christ! Says Paul: *'For though we live in the world, we do not wage war as the world does. The weapons we fight with are not the weapons of the world. On the contrary, they have divine power to demolish strongholds'* (2 Cor 10:3, 4).

I want to suggest seven basic steps in effective warfare against Satan. It may surprise you to know how fundamental they are to your Christian life, because I firmly believe that this is the truth: our power to stand against the wiles of the evil one is implicit in the very fact that we are born again of the Holy Spirit. However, it is true that many believers have failed to realise their birthright, the tremendous potential they have by being in Christ Jesus. I believe we need to ask God to reveal to us just how much we have come into in Christ Jesus – to understand in a real way within our spirits just how tremendous this salvation is in which we stand.

A: Know who you are in Christ

The New Testament is bursting with this affirmation: God has not brought us to birth in Jesus to be defeated. We are not born to fail! In Christ we are born to take authority over every enemy which attacks us and the Kingdom of God. The secret of victory in every area of spiritual warfare, as far as Paul was concerned, lay right here: *'For you died, and your life is now hidden with Christ in God'* (Col 3:3). This is how he begins his instructions to the believers on how to overcome the power of the flesh.

Sometimes when I am leading meetings I ask the audience to look at their feet. This causes amusement, embarrassment and a whole range of responses. But the point becomes clear. I ask them, 'Where is Satan?' The response is always the same: 'Under my feet!' It is a very simple illustration but it makes an important point, because many people live as though *their necks* were under the feet of Satan! But Jesus has crushed his head and on the Cross of Calvary has overcome every principality and power (see Col 2:15). That's why He cried out on the Cross, 'It is finished!' It was not a cry of despair, it was a shout of triumph. He had overcome the powers of darkness and borne all the sins of the world. The victory of the Cross was not achieved in the Resurrection; that was the Father's witness to what had already been accomplished by the Son.

Now we are in Christ. We reign and rule with Him. The reality of this is spelled out by the writer to the Hebrews:

> *In putting everything under him, God left nothing that is not subject to him. Yet at present we do not see everything subject to him. But we see Jesus, who was made a little lower than the angels, now crowned with glory and honour because he suffered death, so that by the grace of God he might taste death for everyone.* (Heb 2:8, 9)

This is the fact of spiritual warfare. In the power of Christ we are involved in the mopping up operations after the main battle has been won. Our power and authority come from that victory. This is why we come against all these powers in the name of the Lord. He is called Jesus, the deliverer and Saviour! His name means 'salvation' and brings salvation and against that name not all the demons under heaven are able to stand: '*Whatever you do, whether in word or deed, do it all in the name of the Lord Jesus, giving thanks to God the Father through him*' (Col 3:17).

B: Put on the whole armour of God

Everybody knows Ephesians 6:10–18, where Paul describes the armour of God for us. It has often been said that the pieces of the armour are mainly defensive but, in fact, every part of this armour is necessary for attack as well as defence.

The old saying tells us the best form of defence is attack.

Certainly in spiritual warfare that is true. You don't want to develop an attitude of sitting waiting around for Satan. We need to get on with the job, and we *have* been given the means to do this. Applying God's armour is an active thing. It requires application and the development of spiritual skills. If we saw this truth it would add so much lustre to our Christian lives. So many believers seem to take the attitude that now they are Christians there is not much more to it than to go to church, pay their dues and do the things that seem right for Christians to do. I don't look upon it like that at all! For me being a Christian is certainly demanding, at times frustrating, but always exciting!

I used to be in business and after that in academic life. In both contexts there was a tremendous lot to learn, explore and become proficient in. We should adopt the same mentality towards our lives as believers. There are so many good things the Holy Spirit wants to teach us if we will take the time to be alert and involved.

I haven't the space to explore every facet of this armour. But take for example, the belt of truth. How do we put on the belt of truth? Well, one thing is certain – we will never be able to put it on if we don't know what it is! If I want to wear a belt with my suit I like to know how this belt fits. I like to test the size of it. I like to know the colour of it. In fact I like to know that it's my belt! To get it I go where I know belts are kept. It's the same with this belt of truth. I feel so many Christians have a vague idea of this spiritual armour. They seem to think that it's just sitting around somewhere and that in some mystical, invisible way we can put it on. But it's not like that. To put on the belt of truth, you need to go where the truth is, and the truth needs to be known, examined, tested and fitted to your life. You see the exciting challenge of this. One thing I am perfectly sure of and that is that I will never exhaust this exploration of the truth of God's Word until the day I pass to glory!

The same is true with every part of this armour. I need to get to know what it is in reality and then go about in practice applying it to my life.

C: Exercise the true power of prayer

In the same passage Paul tells us to 'pray in the Spirit on all occasions'. Now we have taken this phrase, 'pray in the Spirit', and have often interpreted it in terms of the gift of tongues. But I believe that is to limit the meaning of what Paul is teaching us here. Of course praying in tongues is an essential part of 'praying in the Spirit', but it is not all there is to it. To pray in the Spirit is to realise the absolute effectiveness of prayer. I have more to say about prayer in another part of this book, so we only need to notice briefly at the moment that true prayer is a powerful reality.

In spiritual warfare this kind of prayer is important if we are to know how to bind the power of the devil. Jesus said, *'How can anyone enter a strong man's house and carry off his possessions unless he first ties up the strong man!'* (Mt 12:29). This is a terrific picture. That is exactly what I believe spiritual warfare entails – carrying off the possessions of Satan! But the fact is that unless we bind the strong man we cannot carry off his possessions.

It is through the power of effective prayer, where we stand in the authority which we have been given in Jesus, that we bind the enemy. Satan can be bound before he ever starts to cause trouble. We need to remember this important truth. Satan himself cannot be present everywhere, so what we are coming against in the power of prayer in any given situation are spiritual forces which, as we have already seen, have no independent rights or authority of their own.

We can take authority over these forces in the name of Jesus. There is no need for any mumbo jumbo. A simple statement of authority and prayer in the name of Jesus will have the effect of rendering these alien spiritual forces powerless.

D: Use the power of triumphant praise

Paul Billheimer says, 'Satan is allergic to praise, so where there is massive, triumphant praise, Satan is paralysed, bound and banished.' King Jehoshaphat was instructed by the Lord to appoint men to sing to the Lord and 'to praise him for the splendour of his holiness'. It seemed a very unlikely strategy, but it worked wonders and the armies of Ammon and Moab were routed by their own fear and not a sword had to be lifted in Israel, as God had promised: '*You will not have to fight in this battle. Take up your positions; stand firm and see the deliverance the Lord will give you*' (2 Chron 20:17).

One of the most important lessons we have learned in missions is that the period of prayer before a meeting must not be 'just' a prayer meeting. What we are doing is declaring the praises of the Lord. It is this that gives us strength and courage in our hearts and puts the enemy to flight before we have ever started the meeting.

E: Stand in the bond of faith

Paul underlines the importance of faith in spiritual warfare when he tells us in Ephesians 6:16 to take up the shield of faith. Now this is important because the shield that Paul had in mind was not a shield to be used only in individual armed combat. No, it was a great shield that was to be linked together with the shields of fellow soldiers to provide an over-all protection against the enemy as they advanced together against a city. When these shields were held in place they afforded an impenetrable wall against everything the enemy could throw at them.

Now this contains a vital principle in our fight, not only against demonic attack but against the temptations of the flesh, the attacks within our thought life and all the aggression of the flesh. We must not stand alone! We need to stand, taking the shield of faith, in fellowship with other believers we know we can trust and who will stand with us in the heat of the battle. Many a believer has known victory over a certain attack because others have agreed with him in faith and shown real fellowship and suppport in that time of need. This is why fellowship is so important. We need to know who are our allies. Good friends in Christ are important. Value them. Stand with them. Trust them. Know how to stand with each other when the heat is on in these intense moments of spiritual warfare.

F: Be active in your resistance against Satan

Now you may think I have spoken about this already. But I believe we are facing a great challenge, and that is whether we are going to let the devil have it all his own way in this world. I believe that this warfare needs to be fought at ground level. We have already described the steps in the realm of the heavenlies. But there is a need for us to fight on the ground. This is where Satan is and this is where he tries to enforce his rule in the lives and hearts of men.

As we have seen, he not only tries to invade the private lives of individuals, but he wields tremendous power through the structures and systems that man has built for himself on this earth. Today we live in a global village with massive economic and political power structures. Vast amounts of resources and power are held by these structures. Some multi-national corporations hold more clout than many governments. We need to pray about this power and be concerned about how this power is exercised.

One outstanding example of how this can affect the outcome of things is shown through the experience of Tony Campolo. He became aware of the vast resources and power of a particular American corporation. He wondered how he could have a voice into that structure, because there were certain areas of its operation which troubled him greatly. He was directed by the Holy Spirit to buy one share, which gave him the right to speak out at the annual meeting. He spoke about his concern very simply in terms of Christian stewardship. In fact, I think he gave the board a dose of the parable of the talents and applied it to the operation of their business. He challenged them about how they were using their resources. Then he sat down and felt that he had spoken out as the Lord had wanted him to.

About two weeks later he had a phone call from the Head Office of that corporation inviting him to visit them. The outcome of his visit was that they released resources to fund a $100 million project in the Dominican Republic. This project put back into the hands of the local people all the land which was no longer used for growing sugar and provided new housing for every sugar worker in that country. It provided a hospital for every village in the eastern half of the country where this corporation is working and funded schools throughout the whole republic. Such is the power available to those of us who believe in God.

You see, I think we have become frightened that there is no one out there who really wants to listen. We imagine that what we have to say as Christians is taboo to everybody else. That is just not my experience at all. I believe that a real part of this spiritual warfare today is that, under the direction of the Spirit, we are to take such actions as God tells us, to wrest the possessions of the strong man out of his grasp!

In any case when, and if, the time comes for any one of us, we need that resolve of spirit to be like the three men in the Book of Daniel. When they were confronted by the sheer unbending aggression of the world's system they were ready with their repy: *'We will not serve your gods'* (Dan 3:18).

G: Believe in the liberating power of the gospel
Jesus came in the liberating power of the Kingdom of God:

> *'The Spirit of the Lord is on me,*
>   *because he has anointed me*
>   *to preach good news to the poor.*
> *He has sent me to proclaim freedom for the prisoners*
>   *and recovery of sight for the blind,*
> *to release the oppressed,*
>   *to proclaim the year of the Lord's favour'*
>
> (Lk 4:18, 19)

Evangelism is back on the agenda as far as God is concerned! We are not called to be religious story-tellers but to move in the power and operation of the kingdom. Jesus received *exousia* (authority) and *dunamis* (power) from the Father, and He passed these on to His disciples, and He passes them on to us through the Holy Spirit.

Evangelism is deliverance! We have made such a narrow use of this term. But every time a man or woman is saved in the power of God they are delivered from the kingdom of Satan and transferred into the Kingdom of God's dear Son. That deliverance will always mean something in terms of practical life. No man or woman has yet been born again who did not need to be set free, whether it be from habits, thoughts, deeds or demons – certainly from the thraldom and power of sin. Hallelujah! What a Saviour!

Get involved in evangelism. Tell a friend. Tell your neighbour. Tell a workmate. Bring someone to Jesus. It will be the best day's work you ever did! It will do so much for your own spirit, as you will participate in their freedom. Don't just sit there – there's a war on! *Do you not say, "Four months more and then the harvest"? I tell you, open your eyes and look at the fields! They are ripe for harvest* (Jn 4:35).

Chapter 8
Greater Things Than These

1: The Ground of Our Ministry

You are a chosen people, a royal priesthood, a holy nation, a people belonging to God, that you may declare the praises of him who called you out of darkness into his wonderful light. (1 Pet 2:9)

We have all been called as ministers of the New Covenant. God's purpose for every one of our lives is that we should be living in and sharing with others the realities of His Kingdom. Jesus came to declare the Kingdom of God – that is, the rule of God – and to declare the overthrow of the kingdom of Satan. This was the kernel of His conversations with the discipes after His resurrection: *'After his suffering, he showed himself to these men and gave them convincing proofs that he was alive. He appeared to them over a period of forty days and spoke about the kingdom of God'* (Acts 1:3). This is not surprising, because throughout His own ministry Jesus had been manifesting the power of the Kingdom. He acted in the power of the Holy Spirit and when He accomplished mighty deeds He spoke of them as being signs that God's Kingdom was here: *'If I drive out demons by the Spirit of God, then the kingdom of God has come upon you'* (Mt 12:28).

In the parables which He taught He was revealing truths about the Kingdom of God which are not accessible to men in the normal course of events. Although it is clear that even His disciples did not understand them at the time, Jesus left them with teaching which would become their food and drink as they later acted and ministered in the power of the Holy Spirit. We need to remember that the four gospels were written with the benefit of hindsight and the powerful experience of the Resurrection and Pentecost behind them. His teaching is all about the Kingdom of God and is only revealed to those who receive the Spirit of the Kingdom for themselves: *'The disciples came to him and asked, "Why do you speak to the people in parables?" He replied, "The knowledge of the secrets of the kingdom of heaven has been given to you, but not to them"'* (Mt 13:10, 11).

To preach this Kingdom is the great commission of the Church. Jesus declared that it would be proclaimed throughout the whole world before the end would come (Mt 24:14) Jesus spoke very little about the Church during His ministry on earth, but on one of those few occasions He drew a direct link between the foundation of the Church and the witness of the Kingdom. In speaking to Peter He made it clear that He would invest his followers with His own authority and give them the power of the Kingdom here on earth: *'I will give you the keys of the kingdom of heaven; whatever you bind on earth will be bound in heaven, and whatever you loose on earth will be loosed in heaven'* (Mt 16:19). The Church is the servant of the Kingdom. The Kingdom is the proclamation and power of the Church. We are called as heralds of the Kingdom and this is why we need first to receive the power of the Kingdom ourselves.

A: The Kingdom now

I was brought up, as were many other Christians, to look upon the Kingdom of God as something that pertained to the future. This was the day of grace, and the Kingdom would come when Jesus was manifested in glory. Therefore great sections of the Scriptures, and in particular the Gospels, were closed as far as today was concerned. They were labelled 'Kingdom truths', which meant that they would not become relevant until after the Second Coming of Christ in glory and the establishment of the Millennial Kingdom, when we would see and experience all these things in perfection and fulness.

Of course, there is a great deal of truth in this teaching. It is clear that no one would say we are anywhere near the fulness of God in terms of life and power. It is clear that the forces of evil have a field-day in the lives of countless Christian people and that they are governed, not by the power of God's goodness and love, but by the forces of darkness which are hellbent on man's destruction. The greater tragedy is that these people don't realise their bondage, and become willing dupes of this evil system.

But it is equally clear from Scripture that this is not the whole story. Jesus spoke quite clearly in terms of the Kingdom of God having come in His own life and ministry. From the moment that He stood up in the synagogue at Nazareth and read the words from the scroll of Isaiah chapter 61 it is clear that He perceived His ministry in terms of the breakthrough of God's Kingdom here on earth. His works of power, called 'mighty deeds', were, as we have already seen, the sign of God's Kingdom working effectively amongst men and testifying its reality.

When He sent His disciples out two by two to prepare the way for His own visits He gave them this commission: '*Heal the sick ... and tell them, "The kingdom of God is near you"*' (Lk 10:9). He taught His disciples to seek the Kingdom of God and to put it first in their lives. He showed them how faith is the first principle of God's Kingdom and how it releases men from fear and anxiety and brings a new set of priorities. In fact, He gave them the assurance that the Father Himself wanted them to know for themselves the goodness of the Kingdom within their own experience, and He encouraged His disciples to give up everything else for the sake of the discovery of this Kingdom in their lives:

> '*Do not be afraid, little flock, for your Father has been pleased to give you the kingdom. Sell your possessions and give to the poor. Provide purses for yourselves that will*

not wear out, a treasure in heaven that will not be exhausted ... For where your treasure is, there your heart will be also.'

(Lk 12:32–34)

There was high expectation of the coming of the Messianic Kingdom in the Judea of the days of Jesus. The political and religious climate made it a hotbed of rumour and ideas. But the popular notions about this Kingdom were very different from those which Jesus taught and expressed in His ministry. The Jews probably looked for a deliverer who would save them by the might of arms from the hands of the Roman oppressors and who would express His kingship in terms of political and religious power. Jesus was a complete enigma to them. They could see, on the one hand, that He was a man of power and moral goodness; but on the other hand His ideas and practices contradicted their desires and ideals at their very roots. In His conversations with the Pharisees Jesus declared that the Kingdom of God had already come and was in their midst. Once, having been asked by the Pharisees when the Kingdom of God would come, Jesus replied, *'The kingdom of God does not come with your careful observation, nor will people say, "Here it is," or "There it is," because the kingdom of God is within you.'* (Lk 17:20, 21)

B: Three dimensions

The fact is that the Kingdom of God comes to us in three dimensions. The Kingdom *has already arrived* in Jesus. His ministry signalled the tremendous breakthrough of God's Kingdom upon earth and this was witnessed to by the signs and wonders which characterised His ministry. His death on the Cross was the decisive battle in the campaign of God against every power and authority which has ever tried to stand against the Kingdom of God. The Kingdom *comes to us* in the power of the Holy Spirit. In the lives of every believer the Kingdom of God is manifested. Through faith in the name of Jesus we are delivered from the dominion of darkness and transferred to the Kingdom of the Son He loves (Col 1:13). The Kingdom of God *is still to come* and will be manifested fully at the appearing of our Lord Jesus Christ in glory.

This might seem to be a somewhat complex way of looking at the issue, but I believe that it provides a vital and practical ground for our own ministry today. To see that the Kingdom has come in the ministry and victory of Jesus on the Cross provides for us an important platform as we minister to other people. We are not coming in hope but in faith! *Faith rests on the finished work of Christ*. The power of the Kingdom *has been* accomplished. The spiritual battle takes place in every new generation of human beings who are born into the world. We are engaged in this warfare in our own day and age but we are not called to fight the *decisive battle*. We are called to approach people in the sure and certain knowledge that the battle has been won and that the power of the Kingdom is available for them today.

The fact that the Kingdom comes to us in the power of the Holy Spirit underlines an important fact about it. It is not a political Kingdom, or a social Kingdom, it is a *personal Kingdom*. Now what this means is that the Kingdom becomes a reality within the lives of those who open themselves to the King and who bow the knee to the demands of this Kingdom. This means that the Kingdom of God can be related to the life and experience of every individual; that when we speak to people we are bringing something to them that they can comprehend in terms of their own life and can receive for themselves. Some will object to this emphasis on the personal. They will say that I am being far too individualistic in my approach and that I should put much more emphasis on the social dimensions of the Bible's teaching about the Kingdom. True, in the end the Kingdom is more than an individual. But the means into the Kingdom must needs be *personal*. To say that a thing is personal is not the same as saying that it is individualistic. To say that it is personal means that it must be *personally appropriated* – that is, if we are to experience the benefits and power of this Kingdom, they must be received through faith, which is a personal matter.

Today, more than ever, we are seeing the need for people to take personal responsibility for their lives and actions. Where people take personal responsibility it has a *social effect*. This is the truth of the Church. The true Church is made up of those who have become related to Christ personally and through this have become part of His social Body, the fellowship of believers, the Church. The fact that this fellowship bond has such a personal basis in the experience of each member means that there is the possibility of a much deeper commitment and care than if the society was based on a traditional or legalistic basis.

C: Meanwhile

The fact that the Kingdom has not yet appeared in its fulness has a number of important repercussions for life and ministry. It introduces, for example, the tremendous incentive of Christian hope into our discipleship. Christian hope is quite different from the hopefulness that is displayed in the world at large. Such hopefulness is generally based on nothing more than wishful thinking. But Christian hope has its firm basis on the two dimensions of the Kingdom which we have already noted. We have this hope because we *know* that Christ has appeared and has fulfilled His work. Think of the tremendous sense of excitement which must have filled the disciples' hearts after they heard the message of the angels after Jesus had been taken away from their sight in the power of His ascension into glory:

> *They were looking intently up into the sky as he was going, when suddenly two men dressed in white stood beside them. 'Men of Galilee', they said, 'why do you stand here looking into the sky? This same Jesus, who has been taken from you into heaven, will come back in the same way you have seen him go into heaven.'*
>
> (Acts 1:10, 11)

From that moment forward the Church has gone about its task of mission in the knowledge that it operates between the two greatest events the world will ever know – the first and second comings of the Lord Jesus Christ!

This fact also leaves us with some understanding of the

unfulfilled. There are many things we would like to see happen more completely. There are many questions to which we would like to have fuller answers. There are situations in which we long to see more fulfilment and greater happiness: *'Now we see but a poor reflection as in a mirror; then we shall see face to face. Now I know in part; then I shall know fully, even as I am fully known'* (1 Cor 13:12).

It is, also, a strong incentive for our lives as disciples of Jesus. The fact that we live 'between the times' reminds us that we are in this world in much the same way as He was – namely, that we are the forerunners of the fulness of the Kingdom. Every person saved, every healing accomplished, every deliverance effected in the power of the Holy Spirit is a sign of the age to come! *So are our lives.* Jesus described us as the salt of the earth and like the light of a city set on a hill that cannot be hidden. What gives us the power to stand and continue in our lives of holiness as testimonies to the living power of God's Kingdom? John reminds us of the strong incentive of the coming Kingdom within our lives when he says: *'Dear friends, now we are children of God, and what we will be has not yet been made known. But we know that when he appears, we shall be like him, for we shall see him as he is. **Everyone who has this hope in him purifies himself, just as he is pure'*** (1 Jn 3:2, 3).

This three-dimensional reality of the Kingdom of God is of the greatest relevance for our day-to-day witness and ministry in the lives of other people. It means that we can point them to the most decisive landmark for their existence. Jesus has come and declared the Kingdom and through His death and resurrection has established its power and authority. Men and women need live no longer under the thraldom of their own sinful natures, nor under the authority and darkness of Satan. It is the day of release to the captives. It interprets the continuing struggle that every believer faces. This is a fact because we are living between the times. Often the struggle is not so much for ourselves but on behalf of other people. We have not been delivered out of the war zone. We have been called to war and we have been reminded that our offensive is not against human beings but against the vast and powerful spiritual forces which arraign themselves against the Kingdom of God (see Eph 6:10–18).

The fact is that we have been called to minister the Kingdom. The Kingdom has come, the Kingdom is here, the Kingdom is still to come in fulness. Such a perspective should fill us with hope and power as we move in to see God's Kingdom becoming a reality in the lives of those to whom we witness and minister in the name of Jesus.

2: The Pattern for Ministry

In the four Gospels we gain a very clear insight into the ministry of Jesus and into the ways in which He operated in the power of God as He brought the reality of the Kingdom into the lives of men and women. They are not written as exhaustive biographies but have, as their purpose, the declaration of the person and work of Jesus. The incidents which are highlighted are chosen by the Holy Spirit to demonstrate God's truth with regard to Jesus and to reveal the way of salvation to those whom He calls through faith.

John tells us that the reason he wrote his Gospel was to show us who Jesus really was and to lead us to salvation through believing in Him: *'Jesus did many other miraculous signs in the presence of his disciples, which are not recorded in this book. But these are written that you may believe that Jesus is the Christ, the Son of God, and that by believing you may have life in his name'* (Jn 20:30, 31). Luke wrote his Gospel as the first section of a two-part thesis. The first to show how the power of the Holy Spirit was manifested in the life, ministry, death and resurrection of Jesus; the second to demonstrate how this same power carried on working through the life and experience of the first Christians and how it spread right through the world.

This continuum of faith and power is crucial to our understanding of our own witness and ministry. We are called to continue what began in Jesus and what was manifested in the power of Pentecost. Our ministry is a reflection of His ministry and we are given the same power of the Kingdom in which to operate effectively in His saving name.

We can see what this means for us when we look at His ministry as portrayed in the Gospels. It means that we can learn vital lessons from this testimony, which will lead us to understand how we should minister and what it is that we are ministering. The Gospels are unlocked for us when we come to understand that what we are given in them is a paradigm or pattern for our own experience. The Father has left us a witness for our learning so that we can become more effective witnesses in our own lives.

A: Five features

There are five features which characterise the ministry of Jesus and inform our own ministry in a significant way:

(a) **By the Spirit.** The thing that strikes you when you read the Gospels is the fact that Jesus did not operate independently of His Father. Time and again we are given glimpses into the vital relationship between Jesus and His Father and this is expressed by the fact that Jesus Himself operated in the power of the Holy Spirit. It is significant to note that although Jesus was born in the power of the Holy Spirit, He did no mighty deed until after His baptism in the River Jordan. At that time He was endued with the power of the Holy Spirit for the work of His ministry and declared publicly to be God's Son with power.

Jesus Himself acknowledged this fact when He spoke of His casting out of demons: *'If I drive out demons by the Spirit of God, then the kingdom of God has come upon you'* (Mt 12:28). Luke's version of this text (Lk 11:20) expresses the beautiful metaphor which is used in the original Greek to describe the Holy Spirit. There the Spirit is spoken of as 'the finger of God'. What an apt metaphor this is for the Holy Spirit, whose divine work it is to point out to men their need in Jesus. Time and again Jesus emphasised this divine connection between Himself and the Father. John highlights it on a number of occasions in his Gospel – for example: *'Jesus said to them, "My Father is always at his work to this very day, and I, too, am working"'* (Jn 5:17).

(b) **To the poor.** The hallmark of the ministry of Jesus was that it was directed to those who needed it. That is, to those who knew they needed it. The Gospels are filled with incidents of people who had come to recognise their need and who came or were brought to Jesus, to have that need met. Those who are whole do not need a physician, Jesus once said (Mt 9:12). This was a scathing comment on those who felt they were all right and who were self-satisfied with their religion.

The words and works of Jesus were always directed to the poor and needy. This did not always mean those who were materially poor: many of those to whom Jesus ministered cannot be classed in this way. Whether rich or poor in material terms, they had this one thing in common: they were in poor in spirit. Whether it be Zacchaeus, who was probably far from being a poor man in material terms, or the window of Nain, who lost her most prized possession in her son, they came to Jesus empty and needy in spirit and found in Him the answer to that need.

An outstanding example of this is to be found in the Samaritan woman whom Jesus met a Jacob's well near the city of Sychar. Jesus spoke to her about the deepest areas of her life and offered her the satisfaction that only He could bring:

> *Jesus answered, 'Everyone who drinks this water will be thirsty again, but whoever drinks the water I give him will never thirst. Indeed, the water I give him will become in him a spring of water welling up to eternal life,' The woman said to him, 'Sir, give me this water so that I won't get thirsty and have to keep coming here to draw water.'* (Jn 4:13–15)

This feature of the ministry of Jesus is further highlighted by the response which Jesus Himself gave to the disciples of John the Baptist who were sent by John to enquire whether Jesus was actually the Messiah. Jesus answered John in terms that he would understand perfectly as the signs of the outbreak of the messianic age: *'Go back and report to John what you hear and see: The blind receive sight, the lame walk, those who have leprosy are cured, the deaf hear, the dead are raised, and the good news is preached to the poor'* (Mt 11:4, 5).

(c) **Against Satan.** The whole ministry of Jesus, including His life and death, is seen in the Gospels as a direct challenge to the authority of Satan. Satan is seen as the strong man whom Jesus will bind in the power of the Holy Spirit (Mt 12:29). When he has been bound his house can be plundered. The ministry of Jesus is a foretaste of the absolute overthrow and binding of Satan in a day to come. It is a proclamation of the overthrow of the evil one and a sign of his ultimate defeat.

Every mighty deed and healing worked by Jesus is seen as a sign of God's Kingdom and a releasing of the grip of Satan on the lives of men and women. The Cross is spoken of by Jesus Himself as a great judgement on the head of Satan: *'Now is the time for judgement on this world; now the prince of this world will be driven out'* (Jn 12:31).

It is significant that when Mark begins his Gospel the first incident which he portrays after the call of the first disciples by Jesus is that of Jesus confronting the powers of darkness, when he cast the evil spirit out of the man in the synagogue at Capernaum: *'The people were all so amazed that they asked each other, "What is this? A new teaching – and with authority! He even gives orders to evil spirits and they obey him"'* (Mk 1:27). The coming of Jesus into the world is a direct counter-challenge to the power of Satan. He is the 'god of this world' who blinds men to the truth of God and controls their lives through all manner of malevolent spirits and spiritual bondages. The whole of the New Testament shares this witness of the four Gospels, that with Jesus comes the power of God's Kingdom, which is a direct attack on the dominion of darkness. John, writing in his epistle, presents this truth in a very succinct and punchy way: *'The reason the Son of God appeared was to destroy the devil's work'* (1 Jn 3:8).

(d) **For salvation.** We need to remember that the purpose of Jesus was the total salvation of men and women. Time and again when He healed people physically He took them beyond the level of the physical and indicated that salvation was something much deeper. Time and again He told people to go on their way because their faith had saved them! The clear implications of these words is that even if the person had come to Jesus with a physical need Jesus never left them merely at the level of the physical problem. He discerned the root of that problem. He looked into their hearts and He addressed them at their deepest point of need.

This is something we need always to remember for our own ministry today. It is easy to gain a following for the things that people feel are the greatest need. Today we are seeing a boom-time in faith healing, not only in terms of Christian healing but in terms of natural and spiritualisitc healing. There has never been a greater openness to these things, even to the extent of their being received in terms of holistic medicine within the boundaries of orthodox medical practice. Of course, *as Christians we need to offer the ministry of healing as part of the full gospel*. But it is just possible that this high degree of interest in physical healing is expressing a deep-rooted fear in men and women about the question of death.

After all, why do so many want to be healed? Could it be that they are scared to die? In our world death is an ever-present reality. We dress it up and try to cover up its awfulness, but our news screens declare it to us every night and the AIDS epidemic brings the fear of it right to our doors. But for all that, death is and has always been a universal reality in the experience of men. I think it was George Bernard Shaw who said, 'Death is the ultimate statistic: one out of one dies!' The reality of death has come home to millions today. It is a harsh fact that in a world that has more material and technological benefit than the human race has ever known, the fact of death should be more pronounced than ever before.

Jesus Himself lived in a world of death. Life was cheap and death was often violent and tragic. He ministered into this situation. He brought healing to sick people, He brought sight to those who could not see, He brought joy into bereavement when He raised people from the dead. But above all, He addressed the inner heart of man. The gospel is about total salvation. It is not ulitmately about being healed to die again; it is about being born again never to die! Jesus declared: '*I am the bread of life. Your forefathers ate the manna in the desert, yet they died. But there is the bread that comes down from heaven, which a man may eat and not die*' (Jn 6:48–50).

This is the great challenge to our faith and ministry today. We are not called to match the magicians of Egypt with our miracles. Whatever miracles we perform in the power of the Holy Spirit must be those which open the door of a man or woman's life to the saving power of God in an eternal sense. Our fruit for the Kingdom of God will not be measured in terms of the numbers who have been healed, but in terms of those who have been saved. I say this without any thought of criticism of the Christian healing ministry – in fact, physical and emotional healing are a real part of my own ministry. But we need to beware that we are not taking our cue from a world that lives in fear. The devil leads men and women astray by the appeal to the immediate and by playing on their fear of death. As Christians we need to declare, on the one hand, our confidence in the power of God to heal and, on the other, to proclaim our fearlessness of death, which after all, as Leslie Weatherhead once said, is for the Christian believer only a milestone.

(e) **In power.** The Gospels are packed full of examples of the power of ministry of Jesus. For all the reservation I have expressed above, we need to recognise that a true gospel ministry is not only a gospel of words. We need to use words to give the reason for the hope that is in us, but words by themselves are often insufficient evidence for people who have lived in spiritual darkness and bondage all their lives. It takes a breakthrough of the direct power of God to awaken them and alert them to His reality.

This is not the same as playing Satan's tune. It is acting under the direction of the Holy Spirit as He leads us to apply the power of God into specific situations to bring about healing or deliverance so that the person might be free to follow after Jesus. The secret of this ministry, it seems to me, is our direct reliance on the Holy Spirit to guide us in every situation and to bring God's power through us to the person. If we look at the ministry of Jesus we can see this power expressed in two major ways and in several directions.

B: The power of authority

Two Greek words characterise the power ministry of Jesus in the Gospels. The first is *exousia*, which means 'authority' or 'right'. Jesus had the authority and the right to exercise His ministry because He had received it from the Father. We have already seen how close His relationship was with His Father, and He Himself declared a number of times that He never did anything except what the Father told Him to. The people who saw Jesus operate in His ministry were astounded time and again at this authority which He had: *'When Jesus had finished saying these things, the crowds were amazed at his teaching, because he taught as one who had authority, and not as their teachers of the law'* (Mt 7:28, 29).

The second word is *dunamis*, which means 'power'. This word is used many, many times and is translated in the plural as 'mighty deeds'. It is a word which describes the *ability* of a person to do something. It is the same word which is used in Acts 1:8, where Jesus promises this power to those who receive the Holy Spirit. Then they will be able to be witnesses for Him throughout the whole world. Without this God-given power we have not the ability to function in our ministries in relation to other people. This power in the ministry of Jesus is manifested in a number of different ways.

Healing the sick. The healing ministry of Jesus is a declaration of the coming fulness of God's Kingdom, in which there will be neither sickness nor death: *'There will be no more death or mourning or crying or pain, for the old order of things has passed away'* (Rev 21:4). Those who are healed are set free to proclaim the fulness of God's Kingdom. The thing we need to beware of is healing for healing's sake. Every one of those healed or raised from the dead by Jesus lived to die again. But their healing was a token, a sign of the Kings's coming fulness, and a testimony to the real power of God, which sets men free at the deepest levels of their lives.

Casting out demons. When Jesus cast out demons it was a sign of the final and absolute overthrow of Satan. Satan is not equal to the Holy Spirit; he is not omnipresent. He carries out his global work through the agency of demonic powers. The foiling of these forces is the evidence that Satan's power and influence are being undermined in the lives of men and women. Through the Holy Spirit we have absolute power over the demonic powers of the kingdom of darkness: *'When a strong man, fully armed, guards his own house, his possessions are safe. But when someone stronger attacks and overpowers him, he takes away the armour in which the man trusted and divides up the spoils'* (Lk 11:21).

Miracles of nature. God created the world in harmony, beauty and order. As a result of the sin of man Creation has lost the touch of God in these ways. When God viewed His work of Creation He did so with divine satisfaction. Genesis chapter 1 tells us that *'God saw all that he had made, and it was very good'* (verse 31). Under the Fall and the subsequent domination by Satan the created order has been subjected to bondage. Time and again in His ministry Jesus exercised the authority and power of God in the realm of nature. For example, He brings the power of nature back under the control of God when He speaks with power and calms the angry sea (Mt 8:23–27) and He becomes master of the waves when He walks on the water to come to His disciples, who were in danger of being overwhelmed by the storm (Mt 14:22–33).

Raising the dead. On a number of outstanding occasions Jesus brought people back to life. John chapter 11 tells us of the raising of Lazarus; Luke chapter 7 of the raising of the son of the widow of Nain and Matthew chapter 9 tells of the raising of Jairus' daughter.

C: Greater things than these

These important features of the ministry of Jesus provide us with some clues about the nature of our own ministry. It is a ministry of the Kingdom. Jesus Himself said, *'I tell you the truth, anyone who has faith in me will do what I have been doing. He will do even greater things than these, because I am going to the Father'* (Jn 14:12).

It seems incredible that we have been called to share in the ministry of Jesus, but if we take these words seriously then we can expect to be involved in works of power that are even more remarkable than those recorded in the Gospels. When we turn to the Acts of the Apostles we *can* see the works of Jesus being manifested with great power: not twos and threes, but hundreds and thousands coming into the Kingdom of God through the power of the Holy Spirit. Healings and signs and wonders were the hallmark of this outbreak of the power of God, and these caused the world to sit up and take notice of what God was doing. When Paul come later in his mission he could describe it to the church at Corinth:

> *I did not come with eloquence or superior wisdom as I proclaimed to you the testimony about God. For I resolved to know nothing while I was with you except Jesus Christ and him crucified. I came to you in weakness and fear, and with much tembling. my message and my preaching were not with wise and persuasive words, but with a demonstration of the Spirit's power, so that your faith might not rest on man's wisdom, but on God's power.* (1 Cor 2:1–5)

3: The Power of Prayer

'Pray in the Spirit on all occasions with all kinds of prayers and requests.'
(Eph 6:18)

The place to start an effective ministry is the place of prayer. Some readers might be put off by the thought that they have not been called to any spectacular ministry, and all the talk so far about the power of the Kingdom of God may seem too overpowering for them. But I believe that if we can get to grips with the simplicity and power of the gift of prayer we will see that this ministry is open to every one of us. After all, what is ministry but the application of God's power to whatever situation we might find ourselves in? We can all do this as we become confident of the fact that God hears our prayers and will answer them with power. The power does not belong to us but to Him. What He is looking for in us is openness to His working, so that He can work through us and use us in whatever situations He places us in.

It would be a great help if we could immediately reassess our lives and begin to see that we are really *mobile agents of the Kingdom of God!* God wants us to be available to Him and through this prayer ministry to release through us the power of heaven into the lives and circumstances of people around us every day. There is so much we could say about prayer, of course, and there have been a number of very good books written on the subject as a whole. My purpose is not to discuss prayer in a broad sense. I want, rather, to emphasise the place of prayer in our lives as ministers of the Kingdom. Over the past few years I have come to see God's purposes here in a new way. The Father wants us to be so open to the reality of prayer that we will be able, wherever we go, to make a way through to Him on behalf of the people we come into contact with day by day.

We find in our ministry that whereas many people are closed to words and doctrines, they are open to prayer. Think of what can happen if you can introduce the power of God into a situation simply by asking a question or making an offer which opens someone up to that power in a new way!

A: The dynamic of prayer

I found some words of John Wesley the other day which took me by surprise, but they hold a vital secret to the power of prayer in our lives and ministry: 'It seems God is limited by our prayer life – that He can do nothing for humanity unless someone asks Him'. It seems amazing, doesn't it, that God should limit Himself to working through human beings like you and me? And yet He knows what He is doing. He sent His Son in form as a man because He knew that His love needed to be incarnate. Only then could they understand the measure of His love for them and the caring depths of His heart. So it is with us. Through the use of our prayer we can become the power of God for other men and women. It is not then something that is alien and apart from them, but as we come near to them God's power draws close to them and they can experience for themselves the reality of God.

Paul wrote that the things that had been written previously were written for our learning, to give us encouragement and hope (Rom 15:4). Nowhere is this more true than when you look at the Old Testament with regard to the power of prayer. It is amazing to notice just what was accomplished in the lives of men like Abraham, Moses, Johsua, Gideon, Samuel, Elijah, Elisha, David, Daniel and all the prophets through the power of prayer. Such an impact did their testimony make that James recalled it many years later: *'The prayer of a righteous man is powerful and effective. Elijah was a man just like us. He prayed earnestly that it would not rain, and it did not rain on the land for three and a half years. Again he prayed, and the heavens gave rain, and the earth produced its crops'* (Jas 5:16–18). That witness runs like a golden thread right through the Old Testament. Through the power of prayer men and women saw tremendous signs and wonders accomplished: healings, deliverances, supernatural provision of food and water, miracles in nature, as well as the staying of God's hand in divine judgement. Time and again Moses prayed and God's hand was removed from the people in their sin.

There are many instances where prayer is the means by which men and women of God receive God's insight into a situation or are given His word for the moment. Elisha the prophet was noted as the man who knew the secrets of the king of Aram's bedroom. It was through prayer that he received divine direction about what to do in the case of the Shunnamite widow's son who had died (see 2 Kings chapters 4 and 6). You cannot miss the power of prayer in the Old Testament. For these men and women it was not a dead, religious ritual but a living, vital reality which kept them in touch with the power of God and through which they brought deliverance, guidance, salvation and judgement on thousands. There is something very naturally supernatural about the way these men and women handle prayer. For them it was the breath of life and they seemed to keep so readily in touch with God. Even when Abraham sinned by passing off his wife Sarah as his sister to Abimelech the king, he was able to pray to God and bring healing to Abimelech's wife and household (see Genesis chapter 20).

These instances have all been left for our benefit to inspire us to open our own hearts and lives to this power of prayer. This is the secret of a vital and relevant ministry. It is not so much that we strain to achieve what we are not called to be. Rather it is that we use the gifts that God has given every believer and understand the tremendous privilege of bringing God's power directly to bear on every daily situation.

B: The privilege of prayer

The words of Joseph Scriven's hymn seem rather old hat these days, but they remain as true as on the day they were written:

> *What a friend we have in Jesus,*
> *All our sins and griefs to bear!*
> *What a privilege to carry*
> *Everything to God in prayer!*

There is a deep simplicity about the ministry of prayer. Here we are not dealing with all the inroads of a life of contemplation or with the rigours of fasting and intercession. I am speaking of the simple act of bringing someone or some situation 'to God in prayer'.

It is a lovely fact that two of the most important New Testament words for prayer are words that are taken from the simplicity of daily life. There are no heavy religious overtones about them and their effectiveness does not depend on a lot of complicated know-how. They are the words *deomai* and *erotao*. They simply mean to desire something and to ask or enquire about something. I don't want to detract from any significant gifts of prayer or deliverance ministry that some might have, but I simply want to underline the truth that the effectiveness of our ministry with other people may lie in the fact that we take the courage and time to ask them if we can pray with them, and when we do pray, simply bring them to the Father who knows what is best for them.

Jesus said, *'Ask and it will be given to you; seek and you will find; knock and the door will be opened to you. For everyone who asks receives; he who seeks finds; and to him who knocks, the door will be opened'* (Lk 11:9, 10). The secret of this simple prayer of power is our relationship with the Father. That relationship stands, of course, at the heart of our life of discipleship. We don't live in a relationship of fear but of love, and we have been brought into a place of confidence before God. Jesus said, *'You are my friends if you do what I command. I no longer call you servants, because a servant does not know his master's business'* (Jn 15:14, 15).

I have found it a source of great spiritual encouragement and joy recently to realise just what the Father has placed into my hands. It is not dependent on the power of my words but on my relationship with Him. Even in large meetings where I have gone to preach I have found that the most powerful event has been when people respond simply to the invitation to share in prayer. There is a great peace and strength that comes from knowing that we come to our heavenly Father, who wills the best for us and in whose hands we can leave every situation.

C: The responsibility of prayer

It would be nice if we could leave it just at that, of course. But we would soon find ourselves dropping off into slothfulness and inactivity. There is another word that is used in the New Testament for prayer which carries a different feel about it. This is the word *proseuchomai*. This word, and the group of words associated with it, conveys a much greater sense of urgency. It means to pour out or to persist in prayer. This word is used in some surprising contexts. For example it is used in Matthew 5:44, when Jesus tells His followers to pray for those who persecute them. It is used in Luke 18:1, where Jesus is teaching His disciples to pray and not give up. Here we see the idea of persistence in prayer coming very much to the fore. It is used also in Mark 9:29 in the case of the deliverance from the deaf and dumb spirit. Jesus told His disciples that these sorts of spirits could only be cast out through persistent prayer. Some versions of the text, in fact, include the idea of fasting and praying, which only serves to heighten the intensity of the word.

This group of words is only ever used of prayer to God. It is a much more religious term than the other two we have already looked at. But it reminds us forcibly that prayer in this way is not merely an option for the disciples, but a necessity. God looks for it. It reminds us also that our prayer is directed to the Father – it is not an exercise in auto-suggestion – which is why Jesus said we don't need to babble or repeat our prayers meaninglessly.

Significantly, it is this word that is used of the experience of Jesus when He prayed on the mountain and His face was changed with the radiance of God (Lk 9:28, 29).

D: The effectiveness of prayer

There can be no doubt that prayer is the most effective power in our Christian ministries. God has given us a highly powerful tool with which to reach into the lives of other men and women and by which to bring them the healing and releasing power of God. God has chosen prayer as the instrument for the release of His power on earth through believers. Prayer binds the powers of darkness and releases the power of God.

God has a Job Centre with plenty of vacancies waiting for men and women who will give their lives and time to Him for this ministry of prayer. The world is full of needy men and women who are longing in their spirits for someone to come and help them in the name of God. We might need to get rid of some of our jargon and get out of our charismatic hot-houses to find them, but they are there if we will make ourselves available to God and them.

Just look at what can be affected through the power of prayer ministry. The words of Isaiah raise the banner for every person who will answer this call of God:

> *Since ancient times no-one has heard,*
>   *no ear has perceived,*
> *no eye has seen any God besides you,*
>   *who acts on behalf of those who wait for him.*

(Is 64:4)

I suppose we've all heard the old joke about God's telephone number, Jeremiah 333 (33:3): *'Call to me and I will answer you and tell you great and unsearchable things you do not know'.*

The Father is waiting on us to do His will. He wants to accomplish His purposes through our lives. He wants to use us to bring salvation to a dying people. His call through Ezekiel (22:30) was for people who would stand in the gap for others. Our world is full of destruction and is heading for destruction. God wants to use us to deliver men and women from it and to bring them into the Kingdom of His light and power.

Great men of faith have recognised this power of prayer and its significance for the world at large. S. D. Gordon in his book, *Quiet Talks on Prayer* highlights this important fact: 'In its simplest meaning prayer has to do with a conflict. Rightly understood it is the deciding factor in a spirit conflict. The scene of the conflict is the earth. The purpose of the conflict is to decide the control of the earth and its inhabitants.' This is a fact. Every time we pray effectively for another person we are saving them from the control of Satan and delivering them from spiritual bondage. It is another bit of territory claimed for Christ!

E: The exercise of prayer

It will help us in our approach to ministry with another person if we understand the various dimensions which might be involved. This is where we can rely on the Holy Spirit to guide us. The whole secret of effective praying with other people is to be open to the leading and prompting of the Spirit so that He can take us in whatever direction seems best to Him.

We often say that practice makes perfect, and this is true in the areas of prayer ministry. Experience is a great teacher and we will soon become far more acute to the needs of the situation or the leading of the Holy Spirit. There are four levels of prayer that we should take notice of with regard to ministering to others:

Prayer with. This is where we indentify with the other person in their request to the Father and agree with them in faith that their prayer will be answered. Jesus said, *'Again, I tell you that if two of you on earth agree about anything you ask for, it will be done for you by my Father in heaven'* (Mt 18:19).

Prayer for. This is where we have identified the needs of the other person and *bring* them through prayer into the presence of God. This dimension of prayer ministry is particulary helpful in situations where there has been confession and repentance of sin and where the other person needs to be assured of forgiveness: *'Therefore confess you sins to each other and pray for each other so that you may be healed'* (Jas 5:16).

Prayer into. This is where the real act of ministry begins. It is more than standing alongside another person in faith agreement or bearing each other's burdens in the love of Christ. In this prayer we are receiving power from God in a direct way and transmitting that power through our prayer to the other person. There may be elements in this form of ministry which are more man-directed than God-directed. That is, what we say or what we do will often be aimed directly at the person for whom we are praying. There is great direct power sometimes in this form of prayer because, in a sense, we are acting as the go-between between the person and God. Sometimes the prayer will be accompanied by physical manifestations or sensations either on the part of the one praying or the one prayed for, perhaps even in both.

Praying against. Sometimes we are led by the Holy Spirit into an area of spiritual warfare and resistance. Prayer in this situation is more than an address to the Father and probably goes beyond the bounds of the proper use of the word 'prayer'. Nevertheless, there is a strong supplication of spirit and a deep dependency on the leading of the Holy Spirit. The prayer is a movement of resistance against spiritual realities of evil. It may be the presence of demonic power or the influence of spiritual powers of wickedness in the room, area or situation. We will be stirred to a felt need to address these powers in the name of Jesus. It is important to call on the Lord to rebuke Satan and for me to stand as the representative of Jesus rather than rebuking the devil in my own name.

We are speaking here about the ministry potential of every believer, with particular reference to personal ministry within the context of our daily lives. The place to start is by listening to the other person with your spirit. Don't only listen on the outside – that is, to their words and opinions; listen to their spirit. The Holy Spirit will help you hear by imparting those gifts which are needed in the situation. Ask a few simple questions so that you are clear about the direction of your prayer. If it is apparent that you are out of your depth and you need help, then suggest this to the other person, find help, and come back to the situation with the support and confidence of another more experienced Christian.

Don't become a nut! There are some people who turn a ministry into a hobby. They become unbalanced and get to a point where they are unable to have normal social relations with other human beings. They are always looking at them through their 'prayer eyes' and begin to regard other people as 'prayer fodder'. This leads to a failure of sensitivity and lack of dependence on the guidance of the Holy Spirit. On the other hand, if we yield our lives to the Lord every day, we will discover that by His gentle hand we will be led into all sorts of situations that are prepared by the Lord for us to move into prayer ministry. It will be so enriching for us and of great benefit to those with whom we pray.

F: Laying on hands

Should we lay hands on those for whom we pray? My answer is that, in the main, when we pray at a personal level with other people it is useful to lay hands on their heads as a sign of the touch of God into their lives. Many people have not experienced the touch of God's love and your touch will be the means of opening them up to the power of that deeper touch from God. Jesus Himself laid hands on people when the situation was right. For example, after speaking the word of faith to the woman who had been cirppled for eighteen years, He laid His hands on her and immediately she was healed (Lk 13:13).

There are some times, however, when it is not right to lay hands on another person. For example, if you are praying alone for a member of the opposite sex you need to be clear whether the situation is right to lay on hands with prayer. In the wrong situation it could become an opportunity for Satan to use the closeness involved as an occasion for temptation. Again, if there is demonic involvement it is better not to lay hands directly on the other person. The reason for this is because the spirit within the person can feel this restraint and begin to resist in ways that are sometimes violent and frightening. A demonic spirit can be dealt with by the command of Christ more easily than by laying on of hands.

In any event, it is important to be able to claim the covering that is needed for your own spirit in any occasion of praying with others. Ask for the protection of the Holy Spirit and claim the cleansing and protection power of the blood of Jesus. Sometimes it is even helpful to include a song in your prayer ministry which will increase your own faith and will proclaim into the situation the power and authority of the Lord Jesus Christ.

Pray simply and clearly, and if God gives you something to say to the person then say it to them. Remember all the time that prayer ministry is spiritual warfare in action. As S. D. Gordon has said, 'Prayer is insisting upon Jesus' victory and the retreat of the enemy on each particular spot. The enemy yields only what he must. He yields only what is taken. Therefore ground must be taken step by step. Prayer must be definite'.

4: Gifts for Ministry

The Good News translation of 1 Corinthians 12:7 underlines the fact that the gifts of the Holy Spirit are actually ministry gifts. *'The Spirit's presence is shown in some way in each person for the good of all.'* We have not been promised the gifts of the Holy Spirit for our own indulgence or self-display, but that we might be enabled by God as we reach out into the lives of needy men and women around us. The gifts of the Holy Spirit are God's power in action, and they will be released into our lives as we find ourselves in situations that call for those gifts.

This is a tremendous thought to get a hold of : that when we reach out in ministry we are not doing it in our own strength, and God will become directly involved in the situation through the manifestation of His enabling Holy Spirit. This will lift us away beyond the horizontal level of our own weakness and limitation and release us in our ministries into a new dimension of capability and insight altogether. In fact, this is what will make and determine the shape of our ministry in the end, because it will gradually become apparent how we operate in the gifts of the Spirit and what gifts find more ready expression through us than through someone else. The style and application of our ministry will be shaped by how the gifts of the Spirit operate through us. Nevertheless, we should remember that it is open to any Christian to ask for the appropriate gift for the situation, even if it is in an area in which we normally do not operate. The Father's intention is to bring His power for salvation and healing into the lives of men and women, and He will not withold the capability to do that if we ask Him with a clean heart and the right motives.

A: Trinitarian gifts

Paul teaches about the gifts of the Holy Spirit in 1 Corinthians chapter 12. Before he goes on to speak about the gifts in particular he discloses to us the tremendous fact of the unity of action of the Father, Son and Holy Spirit in this area. In fact, it might be more proper not to speak about the gifts of the Spirit so much as the gifts of the *Father, Son and Holy Spirit!*

If you look at verses 4–6 you will see what I mean. Paul uses three distinct phrases in these verses which build up one on the other. I used to think that he was speaking about three distinct subjects until I saw that he was really expounding the truth about spiritual gifts. One word recurs in each of the three distinct phrases: *different*:

'Different kinds of gifts, but the same Spirit.' This demonstrates the source of these gifts within our experience. The Holy Spirit is the bringer of the gifts in a direct sense.

'Different kinds of service, but the same Lord.' This demonstrates who is being served by the operation of these spiritual gifts and who it is that determines in which direction the gifts will operate – namely, the Lord Jesus Christ.

'Different kinds of working, but the same God works all of them in all men.' The root word is *energemata*. The idea is of energy and power, but of energy working out towards a purpose. The phrase demonstrates the purpose for which these gifts operate – namely, to fulfil the will of the Father in every situation.

This brief survey reveals to us an important truth which undergirds all our ministry. It is not so much that we exercise the gifts of the Spirit; rather we are engaged in the power and operation of the triune God!

B: Various gifts

Paul lists nine gifts in this chapter which are significant for the operation of our ministry.

Message of wisdom (literally, 'word of wisdom'). This is the very basis of our approach to other people in ministry. Without the gift of God's wisdom we will find ourselves blundering into situations, making the wrong judgements, taking hasty and irrelevant action and perhaps leaving a trail of misunderstanding and hurt. God's wisdom is the ability to see things as God sees them and to gain an insight into the heart of the matter in such a way that we will know what it right and what to do within the particular context. The NIV translation gives the impression that this word of wisdom must always be a message which will be given to another person. This is not the case. The word of wisdom may be a word received by the person ministering directly from the Lord into their own spirit which will bring the insight and understanding that is essential for the moment.

Message of knowledge. Knowledge is also a gift of understanding, but a word of knowledge is more likely to be shared with the other person concerned in a direct way, because it will often contain elements which will uncover the truth for you both and enable much deeper areas to be touched than were previously accessible to the Holy Spirit. This is the truth of Hebrews 4:12 in action, where the Word of God is sharper than any two-edged sword and divides right into the very heart of a person and lays their thoughts and attitudes bare before God.

The gifts of wisdom and knowledge often operate together, because it takes the first to know how to handle and apply the second.

Faith. We have already looked at faith in depth in another section of the book. Suffice to say here that faith is the gift which brings assurance and confidence into a ministry situation. Through the gift of faith we gain the certainty of what God intends to do and are given the power to believe with expectation that this will happen.

Gifts of healing. The word is in the plural because there are many different gifts of healing which are given relative to the many different illnesses and traumas which people suffer. It is not uncommon for a person to have a capacity for healing in a certain range of illness or in relation to particular emotional needs.

Miraculous powers. A miracle is something beyond the process of spiritual healing. It is an event which relies utterly on the direct intervention of God and which produces results that manifest the extraordinary power of God. In this category I would include such occurences as raising the dead, or the replacement or growth of limbs which are missing, or the sort of powerful deliverances through angelic intervention that we hear about in the Acts of the Apostles.

Prophecy. Paul tells us in 1 Corinthians chapter 14 that prophecy is for the upbuilding of the Church. Prophetic utterance is very direct and contains within it the need for a response. Agabus, for example, was a prophet in Antioch who stood up and warned the Church of the forthcoming world famine, an event which we know from history occurred during the reign of Claudius in 49 AD (Acts 11:28). The effect of a word of prophecy can be of great benefit in the life of an individual to whom we minister: *'Everyone who prophesies speaks to men for their strengthening, encouragement and comfort'* (1 Cor 14:3).

The ability to distinguish between spirits. This is the gift of discernment. We are told by John in his first Epistle to test the spirits and see if they are of God. It is by means of this gift of spiritual discernment that we can best know what sort of spirit we are dealing with in any given situation.

Different kinds of tongues. The gift of tongues is very important in the ministry situation. It is not so vital that we bring a message in tongues to the other person concerned. In 1 Corinthians 14:2 Paul reveals to us the true value of the personal gift of tongues: *'Anyone who speaks in a tongue does not speak to men but to God. Indeed, no one understands him; he utters mysteries with his spirit'* (or 'by the Spirit'). Personal exercise of the gift of tongues opens us up to the Word of God. The gift of tongues can also be the means by which we are opened up to other gifts. For example, as we pray in tongues in our spirit we become very sensitive to God's will in the situation and to His direction as to what is right to do in ministry.

Interpretation of tongues. This gift is usually more appropriate in a corporate setting where the Spirit responds through interpretation to the exercise of the gift of tongues. What comes is the dynamic equivalent of what is said in tongues. It is not a translation; indeed, it could rather be classed as a response. The tongue is used by the Spirit to draw attention to the fact that God wants to speak, and heightens expectation. The interpretation gives the word from God so that everybody can understand, judge and act on what is said.

The exciting thing about these gifts of the Holy Spirit is that they are gifts which are given to be given away! That is, we are given the spiritual capacity so that the power and life of God will become real in the lives of other people. So often the freshness and vitality of these spiritual gifts have been lost because we have used them to wrong ends. They are not given to be kept locked up in the church. Neither are they given to be paraded at special charismatic services where so often the value of the meeting will be judged by whether or not there was an operation of a gift or gifts.

It is clear, of course, that any healthy local fellowship will be walking in the fruit of the Holy Spirit and manifesting the gifts of the Spirit in its witness and worship. But the gifts are given for our ministry into the lives of other people. It is through these that we are equipped by God to do His will. Without the gifts of the Holy Spirit we are living and working at the level of our own natural capacity and strength. And the Father's purpose is that we move on in our understanding and operation of the gifts. There is more to this question than tongues and prophecy. What a wonderful panoply of gifts the Father has made available to us in Jesus through the Spirit! They are the gifts for giving, and when we operate in their reality and power we are exposing people, with all their deep needs, to the effective ministry of the Kingdom of God.

5: Moving into Ministry

There are a number of important areas to be taken into account as we prepare to move ahead into ministering to other people. We bear a very important message and are the channels of the living power of God. It is important to say that, as far as Christian ministry is concerned, the medium is not the message. We do not preach ourselves, as Paul said, but Jesus Christ as Lord. Nevertheless, we can enable the effectiveness of our ministry or else inhibit it if we fail to pay attention to those areas in our lives which affect how we present ourselves to other people.

A: Personal factors

We need to begin by taking into account certain factors which are of a very personal and basic nature. We can have every spiritual gift and know how to move in power in the lives of other people, but all of that can be negated through a careless stewardship of our lives and personal appearance.

When we minister to individuals we invariably find ourselves in close proximity to them. This means that they become aware of us in a very immediate sense. Cleanliness, as they say, is next to godliness. Many a person has been adversely affected in a counselling or ministry situation because the person who was ministering to them failed to take due care in the area of tidiness and personal hygiene. There is no more potent counter-balance to the work of the Holy Spirit than 'B.O.'! Bad breath, tooth decay, body odour, smelly clothes, greasy and unkempt hair, dirty collars and unkept or dirty fingernails are all put-offs as far as the person receiving ministry is concerned. For one thing, they demonstrate a lack of discipline and authority in our own lives. There is little point in bringing a word from God into the life of another person if our own appearance tells them that we could do with a word from God ourselves!

It is in this area also that some of our bad habits catch up with us. Smoking is the outstanding example. The smell of stale cigarettes on the breath or clothes is a killer to victorious ministry. The sad fact is that most folk who indulge in smoking don't realise the degree to which the smell and general fug hangs around!

Of course, it is just as possible to go to the other extreme and present ourselves in such a way that other people feel they are talking with mobile outpost of Coty International. Balance is needed, and our dress and manners should be such that we are able to enter into any situation without embarrassment or unease.

Another important factor is the need to become aware of who or what we really are. Self-awareness is a great gift of the Holy Spirit. The reason for this is that our personality traits can get in the way of our ministry if we have not become aware of them. We all have different personality traits. It is not necessary to get rid of them all; indeed, the Lord may show us how to employ some of them to the benefit of the work He has called us to. The greater likelihood is that we will live in ignorance at this level and fail to realise that we are damaging the ministry or other people's reception of the work of God through us.

The practice of our ministry calls for life-discipline and personal training. These things usually start, not in public, but in the deeply personal and private areas of our lives. If we apply the discipline of the Spirit in these areas we will soon know how to bring that discipline into the lives of others through the ministry God gives us for them.

B: Spiritual factors

God will anoint us for our ministry. It is open to every believer to know the anointing of God in his or her witness to other people. As we have seen already, the gifts of the Spirit are at our disposal to make us effective in whatever situation the Father places us. We can describe this empowering of God for different situations as an *occasional anointing*. The word 'occasional' has nothing to do with how often this happens but points to the variety of ways in which God empowers His people for ministry day by day.

It may be, however, that our ministry takes on a more

permanent character. This means that we find ourselves involved in a certain ministry on a regular basis and that this amounts to a specific call by the Lord to this ministry. It is worth noting certain basic principles of this call and anointing by God:

Find it. God does not appoint without anointing. As we move ahead in ministry we will begin to find that our hearts are drawn in certain directions and we will discover that we exercise one gift with more authority than we do others. These are all indicators that God is giving us a ministry in this particular area. There is a great spiritual satisfaction in perceiving where your gift and ministry lie, and in exercising that gift more and more effectively as time goes on. These may not be spectacular things but may be quiet and wholesome in their effect in the daily lives of other people whom God brings across our path.

Polish it. We polish our gift through practice. We polish our gift and anointing by learning from others with similar and more developed gifts and anointings. Listen and be ready to learn from others, but don't be caught in the trap of trying to copy them! The gifts of the Holy Spirit in ministry should be held in trust and guarded and made more productive through proper use and development. Otherwise the anointing will fade and the gift will atrophy and eventually disappear.

Relax into it. I don't mean that we should take the gift for granted or become sloppy and negligent. But one of the greatest threats to wholesome ministry is the intensity which Satan wants to introduce into our ministries. This comes from a number of sources. One is the danger of always comparing ourselves with other people and thereby falling into a trap of developing a competitive spirit. Another is that of thinking too highly of ourselves and our gift. Paul warns against this when he writes to the church at Rome and exhorts the believers there to have a right and proper estimate of themselves and their gifts (see Rom 12:3–8).

Keep it. It is God's power, not yours. The most dangerous thing is to presume on it. Anointing is not the same as natural talent inasmuch as it may go away at any time God wants to withdraw it. Zedekiah the prophet found to his dismay that he had no monopoly on the Spirit of God. When he presumed on the Spirit of God he found that he had no longer any true word from God and that the Spirit has passed to Micaiah (2 Chron 18:23). To remain in the anointing we need to remain where God is. We need to walk in our ministries humbly, gratefully and above all *innocently* before the Lord. We do not minister by magic or human power but only as we make ourselves available to the empowering of God Himself.

C: Negative factors

Other factors can very quickly rob us of our effectiveness in ministry. There are certain times and circumstances when you should refrain from ministry because the other things that are going on in your life will vitiate the purity of God's power to such a degree that it will become corrupt and potentially harmful to the other person. We need to bear in mind the fact that when we minister, the other person gets a dose of what we are as well as of the power of God. That's all right as long as the percentage of us is limited and benign. But when other elements are out of true in our lives, it may be better to refrain from ministering to another person until the situation changes or improves. Here are some of the most common factors which can prove negative in our ministry:

Tiredness. Sometimes, of course, you will need to minister no matter how you feel, but in the main it is better not to minister at a costly level when your own physical and emotional resources are low.

Active or unresolved sin. Nothing so prevents the flow of the power of God as the lack of liberty in one's spirit which sin brings. This, of course, is where ministering to others presents such a continual challenge to one's own life and lifestyle, because sin clouds our conscience and we cannot come to the Father with a clear heart and confident spirit. This destroys the effectiveness of ministry into another person's life. The amazing fact is that God still blesses people despite our imperfections, but that just proves the grace of God and does not relieve us of the reponsibility to be clean vessels fit for the Master's use.

An aggravated spirit. The devil will try to ensure that there are many factors which cause irritation within our spirits. We are indeed very vulnerable to this sort of attack when involved in active ministry to other people. We need to cut ourselves off from the source of aggravation, and re-establish the peace of Christ in our hearts. If we try to minister out of a disturbed spirit we will find ourselves making wrong judgements and demonstrating hasty and hurtful reactions to people who need our help.

Self-consciousness. It is helpful to minister along with another more experienced person to begin with. This means we can learn a lot more and overcome any feelings of self-consciousness we might suffer from. The wrong kind of self-consciousness can rob us of our spiritual authority and confidence in the situation.

Emotionalism. I do not mean that we should never show emotion. Often, in fact, there is a good degree of emotion involved in personal ministry. This is particularly true of the other person who may display emotions of grief, joy, exuberance, excitement, awe and so on as a result of what the Spirit does in them. But it does mean that we will not be governed by emotion. Often when we feel least, God will do the rest!

Narrow-mindedness. This may seem a strange thing to say, but what I mean is that sometimes our own presuppositions can inhibit the liberty of the Holy Spirit. If we are always looking for the same thing to happen or expecting to move in the same patterns of ministry, we may miss the new thing that God wants to do this time.

Unbelief. Even Jesus Himself was unable to perform many mighty deeds where unbelief was rampant (e.g. Mt 13:58). We can find ourselves beating our head against a brick wall if we don't exercise discernment about the context within which we are ministering. There needs to be faith for it to be effective. Faith needs either to flow through your heart or through the other person's heart. *Without faith*, as Hebrews teaches us, *it is impossible to please God.*

D: Into practice

It is helpful to go into any ministry situation with some clear and simple principles of action before our eyes. In the end, we all need to understand our own ministries and recognise how they operate. Experience is the greatest teacher of all. But there are certain basic ground rules which will provide a starting point for us:

Use your eyes. Always pay attention to what you see. Obviously, therefore, you must keep your eyes open while you are praying. Ask the Lord to help you see what is really there. How a person looks and acts can tell you a lot about where their needs really lie. Their body language can either confirm or deny their words, so it is important that we are watching for the message that comes through everything that the person is.

Use your ears. It is important in a personal ministry situation to make a brief enquiry of the person about their need. Let the Holy Spirit guide you in the questions you ask because it will amaze you how much there is to be learned once the Spirit of God opens up a person's life. But don't let the other person rule the roost. People will sometimes talk themselves out of letting God do His work in their lives or, even worse, talk themselves into ever deeper bondage to demonic influence. In your enquiry it is always helpful to get to know if the person has been or is being ministered to by someone else. The Holy Spirit will show you whether the person needs to talk the problem out at length or not.

Exercise your spirit. It is important to remain open to God at all times. This means keeping your spirit active and alert and paying attention to anything that God might be saying to you within your own spirit. Impressions of the spirit and pictures in your mind may be important and Scriptures which God brings to your memory can prove a vital aid in hitting the right spot with the other person. For all this to happen it is important to learn to exercise your spirit while at the same time paying attention to what is happening in the other person. I find praying in the Spirit important at this point. I can exercise my spirit by praying in tongues under my breath, so to speak. I find my spirit is quickened and enlivened and the Holy Spirit is able to work in me and through me according to the principles of Romans 8:26, 27.

Be honest and clear. There is a great need for integrity in personal ministry. Any attempt to manipulate the situation can be disastrous for the person being ministered to. There is no need to feel under pressure to minister in any particular style – 'to thine own self be true'! Jargon and other people's style of ministry should be avoided like the plague unless the Spirit has led you into that approach in ministry for yourself. There is a wonderful variety in the ways in which God works and you will find it very encouraging and confidence-building when you become aware of how He wants to work in an individual way through you.

Be simple and direct. Clarity is important so that you and the other person both know what is being said and what is being done. It is also very important that they know what is being asked of them, because the nature of their response will depend to a large degree on the nature of their understanding. Sometimes the Holy Spirit will lead you in a very quiet way, at others He will come with great authority and power and on those occasions it may become quite noisy! But there is no virtue in noise for noise's sake. We are ministering in the power and authority of the Lord Jesus Christ and that is the ground of our power. We don't need to be like the old preacher who was unsure of the soundness of his argument in his sermon. He pencilled a reminder for himself at the side of his notes: 'Argument weak here, shout louder'!

Expect results. Look for some change. Ask the person how they are feeling or what they have experienced. If you have prayed for some inner spiritual gift such as the peace of Christ then expect to see the effects of that peace on the person's face. It is important to teach folks not to lean on their feelings but to rest on the word that God has given them through the ministry. Nevertheless, when we are asking the Father for concrete things there should be some sign or token that the prayer has been granted. The more we look for these things to happen the more we will recognise the signs when they do.

Leave positively. It is important to leave the ministry time on a postitive note. This may take the form of a word of encouragement, direction, or even warning. If you feel that it is necessary follow up the time with another session of ministry then be sure to leave the door open for yourself. Make an appointment or at least get a firm agreement of spirit that the person will meet you again.

Ongoing support. I find that a small book or booklet is often helpful to give the person some practical touchpoint for the time immediately following the ministry. On the other hand, you may be able to recommend a tape which they can listen to or some other spiritual aid that will sustain them as they seek to follow the Lord for themselves.

All these are points which will be learnt with time and experience. But above all, remember that we minister the Lord and His power: *'We have this treasure in jars of clay to show that this all-surpassing power is from God and not from us'* (2 Cor 4:7).

Chapter 9

God in the Present Tense

1: The Personal Spirit

It may seem unnecessary at this point to focus especially on the work of the Holy Spirit as if it were a new subject, because that has been the foundation and backbone of everything I have said so far. Over the past few years many books have been written about the Holy Spirit and it would be impossible to do justice to these great truths within the scope of a few pages. However, I do want to highlight features of His work which have been important in my own life and ministry over recent years and which are important to our lives as disciples of Jesus.

A: Person to person

When we speak about the Holy Spirit we are speaking about a Person. The Holy Spirit is God. God is Person with a capital P. He is not a vague influence or a mystical idea. It is from Him that all our personhood flows. In the words of Paul: *'I kneel before the Father, from whom his whole family in heaven and on earth derives its name'* (Eph 3:14, 15). He is Person, we are persons. This means that we share something very important in common, as we will see later. The Holy Spirit is Person and that means He can communicate and make Himself real to us. This is not a matter of visibility – that is, we cannot necessarily *see* Him, but He is real and He can make a great impression on our lives through our inner being.

We are like that with each other. It is true that our superficial contact with each other depends, among other things, on sight. But our deeper and more lasting encounters with each other depend on far more profound and enduring contacts in the deeper reaches of our inner man. It is when our spirits are stirred that something profound takes place which makes its impact in a lasting way.

As persons we have this tremendous capacity for opening or closing our inner beings to each other. We do it every day of our lives. Whether we are meeting people or watching television or just responding to objects and circumstances, we open or close ourselves as feels appropriate, and to that extent we are affected by whatever the influence is.

Just imagine for a moment that you are walking down the street. Here comes someone you know and, to be truthful, you can't stand him. What do you do? You don't just ignore him and cut him dead. As he comes up and greets you, you respond with your own greeting. You ask him how he is, discuss the weather and share some trivia about the family or holidays. You shake his hand and smile. But all the time you have decided that he won't be allowed to penetrate behind the enamel of your front teeth! You see, although some exchange has taken place, no deep personal encounter has been allowed to happen because you have decided in advance to keep yourself closed to that possibility.

On the other hand, imagine the very same street at another moment. Here you see someone coming in the distance whom you admire greatly. One minute in their company and you feel done good to. They come to greet you with the same handshake, the same conversation, perhaps the very same subjects, but something very different happens. It is as though a deep spiritual meeting takes place. You open yourself in an inward way and so does this other person. Perhaps it is only for a minute, and then they go their way. But as they go it seems as though part of you goes with them. Certainly you feel that they go with you. A meeting has taken place, person to person. Our friendship and openness to someone like that is dependent on far more than this fleeting moment. There is a depth of personal encounter that is greater than normal and a commitment of spirit that goes beyond the ordinary.

Now consider this. God is *Person*. He has the very same capacity to open Himself into a situation or to withold Himself from it. In fact, our capacity to do this is a pale shadow of His. And the Holy Spirit *is* God in the present tense, right inside our life situations, communicating with us, opening Himself up to us and looking for us to open ourselves to Him in response.

The truth is that He works in ways not unlike our own, which should not surprise us if we are connected to Him as our Creator! It's like this. Those deeper encounters between human beings usually depend on seemingly small things to begin with. A fleeting glance, one warm word, a smile in our direction, something that makes contact in a personal way and opens our hearts to the possibility of deeper contact. So it is with God. He will speak in quiet, personal ways. Sometimes He has a special word for us. It may come through something we hear or read, perhaps in the Scriptures. Often He whispers to us in our circumstances, sometimes He shouts to us in our pain. God is not short of ways to make us aware that He has something to say. He is Person and He speaks to us personally.

B: Living water

The Bible uses another way to describe the Holy Spirit. It uses the image of *living water*. Jesus Himself used that picture when He said, '*Whoever believes in me ... streams of living water will flow from within him*' (Jn 7:38). By this He meant that every believer would know the reality and power of the Holy Spirit, bringing life right into the centre of their being and strength into their lives. Indeed, the Bible makes is clear that without this reality we can never live in the power of God or know God's strength for our daily lives. The presence of the Holy Spirit in our lives is a great gift from God which God sees as absolutely necessary for the full enjoyment and fulfillment of our human existence.

I often think of it like this. Our lives are like drinking

glasses. These are made for a specific purpose: to hold water so that we can drink. It comes as a surprise to many people to realise that the chief purpose of their lives is to hold God! Yes, that is why we are created. God made us to be the channels and expressions of His life here on earth! He made us to live in that power, to work in that power, and to operate with that power for the good of the whole of Creation! Read the first two chapters of the Book of Genesis and you will see that what I am saying is true. God began with a great plan for the human race that went horribly wrong because man failed to appreciate the tremendous privilege God has given him. Our sin has made us leak! We can no longer hold the power of God in our lives because we are spoiled vessels! And God can't refill us with the living power of His Holy Spirit until something happens to us.

Think of a glass that is *dirty and stained inside*. You would never use a glass like that to give anybody a drink of water, would you? The glass needs to be washed thoroughly and rinsed clean before it is usable. It's just the same with our lives. Many people know nothing about the power of the Holy Spirit inside them because their lives are like dirty glasses. They need to be made clean before they can be filled. The Holy Spirit is clean water. God has made it possible through Jesus for our lives to be cleansed of all their filth inside. Some of us look spotless on the outside but all of us need cleansing deep inside our hearts. The Bible tells the truth when it says: *'The Lord does not look at the things man looks at. Man looks at the outward appearance, but the Lord looks at the heart'* (1 Sam 16:7).

Or maybe the glass *has a crack in it*. We would never dream of giving someone else a drink from a cracked glass. We would throw it away. But the tremendous thing is that God never throws His cracked glasses away! No, He heals them! Many people feel unable to open themselves up to anything or anybody because they are acutely aware of their cracks. Life and circumstances have often dealt them severe blows to such a point that they seem unable to recover. God has a tender way with such people. In His power He can touch them and

and make them whole. We see this in the ministry of Jesus. He said, '*It is not the healthy who need a doctor, but the sick*' (Mt 9:12).

Right throughout His ministry on earth Jesus healed those whose lives were cracked by sickness and pain, loneliness and hurt. He was able to bring them the power of God and heal them, and when they were healed He was able to send them away in the power of God with a new strength so that they no longer needed to live in their infirmity. This is what God wants to do for each one of us. He brings us healing and forgiveness in the Cross and the Resurrection and then fills us with His life and power through the Holy Spirit.

Glasses are *made to be filled*. A glass that has never held water has never fulfilled the purpose for which it was made. We are made to be filled. People who have never known the fulness of God's power through the Holy Spirit in their lives have, likewise, never fulfilled the purpose for which they were created. *You were made to be filled with God.* He is waiting to fill you.

Of course, you can never fill a glass that stays upside down all the time! You may pour water until your face turns blue, but if the glass remains upside down all the water in the world will never fill it. So it is with us. We need to be open for God to fill us. We need to be right side up. There needs to be that willingness in our spirit to receive the Spirit of God. Just as we *invite* other people into our lives at that deeper level, so we also need to *invite* the Holy Spirit into our lives at that same level. He will not force His way in, for He is a gentleman.

C: Unlimited power

Here are four important reasons why we all need the power of the Holy Spirit in our lives:

(a) **Power to become.** Without the power of God in us we can never become sons of God. Some people imagine that because we are all born naturally into the world we are thereby children of God. That is certainly what God meant to happen. But we have all lost our way. Mankind does not live in recognition of its true Father. In the words of Isaiah:

We all, like sheep, have gone astray,
each of us has turned to his own way.　　　(Is. 53:6)

But God has made a way back for every one of us. The Holy Spirit's job is to bring us home to God. He awakens us to our spiritual need and points us to God's way back through Jesus. John tells us in his Gospel: '*To all who received him (Jesus), to those who believed in his name, he gave* **the right** *to become children of God – children born not of natural descent, nor of human decision or a husband's will, but born of God*' (Jn 1:12, 13). Now the words 'the right' in that verse translate the important Greek word, *exousia*, which means 'power' or 'authority'. With the power of God's Holy Spirit working in us we can do what we could never do by ourselves. We can become God's sons and act and live like a member of His family.

I believe this to be a most important point to make. Sadly, I have come across people who claim to have known the baptism of the Holy Spirit but who seem to show very few signs of having been *born again* in the power of the Spirit. The Holy Spirit is not sent only to warm up our church tradition, nor indeed so that we can all enjoy the gift of tongues, at least not primarily. The Holy Spirit is sent first to stir our hearts towards God and then to turn our eyes to Jesus. This leads to us to turn to God in repentance, and then the Holy Spirit brings faith to birth within us so that we can believe in Jesus and receive all the benefits of His death and resurrection. Only when we are 'in Christ Jesus' can we claim to have become Christians or sons of God in the full Biblical sense.

(b) Power to be. The Holy Spirit's dwelling in us also means that we have the power we need for our daily living. It is a great thing to be born again in the power of the Holy Spirit, but even those of us who have been Christians for many years know how difficult it is to keep up the standards that God wants us to have in our everyday lives. God wants us to know His power so that we can live a life of faith and become examples to others of what it means to live the new life of Jesus day by day. This is one of the main reasons why He offers us the power of His Holy Spirit in our lives.

We all know the weakness of our flesh. This is why the prayer of the Apostle Paul is so real for every one of us: *'I pray that out of his glorious riches he may strengthen you with power through his Spirit in your inner being'* (Eph 3:16). But the tremendous fact is that we are not alone. God has opened to us the channel of divine power. Imagine this: God Himself wants to dwell in my heart! That seems amazing and to some people almost heretical. But that is the clear statement of Scripture. It was on this matter that Paul challenged the Christians in Corinth, who were having difficulty precisely at the point of their daily living. Like us they had to live in a demanding world; like us they were open to every temptation of the flesh: *'Do you not know that your body is a temple of the Holy Spirit, **who is in you**, whom you have received from God?'* (1 Cor 6:19).

(c) **Power to overcome.** Every Christian believer lives in a war zone. We can't escape that. Choosing to follow Jesus is choosing to change sides. Before we were Christians we were on the side of Satan. It's a sad fact that most people who are not Christians don't realise this. The Bible makes it clear that every human being is governed at a spiritual level by some power or other. If we are not living with Jesus as our Lord then we are surely living under the domination of some other spiritual power: *'As for you, you were dead in your transgressions and sins, in which you used to live when you followed the ways of this world and of the ruler of the kingdom of the air, the spirit who is now at work in those who are disobedient'* (Eph 2:1, 2).

When we become Christians the war really breaks out! Satan tries to throw everything at us to prevent us from following Jesus. In fact, it may seem as though the warfare is much tougher after we believe, and that is probably right. *The great difference, of course, is that we are now on the winning side!* God makes His power available within us so that we have the strength and the know-how to defeat the devil. Listen to what the New Testament says about the subject: *'You, dear children, are from God and have overcome them, because the one who is in you is greater than the one who is in the world'* (1 Jn 4:4).

(d) Power to share. The Holy Spirit came with great power at Pentecost. When the disciples were all together in one place the whole house they were in was filled with the noise of a mighty wind, and what seemed to be tongues of fire came and rested on every one of them. What an experience that must have been! But before it happened they had met with Jesus, risen from the dead. He spoke with them over a period of forty days. That was long enough for any suggested hallucination to wear off! One time when He spoke with them He explained the purpose of the coming of the Holy Spirit in power: *'You will receive power when the Holy Spirit comes on you; and you will be my witnesses in Jerusalem, and in all Judea and Samaria, and to the ends of the earth'* (Acts 1:8).

Now the word for 'power' in this scripture is different from the one we noticed before. This is the word from which we get our English word 'dynamite'. That's power! You see, the Holy Spirit was coming like dynamite, and because of that the disciples were going to *be* dynamite. Read the rest of the Acts of the Apostles and you will see that this is exactly what happened. It was dynamite! They went all over the world, and wherever they went, God's Kingdom came with power.

This is what God wants today! He wants our lives to be so filled with the power of the Holy Spirit that *we* will be dynamite. He wants us to be witnesses to the life of Jesus – not only that we *speak* about Jesus but that we *become* Jesus to other men and women. What I mean is that when we speak and pray and touch people in the power of the Holy Spirit it will be as though Jesus was with them. That is exactly what Jesus Himself said would happen. *'I tell you the truth, anyone who has faith in me will do what I have been doing. He will do even greater things than these, because I am going to the Father'* (Jn 14:12).

D: Gifts and Fruit

There's more to it than even this. God doesn't want only to do great things through us. He wants to give great things to us.

(a) Many-splendoured gifts. The 'gifts of the Spirit' are supernatural endowments of God. We don't do anything by 'natural' talent in the Kingdom of God. Even those gifts which we are born with need to be surrendered to God before He can use them fully to His glory. But the Holy Spirit is the One who equips us to be able to do God's will and to worship and serve Him: *'Now to each one the manifestation of the Spirit is given for the common good'* (1 Cor 12:7). The Good News Version puts it like this: *'The Spirit's presence is shown in some way in each person for the good of all.'*

The list of gifts in 1 Corinthians chapter 12 helps us to understand more clearly just what a terrific thing God wants to do in us. Today we have got caught up to a large degree with the gift of tongues, and frequently I am asked whether every Christian can or should speak in tongues. Now the gift of tongues is a marvellous gift and is useful in a number of very important areas of spiritual life. For example, in private prayer tongues take us into the very heart of God. Very often the Holy Spirit enables our prayer and intercession to happen at a much deeper level than would be possible by our using only our native language. In praise, tongues enable us to worship God and express our admiration and wonder far more deeply than the limitations of our mother tongue. Very often when the Body of Christ meets together the Holy Spirit will bring a direct word from God through the medium of tongues and interpretation. In fact, I1 Corinthians chapter 14 makes it clear that there should be no message in tongues given for all to hear unless the interpretation follows.

But when I am cornered into giving my opinions as to whether all Christian *must* speak in tongues, I am reminded of the words of a Roman Catholic teacher called Simon Tugwell who said, 'All may, some do, others should.' I believe every Christian can speak in tongues and that the gift of tongues is a great benefit in Christian living. But there are other gifts of great importance and God wants us to be just as open to receiving these through the indwelling power of the Holy Spirit.

Think of the power that would be seen in the Body of

Christ if we asked the Holy Spirit to make these gifts real among us: wisdom, knowledge, faith, gifts of healing, miracles, prophecy, discernment of spirits, tongues and interpretation. And after these we need to go on with the list of gifts to be found in Romans chapter 12! The Father has ensured that His children will lack nothing they need for fulfilling His will and purpose and for witnessing to the power of Jesus here on earth.

(b) **The fruit of the Spirit.** Just as important as the gifts of the Spirit is what the New Testament describes as the fruit of the Spirit. This fruit of the Spirit is the evidence in our lives of the work of the Holy Spirit in changing us into the nature of Jesus.

The testimony of our lives is very important. The problem with the Christians at Corinth was that they laid great emphasis on the *gifts* of the Holy Spirit while ignoring the need to display the *fruit* of the Holy Spirit in their attitudes and practices.

Fruit is beauty. And God's fruit in our lives by the Holy Spirit is real beauty in a world of degradation and ugliness: *'The fruit of the Spirit is love, joy, peace, patience, kindness, goodness, faithfulness, gentleness and self-control. Against such things there is no law'* (Gal 5:22, 23). The Holy Spirit plants the seed for God's beauty in our hearts. It is up to us to respond to Him and open ourselves more and more to His holy influence so that we become more and more like Jesus in our actions and attitudes.

2: Spirit of Holiness

We have already seen that there is that about the Holy Spirit which corresponds to and communicates with the spirit of man. So there is that which corresponds to the character of God. Of course, we will not be surprised at this when we remember that the Holy Spirit is God.

The Holy Spirit reveals to us the nature of God. God is holy. Holy is *what* God is *in Himself*. Holiness is intrinsic: apart from the self-revelation of God we can never know what holiness means. When a holy God reveals Himself, what we see is *glory*. Time and again this is illustrated for us in the Scriptures. For example, when Moses went up the mountain to receive the Law the glory of the Lord settled on Mount Sinai and appeared as a consuming fire (Ex 24:16, 17). Similarly, the glory of the Lord appeared time and again in the tabernacle and during the wilderness journey of the Children of Israel (e.g. Leviticus 9:23). The same thing happened when Solomon dedicated the temple in Jerusalem (1 Kings 8:11).

This is the very language which is used at the beginning of John's Gospel of the coming of Jesus into the world: '*The Word became flesh and made his dwelling among us. We have seen his glory, the glory of the One and Only, who came from the Father, full of grace and truth*' (Jn 1:14). It is as we see the glory of God that we begin to comprehend something of the nature of God. He is wholly Other. He is different. And His aim is to make *us* different!

Nowhere is this *process* of holiness better expressed than by Paul in 2 Cor 3:18 – '*We all, with open face beholding as in a glass the glory of the Lord, are changed into the same image from glory to glory, even as by the Spirit of the Lord*' (A.V.). We cannot share in the holiness of God unless we see the glory of God!

A: Encounter with God

There is no more powerful testimony to the revelation of the holiness of God and the impact it can make on a person's experience and life than that of Isaiah. Every time I read the words of Isaiah chapter 6 I feel the depths of his experience:

In the year that King Uzziah died, I saw the Lord seated on a throne, high and exalted, and the train of his robe filled the temple. Above him were seraphs, each with six wings. With two wings they covered their faces, with two they covered their feet, and with two they were flying. And they were calling to one another:

'Holy, holy, holy is the Lord Almighty;
  the whole earth is full of his glory.'

At the sound of their voices the doorposts and thresholds shook and the temple was filled with smoke
  'Woe to me!' I cried, 'I am ruined! For I am a man of unclean lips, and I live among a people of unclean lips, and my eyes have seen the King, the Lord Almighty.'
  Then one of the seraphs flew to me with a live coal in his hand, which he had taken with tongs from the altar. With it he touched my mouth and said, 'See, this has touched your lips; your guilt is taken away and your sin atoned for.'
  Then I heard the voice of the Lord saying, 'Whom shall I send? And who will go for us?
  And I said, 'Here am I. Send me!'

These words of the prophet Isaiah portray an experience of God that few of us have ever known. It is so deep, so rich and powerful, so absolutely challenging to all of life. It is to be touched by God's fire, to know that you have escaped from death under the blazing glory of Almighty God. There is a depth about this experience that we sorely need to perceive for ourselves today.

I don't know how you explain words like these of Isaiah chapter 6. They go beyond understanding. For me it seems that the prophet is trying to express something that defies expression. It is almost as though there are no adequate words to describe the prophet's experience. Apart from the help of the Holy Spirit, how can you possibly describe an event like this?

There was a moment in my own life when those words

became absolutely real for me. I entered in some small measure to an encounter with God in the living power of which Isaiah speaks and, even now, years later, although I have denied it many times in my actions and sins, that experience lives vividly in my heart and mind. In fact, it would not be saying too much to claim that it has become the very foundation of my whole life and work.

God's heart-desire is that we should enter into a depth of experience and understanding of Himself that few of us every really reach. This experience of the holiness and power of God is open to all believers who will open their hearts and seek Him. It is not the exclusive or secret experience of members of some sect or mysterious cult. It is an experience of the depth of God. This is what we all need. We need to be taken into the heart of God. We need to see the purity of His heart, to know the love of His heart, to become aware of the jealousy of His heart – not the petty jealousy of human experience but divine jealousy, the jealousy with which God is passionately concerned for holiness, righteousness, justice and love, the very cornerstones of His nature. We need to feel His heartbeat, so that our own hearts will beat with it. We need to feel the size of His heart, its largeness and breadth, so that we will be delivered from being men and women of a small heart. We need to comprehend as God comprehends, and feel His passion for the exiled and lost.

B: Consuming fire

We need to know His fire. That is what Isaiah knew. He met the fire of God, and it almost killed him. He was burnt in his vision of God. When you read it you know it was not just a dream, but a profound inward experience of the reality of God in all His awesome power which left the prophet as good as dead. It burnt the dross out of him. Only the purging touch of the angel in the mercy of God saved him. But for that touch he would have been finished. This is what we need in our discipleship. We need to know that we have come to the absolute end. We need to come to the realisation that but for the grace and mercy of God we would have died.

Too much modern experience is of our own making. It leads to triviality and self-centredness. The reason why so many of us need to go on having ministry after ministry for our supposed needs and bondages is because we have never touched the altar of God. Those who have touched the altar of God find their bonds are burned away. That is what is involved in a proper conversion, not just some superficial ritual whereby we give our hearts to Jesus but know little of His power or holiness. It is the sight of the holiness of God which challenges everything of the old life and consumes it in the blazing fire of God's presence. I believe nothing less will suffice to deliver us from the man-centred, problem-orientated religion into which we have fallen nowadays. The Holy Spirit does not come to lead us back into our mother's womb, as Nicodemus suggested (Jn 3:4). The Holy Spirit comes to lead us into the heart of God. That is where the birth takes place. We need to catch such a vision of God in Jesus through the Spirit that we are so radically changed that the old life no longer carries the appeal or power it had.

Jeremiah the prophet was given the word of the Lord. It was first spoken to a people in captivity and today the Holy Spirit wants to declare it into your captivity: '"You will seek me and find me when you seek me with all your heart. I will be found by you," declares the Lord' (Jer 29:13, 14).

C: Baptism of fire

When I hear people speaking of being baptised in the Spirit, or what that meant for them, I sometimes wonder if we are talking about the same thing. For me it is a baptism of fire. It is a face-to-face encounter with the reality, holiness and power of God. It is not some little movement of joy which leads to my being able to speak in tongues or some such gift. I really believe that some of our explanations have led people to seek the gift instead of the Giver!

God starts the process by causing divine dissatisfaction in our hearts. We don't seek God just from cold. It is not in us to turn to God and seek Him with all our hearts (Rom 3:11). The stirring within us is done by the Holy Spirit. We may not recognise it as the hand of God, but God begins to work by many different means to rouse us from our contentment with things as they are. It is impossible to say how God will move in your life. I now know how He worked in mine but I can't say how He will work in yours. He knows you and He knows how you live. He has more ways of dealing with people than there are people to be dealt with. But move He will.

In my own life He worked for over two years. At the time I was a young aspiring minister. I had gone from college with good grades in my study and had become the minister of a university church and had started research for a Ph.D. But very soon God began to work in my life. He surrounded me with people who challenged me greatly. I saw things in the lives of other people which I knew were not in mine. I began to long deeply for effective power in my daily ministry, particularly among the students. I know that the old formulae and words would never work by themselves. No matter how good and true they were, they needed to be clothed in power. I began to feel depressed and dissatisfied with life as it was.

To most people on the outside this would have seemed crazy. I was in a priviledged position and with my cards played right (and carefully) I could have made the grade in my denomination and college as well. But you know, when your heart is out of sorts nothing else is at peace either. It's hard now to describe those days except to say that I became increasingly aware of my need for something I did not have.

What happened was in a way really very simple. I was invited by a minister friend of mine to attend a special conference being held for clergy and leaders where the theme was Holy Spirit renewal. I can't recall what the precise title was or anything like that, but I remember there were about thirty people there, nearly all Scottish Presbyterian and pretty staid. The meetings were held in a room on the first floor of the conference centre whilst the dining room and other facilities were on the ground floor. That is only important because it became an integral part of what happened. Actually I remember very little of the first two days of the conference. It seemed all right and fairly harmless until the final evening.

The conference was going to finish the next morning with a celebration of Holy Communion.

D: The hand of God

It is that last night I remember so vividly, however, An Anglican priest was due to speak. He chose for his text Isaiah chapter 6. It is not that I remember much of what he actually said; it is more that I remember what he was. That priest is now with his Lord in glory but I doubt if he is very much different from what he was that night! It was almost as though the glory of God shone through him. He was so simple and yet so profound! There was a shining about him. I knew as I watched him that this man was living in the good and richness of what he was sharing. In fact he was a living presentation of the message.

I was sitting in a Parker-Knoll-type chair with a low seat and open wooded arms. I felt the hand of God come on my life and the more the preacher spoke, the lower I seemed to sink into the chair. There was no conviction of any particular sin. I felt as though a tremendous heaviness had descended upon me through the roof, as though the whole world had come to rest on my head. I had never known darkness like that. By the time he had finished I felt as though I had disappeared down through the chair onto the floor. I felt as though I was sitting on the floor or even below it. It was an amazing sensation which I find hard to put into words.

The man finished and I have no doubt led the congregation in some sort of prayer. When he had finished everybody else took off downstairs to have their bedtime hot drink, but I was left in the room. It was as though no one else had noticed. They all just left.

The darkness of the night drew in and I was still sitting there. After a while two people came back upstairs. One was the friend who had taken me there, the other the leader of the conference. They came and looked at me where I sat. Nothing was said that I remember but it seemed evident to them that something deep was afoot. They prayed with me and laid hands on my head and then led me downstairs to supper. I sat with my hot chocolate, feeling as though I had just had a near miss with a nineteen ton double-decker bus! I knew firsthand what Isaiah meant when he said he was lost and ruined. I felt as though my personal inner world had come to an end. At the same time I knew this was because I had become aware of something new about God – His holiness and power, His purity and judgement. I had an overwhelming sense of the light of His presence – not the sort of light that makes you feel light, but the kind of light that makes you feel your own darkness. The brighter the light shone, the more I felt myself retreating into the darkness. I was overcome with the darkness that is sin, in the presence of absolute purity.

E: The touch of God

The touch of those men on my head must have been for me like the angel's touch for Isaiah. I felt the tide turning. I felt the trembling rising in me as I realised I was being permitted to live and not die. Much later I came across a verse in the apocryphal Book of Ecclesiasticus. It says: 'As is his majesty, so too is his mercy.' Praise God, there is only one thing as great as the majesty of God and that is His mercy. His love overpowers His wrath in the hearts of those who turn to Him.

I went to bed feeling like that, all trembling and faint. But the next morning when I awoke I went over to the window and pulled back the curtains just as the sun was rising over the hills. It was as though the sun of righteousness had risen with healing in its wings (Mal 4:2). I was a new creation. It was like being born again all over again! In fact there were depths to this new experience of God which I had never known before in my whole Christian life. It was as though a fire had been kindled in my heart. Instead of being consumed by it I had caught it. I believe that is the fire of the Holy Spirit.

After the Communion service which followed later that morning I set off in my car to return home. That was a journey I will never forget. There have been many discouragements in my Christian life and Satan would dearly love for us to be consumed by these things, so that we would falter in our confession of Christ. But I could almost say that this journey was worth every discouragement. I have never known such holy joy as in that car. The Holy Spirit brought songs into my heart and onto my lips that I had never known. Even the sheep on the hills seemed to watch in amazement! The following Sunday morning I stood up in my church to preach and found that I could do nothing but share what God had done. It was the start of a completely new and radical phase of my ministry in which many other people found the power of God.

F: Flames of fire

It was in tongues like flames of fire that the Holy Spirit appeared at Pentecost. The movement which set the disciples on their feet and sent them out into a lost world was no small movement of personal blessing. It was a mighty insurgence of a holy God. They came to understand for themselves in that moment all that had been revealed in the life and work of Jesus but which they had never fully grasped before. The Spirit of truth, power and holiness had come to abide within their hearts and to set them on fire for God.

This is what Jesus said: '*I have come to bring fire on the earth, and how I wish it were already kindled!*' (Lk 12:49). God wants to kindle that fire in the hearts of all of us. Don't be content with a day of small things. Let God work within you. Let Him stir up a thirst and heart's desire for something more. Seek Him with all your heart and you will surely find Him. There are, I believe, four simple but important steps to our finding God in this way:

Thirst. God deals with thirsty people. He will bless those whose hearts are really after Him and who unreservedly will allow Him to work in their lives. Let God speak to you. Let Him stir up in you that heart's desire that is so vital to the fulfilment of His purpose.

Openness. Be willing for God to do in you whatever He needs or wants to do. I found this to be the greatest struggle of all. My human pride and my theological presuppositions conditioned me against allowing God to have His way in my life. All of us have factors within our lives and personalities which militate against our giving ourselves away to God. It is these things which will be challenged and sometimes the battle in our wills will be violent until we surrender ourselves to the hand of God.

Receive. Throughout the Scriptures we are encouraged to receive from God the good things He has for every one of us in Jesus. We receive these things by the present work of the Holy Spirit within us. The Holy Spirit is the bringer of every good and perfect gift from God. This is a great truth, that the very Spirit who stirs us up and convicts us of our sin is the same One who brings and administers to us every mercy of God. We just need to ask Him: *'If you, then, though you are evil, know how to give good gifts to your children, how much more will your Father in heaven give the Holy Spirit to those who ask him!'* (Lk 11:13).

Obey. Knowing the touch of God on your life in this way is only the first step. The harder thing is following it through. When I look back on my life I can truthfully say that the toughest thing has been in remaining obedient to the heavenly vision. Many times Satan has attacked the reality of it. Many times my life and actions have seemed to be a standing denial of it. There is great responsibility laid on those who have known God in a measure like this. Praise God we are not left to bear that responsibility alone. The Holy Spirit who brings us to the blazing light of God and the Holy Spirit who brings to us the amazing gifts and mercy of God, is the same Holy Spirit who is sent by the Father to dwell in our hearts and lives, to keep us in that experience and knowledge of God.

3: Spirit of Witness

The point of sale for the Holy Spirit is the testimony of our lives. This is the bottom line as far as ordinary men and women are concerned. Most people have been put off by the pomp and, as far as they are concerned, the unreality of organised religion. Sadly, they often claim to have been put off by the lives of the professing Christians they have met. This is the great challenge of our own day: can Christian faith be seen to be credible in the lives of ordinary men and women? In a world that lives under fear and is threatened by disease and violence, does believing in Jesus make any difference? In the recent history of the human race there never has been a more urgent moment for the power of the Holy Spirit to be demonstrated in real-life terms.

So much of our modern evangelism, particularly amongst young people, has been a copy of the world's own way of doing things in the name of communication. This is the moment for something *different*: for lives that are different, for attitudes that are different, for values that are different, for relationships that are different. By 'different' I don't mean freakish. We need to be different in goodness, different in care, different in loving, different in standards, different in life – not different in a negative sort of way but different in a positive way. That was the secret of Jesus: He was different in a positive way – so different that they did not know what to make of Him. He wasn't a religious freak, He was a real man. His difference compelled men and women to follow Him, and at the same time His difference repelled those who hated goodness and the love of God. In the end it forced them to a choice. Some followed Him, the others crucified Him, but even those who crucified Him could not deny the testimony of His life. Perhaps that's why we are not so keen to be His witnesses – we are frightened about the repercussions of our testimony.

Every believer is called, nevertheless, to be a living witness to the life and power of Jesus in the day in which they live. Many people will never enter a church or open a Bible, but they see our lives before them every day we meet them.

Michael Green is right when he writes in his book, *I Believe in the Holy Spirit*:

> *There can be no doubt from a candid examination of the New Testament accounts that the prime purpose of the coming of the Spirit of God upon the disciples was to equip them for mission. The Comforter comes not in order to allow men to be comfortable, but to make them missionaries.* (p58)

This is exactly what Jesus said before He ascended into glory: '*You will receive power when the Holy Spirit comes on you, and you will be my witnesses in Jerusalem, and in all Judea and Samaria, and to the ends of the earth.*' (Acts 1:8).

This is not only a word for the big guns of evangelism with their structure and organisation. It is the promise to every believer who will open his life to the operation of the Holy Spirit in fulness. This is a tremendous fact: we have been called to be the witnesses of the Kingdom of God. Michael Green again:

> *The message is clear. All disciples are expected to bear their testimony to Jesus. That is what the Holy Spirit is given them for ... The witness attests his own experience: he does not necessarily preach ... Witness in the New Testament is neither the silent churchgoing that passes for witness among many Christians, nor the sickening self-advertisement that often results when a believer 'gives his testimony'; but simple, factual reference to the historical Jesus, his death and resurrection, his gift of the Spirit, and his present availablity and power.* (pp67, 68)

Witness is not only *demonstration*, it is *explanation*. Pentecost was a great demonstration of the outpouring of the Holy Spirit but it gave rise to questions which demanded an answer. The people wanted to know what this power was and how it was that men and women they knew seemed to have a new capacity and joy in their lives (see Acts 2:7–12). Peter stood up in the power of the Holy Spirit and gave an answer to the questions which were raised by the manifestations of the Spirit in the lives of the disciples: *'Then Peter stood up with the Eleven, raised his voice and addressed the crowd: "Fellow Jews and all of you who are in Jerusalem, let me explain this to you; listen carefully to what I say. These men are not drunk as you suppose. It's only nine in the morning!"'* (Acts 2:14, 15). This is the secret of personal witness. It is not the intensity and often unreality of sallying forth armed with a bunch of tracts, ready to run every unsuspecting soul to ground. I am not saying there is no place for this sort of effort, but the real power of personal witness is felt where the reality of the love and power of Jesus through one person raises questions in others.

This kind of testimony has been at a discount in many churches for years. We have suffered a total lack of confidence at this level of personal witness. Christians have lost the art of being 'naturally supernatural' in their daily relationships and involvements with other people. I have heard it said that it is the life that counts. It is not so much what we say as what we are. Of course, like every effective lie there is a good measure of truth at the heart of this one. After all, this is what this book is all about: it is the life that counts! But there's more to it than that. The trouble with that argument is that when time is taken to examine the lives in question there is often very little evidence of a dynamic and personal experience of God within them. In many cases middle-class decency seems to have taken the place of the power of the Holy Spirit. The Moonies and loonies have had a field-day because of our failure of nerve. We have become reticent about wearing our religion on our sleeves lest we be labelled extremists or nuts. Modern theology has riddled many dear people with doubt and uncertainty to the point that many no longer have any clear idea what they believe.

A: Now it's your turn

I was very moved one time by the challenge which Bob Humburg, leader of the Glaubenszentrum in North

Germany, brought to his students. He reminded us of the continuous reality of God's testimony throughout the centuries. There never has been a time when God was without witness. We know of those who have become famous and noteworthy, but imagine the millions of unsung believers who have borne witness, through their lives, to the power of God in Jesus. I felt the power of God's Word into my own life that night. What a thrill to see our lives in that perspective! Bob simply challenged us with these words: 'Now it's your turn!'

I believe it. It is our turn. What an awesome thing it is to see our lives like this. I recalled the words of Mordecai to Queen Esther when he sent his messages to her: '*And who knows but that you have come to royal position for such a time as this?*' (Esther 4:14). We have come to a Kingdom for a time like this. As Peter says: '*You are a chosen people, a royal priesthood, a holy nation, a people belonging to God, that you may declare the praises of him who called you out of darkness into his wonderful light*' (1 Pet 2:9).

What an even more awesome thing it is to remember that if we fail in our witness, our generation might have no other witness. To make this more particular: if our lives don't witness to Jesus in the power of the Holy Spirit, maybe those people who are near to us every day may receive no other direct witness to the goodness of God. We are not at liberty to speculate on the ways of God and what alternative plans He may have. We have been born to this: to bear witness to the power of Christ in our lives. It may not seem as though many want to listen, but our experience with The King's Coach in the market place convinces us otherwise. There are many, many people who will never hear a sermon or open the Bible for themselves, who are longing to hear a word that is relevent to their own needs. That word is your life and mine!

B: The Spirit helps us

There are a number of fundamental areas in which we can be sure of the help of the Holy Spirit. Personal witness does not, in the first instance, depend on expertise, but on openness. Personal witness is not preaching or even giving a public testimony. It is living our lives in daily openness to God and allowing the reality and love of God to flow from deep within us into the lives of those people with whom we come in contact. Jesus said that the power of the Holy Spirit was like living water which flows out of the innermost being of every person who believes in Him (Jn 7:38, 39). We need to be open to whatever God wants to do through us by His Spirit and willing to look upon our whole lives as the arena within which God can do His work.

(a) **Experience.** Our testimony grows out of our experience of Christ. There is no real vital truth apart from *experienced* truth. This does not mean that experience is the arbiter to truth. Some things remain true whether or not we experience them. For example, it remains true that Christ died for my sin whether or not I experience it. But it is not effective in me unless I *do* experience it. It is my experinece of the truth which makes it real and powerful in my life. That is what Jesus meant when He said, that we would know the truth and the truth would set us free (see Jn 8:32). This is the very heart of discipleship. A disciple is a person who follows the truth, not as a mere philosophy or ideology, but as a life-changing reality, through a personal relationship of faith and commitment with the One who described Himself as the way, the truth and the life. This is the difference between a person who can repeat the story of Jesus and a person who says, 'I know'. Paul makes the point when he writes to Timothy: *'I am not ashamed, because I know whom I believed, and am convinced that he is able to guard what I have entrusted to him for that day'* (2 Tim 1:12).

The Holy Spirit brings us experience of God. He makes real within our lives the forgiveness and freedom which come from the work of Christ for us. He releases within our lives God's power, by which we are able to live and act in the reality of the Kingdom of God. This is why the process of conversion and commitment is so important because we then become truly aware that we have turned away from an old way of life and have entered into the reality of a new life in Christ. There is nothing so powerful as the testimony of a new life in Christ. For many who never enter a church or read the Bible our lives will be the first and most immediate witness to the power of God they may ever know. As someone once said, our lives are probably the first Bibles that many people ever read.

Ask yourselves what you know of God. Examine your experience of God. What personal testimony can you give to the saving power of God within your life, or how have you known the help and strength of God through the Holy Spirit in the circumstances and events of your life? The material for personal testimony is built by the Holy Spirit into the very fibre of our own experience of life with Christ.

(b) Assurance. The Holy Spirit is Himself first and foremost a witness. He is first a witness to Jesus Himself. It is the Holy Spirit who points us to Jesus and who reveals the meaning of the life, death and resurrection of Jesus for us. Jesus said that this would be the great work of the Spirit: *'When he, the Spirit of truth, comes, he will guide you into all truth. He will not speak on his own; he will speak only what he hears ... He will bring glory to me by taking what is mine and making it known to you'* (Jn 16:13, 14).

But the Holy Spirit is also a witness within us. This is the ground of our assurance and confidence as believers. Paul underlines this truth when he says, *'The Spirit himself testifies with our spirit that we are God's children'* (Rom 8:16). When he speaks of this fact again in his letter to the Ephesians, Paul uses a beautiful image to make his point. He uses the metaphor of an engagement ring given between two lovers as the symbol of the certainty which the Father brings to our hearts through the witness of the Holy Spirit. Paul speaks of the Spirit as being a *deposit* which is the guarantee of even greater things to come. The word meaning 'deposit' comes from an original Greek word which also means 'engagement ring': *'Having believed, you were marked in him with a seal, the promised Holy Spirit, who is a deposit guaranteeing our inheritance until the redemption of those who are God's possession'* (Eph 1:13, 14).

Here lies the true secret of effective personal witness. It is not something that is hypertensive and filled with anxiety but rather bears witness to this relationship of confidence and trust that exists between the heavenly Father and His new-born child.

(c) **Boldness.** One of the most outstanding features of the Book of Acts is the freedom with which the early Christians testified to Christ. One word crops up time and again in Scriptures such as this: *'Now, Lord, consider their threats and enable your servants to speak your words with boldness'* (Acts 4:29). They spoke and acted with a boldness that did not come from themselves but was the result of the work of the Holy Spirit within their hearts. This was not a boldness that grew out of arrogance or aggression. In fact, the original Greek word has nothing to do with attitudes like these. The true meaning of the word is highlighted later in the New Testament by Paul: *'Pray also for me, that whenever I open my mouth, words may be given me so that I will fearlessly make known the mystery of the gospel'* (Eph 6:19).

Jesus had promised His disciples that they need have no fear whenever they were called to give an account of themselves on His behalf, because it would be given them in that very moment what they should say. The Book of Acts bears eloquent witness to the fact that the Holy Spirit gives the words and the power to those who will witness faithfully to what Jesus means to them. Some people would like to make witnessing a matter of personality, as though some are called to it more than others because they are more extrovert. I am sure that God will use our personalities in His service. After all, one of the main reasons He made Christians all different is because the world is full of different types of people. There are people whom you will reach at a personal level whom I could never touch, and vice versa. But Holy Spirit boldness has nothing to do with personality: it has to do with openness and with being willing to allow God to speak through you in every situation.

(d) **Understanding.** For some people the problem is fear. They are afraid to share their faith and experience of God with other people because they lack confidence. This fear rises out of ignorance – that is, they don't feel they know enough to be able to handle questions or difficulties which may result from the testimony. I remember suffering from the very same syndrome sometimes when I was in business. Part of my job was to give a presentation to hospital medical teams on the latest medicine my firm had produced. This was all right when I had taken the time to prepare and become acquainted with every aspect of the product. Then I could answer all the questions and deal with any difficulty which arose. But on those occasions when something had prevented me from being as prepared as I should have been it was very different. I lost my sense of confidence and was always concerned in case the conversation should lead me into areas where my ignorance would become apparent.

There are two simple steps you can take to deal with this fear.

First, start where you are. A testimony is a testimony – that is, it is a witness to what you have come to know of God within your own life. People don't want a theological treatise, and it is likely that Satan will try to paralyse you with fear about questions that other people will never ask you anyway. The man whom Jesus healed of blindness experienced such questioning. The enemies of Jesus interrogated him after he had been healed and tried to trap him with arguments that went far beyond his experience. In the end the man exclaimed what he knew for certain: *'One thing I do know. I was blind but now I see!'* (Jn 9:25). You know something that no one else in the world knows: what God has done for you in Christ and through the power of the Holy Spirit.

Secondly, be determined to move on from where you are. The Holy Spirit Himself is your teacher. You will be amazed at how much you can grow in your understanding if you take time and effort with the Scriptures. Paul reminds you of the help that is available to us from the Holy Spirit in this: *'We have not received the spirit of the world but the Spirit who is from God, that we may understand what God has freely given us. This is what we speak, not in words taught us by human wisdom but in words taught by the Spirit, expressing spiritual* *truths in spiritual words'* (1 Cor 2:12, 13). There are available to us today a huge number of aids to our spiritual understanding. The Lion range of books, for example, is full of interest and colour and will provide a backcloth to our own experience of God. The list of books and tapes which are available is almost endless and no believer need be without the sort of help and support they need to move forward in their understanding of the things of God. For many of us it is a matter of the will, not of the intellectual or spiritual capacity. We need to be willing to give our time and minds to the Lord and to leave aside some of the trivia with which so many folks fill their lives.

(e) **Capability.** I have spoken elsewhere about the gifts of the Holy Spirit. But nowhere are they more relevant for our own lives that in the area of witness. The Holy Spirit not only gives us the power to speak, but through His gifts of wisdom and discernment, shows us when and how to speak in any particular situation. We all live under the shadow of a great commission to go and make disciples of all nations, but we are not left to ourselves in the task. Jesus promised His first disciples that He would always be with them and He is always with us, giving us power and guidance through the Spirit whom He has sent to enable us everyday in our witness to Him.

(f) **Opportunity.** Another of the outstanding features of the Book of Acts is the way that the Holy Spirit leads men and women into areas of effective witness. He is always taking the initiative in opening the right doors where He has prepared the ground for the reception of the gospel. One of the clearest examples of this is the experience of Philip, who is told by the angel of the Lord to take the road south to the desert. On the way he meets the Ethiopian eunuch who is just ready to listen to the testimony that Philip has to give him (see Acts chapter 8). Another is the case of Peter, who through the direction of a powerful dream is led to share the message of Christ with the gentile Cornelius, an event which determined the spread of the gospel throughout the world in a most definite way (see Acts chapter 10). Paul's whole life was directed by the Holy Spirit in this way and he became very open to the leading of the Spirit in every circumstance. Even when he was thrown into jail at Philippi he was ready to see the hand of God in it, and we all know how he ended up leading his jailer to Christ. Later, when he was writing from his house-imprisonment in Rome to the same Philippians, he could remind them that the things that had happened to him had served to advance the cause of the gospel (see Phil 1:12).

So it will be for us if we open our lives to the influences of the Holy Spirit. Life takes on a new dimension altogether when we are prepared every day to follow the leading of the Spirit on every occasion.

Our whole life is an opportunity, and if we will open ourselves to the possibilites of the Holy Spirit we will be surprised at how many opportunities we are given to share what our faith in Jesus means to us. This does not mean we need to always straining to barge into people's lives; it means that we need to follow the Lord as He opens the door by His Spirit. Witness means many things. At one time it will mean making a clear statement about what we believe and why; frequently it will mean we are the outlet for God into the situation, demonstrating His love and power through our attitudes and concern for other people. In any event, it is not a witness to ourselves but to the loving power of the Lord Jesus Christ. Paul reminds us of that when he writes: *'For we do not preach ourselves, but Jesus Christ as Lord, and ourselves as your servants for Jesus' sake'* (2 Cor 4:5).

(g) **Love.** It is the love of Christ that compels us to be His witnesses. We are not driven by fear, guilt or condemnation. All these have been removed through the forgiving power of the love of God. Because we have come to know the reality of God's love in our own hearts and lives we want as many others as possible to share this same gift: *'For Christ's love compels us, because we are convinced that one died for all'* (2 Cor 5:14).

People *feel* the reality of love like this. It is not something that rises from our own human nature but is, again, a product of the work of the Holy Spirit in our hearts. Paul, when he writes to the Romans, reminds us that this love is poured out into our hearts by the Holy Spirit (see Rom 5:5). It is the power of this love at work within us which transforms our testimony into something more than words: *'This is how we know what love is: Jesus Christ laid down his life for us. And we ought to lay down our lives for our brothers ... Dear children, let us not love with words or tongue but with actions and in truth'* (1 Jn 3:16, 18).

C: The healing of the nations

Ezekiel ends his great prophecy with a tremendous vision of the renewing power of the life of God. He pictures it as water that is flowing out from the temple of God. The further this water flows, the deeper it becomes, and wherever it goes everything becomes fresh. It is like a great river of life that flows from the heart of God: *'Fruit trees of all kinds will grow on both banks of the river. Their leaves will not wither, nor will their fruit fail. Every month they will bear, because the water from the sanctuary flows to them. Their fruit will serve for food and their leaves for healing'* (Ezek 47:12). What a terrific picture this could be of our lives! Fed and nourished by the flowing water of the Holy Spirit of God, who produces His fruit in our lives so that we become the source of life and healing for those we encounter day by day.

4: The Fellowship of the Spirit

The Fellowship of the Spirit is not the name of a church in the New Testament. It is an attitude of heart and mind. It is the expression of a bond in Christ Jesus between Christian believers that goes far deeper than the natural ties of family or friendship. It is one of the greatest challenges to our lives as Christians today. We live in a world of tremendous spiritual flux where nothing seems to be the same for long and in which we are called upon to interact with people from many different backgrounds and places. As Christians we are not on our own. We have been born by faith into a tremendous world-wide family of believers who are joined together not by race, colour or convenience, but by the blood of Jesus. Paul spells out the reality of this when he writes to the Galatians: *'You are all sons of God through faith in Christ Jesus, for all of you who were baptised into Christ have clothed yourselves with Christ. There is neither Jew nor Greek, slave, nor free, male, nor female, for you are all one in Christ Jesus'* (Gal 3:26–28).

When the New Testament expresses this unity which we have together, it uses phrases such as 'in Christ' or 'in Christ Jesus' rather than terms which explicitly relate this unity to the work of the Holy Spirit. The fact is that we are one because of what God has done in Christ. Paul reminds us in Ephesians chapter 1 that God purposed this in Christ for us before the world began.

The New Testament speaks on only two occasions about this fellowship in terms of the Holy Spirit. The first is in the words of the benediction which we have all come to know so well from the end of Paul's correspondence with the church at Corinth: *'May the grace of the Lord Jesus Christ, and the love of God, and the fellowship of the Holy Spirit be with you all'* (2 Cor 13:14). The second is from an equally well-known passage of Scripture – that is, Paul's exhortation for unity in Philippians chapter 2: *'If you have any encouragement from being united with Christ, if any comfort from his love, if any fellowship with the Spirit, if any tenderness and compassion, then make my joy complete by being like-minded, having the same love, being one in spirit and purpose'* (Phil 2:1, 2). Those words of Paul, *'if any fellowship with the Spirit'*, are better translated something like: 'if the fact that you all participate in the same Holy Spirit means anything'. Paul is appealing in strong terms to the fact that we are what we are because of God's work in us through the Spirit. This is what we have in common and our unity should not depend on taste or discrimination but on our common experience of the life of God through His Spirit.

It is important to notice that although the words are used on these two occasions only, the idea of oneness and sharing between the believers because of their common bond in the work of the Holy Spirit, runs like a golden thread throughout the New Testament.

A: The heart of fellowship

There are seven areas in which the New Testament stresses the work of the Holy Spirit in the common life which believers share, and an examination of relevant scriptures will demonstrate what is involved in this fellowship of the Spirit. We might think of these areas as a diamond with seven important facets, which we can present as shown in the diagram on page 343:

(a) **The love of the Spirit.** Paul writes: *'I urge you, brothers, by our Lord Jesus Christ and by the love of the Spirit, to join me in my struggle by praying to God for me'* (Rom 15:30). Elsewhere Paul connects the idea of love with the work of the Holy Spirit when he is speaking about his relationship with fellow believers. In Colossians 1:8 he acknowledges the love which the Colossians had for him in the Spirit and in 2 Corinthians 6:6 he commends himself to his readers *'in the Holy Spirit and in sincere love.'*

At the heart of our relationship as believers, then, stands the love of God. This is not a love which grows out of natural affection or liking for each other, but is rather a love which is produced within us by the direct work of the Holy Spirit: *'Hope does not disappoint us, because God has poured out his love into our hearts by the Holy Spirit, whom he has given us'*

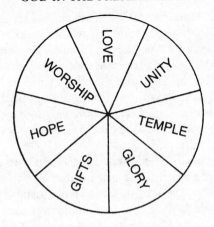

(Rom 5:5). Jesus said that it was the reality of this love which would be the hallmark of our discipleship in the eyes of other people (see Jn 13:35).

(b) **The unity of the Spirit.** The dynamic equivalent of Galatians 3:26–28 which, as we have seen, stresses the fact of our unity through faith in Christ, is 1 Corinthians 12:13: '*For we were all baptised by one Spirit into one body – whether Jews or Greeks, slave or free – and we were all given the one Spirit to drink.*' This unity is something that grows out of the fact of our salvation in Christ Jesus. We are one because the Holy Spirit has acted in each one of us to bring us into the reality of Christ's life through the gift of faith. This salvation has been sealed by God in the blood of His Son: '*He came and preached peace to you who were far away and peace to those who were near. For through him we both have access to the Father by one Spirit*' (Eph 2:17, 18). It is a unity which is precious and needs to be guarded and persevered in when necessary. Paul exhorts his readers to do all they can to promote and preserve the unity of the Spirit: '*Make every effort to keep the unity of the Spirit through the bond of peace*' (Eph 4:3).

A practical example of how this principle applies to daily

life surfaces in Romans 14:13–23, where Paul tackles the problem of differing views on food and what should be regarded as clean or unclean by the believer. Paul argues that there are more important principles with which we should be concerned and that, in areas like this, we should be free to leave each other to decide without letting it disrupt the reality of fellowship with one another: *'For the kingdom of God is not a matter of eating and drinking, but of righteousness, peace and joy in the Holy Spirit.'*

(c) **The temple of the Spirit.** Closely allied to this truth of the unity of the Spirit is the picture that is used a number of times in the New Testament of believers being built together as a holy temple to the Lord. In Ephesians chapter 2 Paul uses the picture to underline the importance of our unity in Christ and to make the further point that we have become, through this unity, *the dwelling place of God on earth*. The temple or house of God is also the place of service, offering and praise, and this is precisely the truth which Peter highlights when he says: *'You also, like living stones, are being built into a spiritual house to be a holy priesthood, offering spiritual sacrifices acceptable to God through Jesus Christ'* (1 Pet 2:5).

The significance of this building as far as God is concerned is made clear in 1 Corinthians chapter 3, where we are exhorted to be careful how we build on the foundation that has been laid. It is no light thing to play fast and loose with the temple of God, and we will all be held accountable before Him as to what we have done with His precious dwelling place: *'Don't you know that you yourselves are God's temple and that God's Spirit lives in you? If anyone destroys God's temple, God will destroy him; for God's temple is sacred, and you are that temple'* (1 Cor 3:16, 17).

(d) **The glory of the Spirit.** These ideas flow into one another like a running stream. The temple is the place of God's dwelling, as we have seen, and the amazing fact is that God has chosen to dwell in us! Where God dwells His glory is seen, and this is the next truth which the Scriptures teach us about the fellowship of the Spirit: it is a fellowship of the glory of God. Peter uses the phrase 'the Spirit of glory' within the context of our suffering for Christ: *'If you are insulted because of the name of Christ, you are blessed, for the Spirit of glory and of God rests on you'* (1 Pet 4:14).

The idea is expanded even further when Paul speaks about the transforming work of the Holy Spirit, who enables us first to behold God's glory in Jesus and by that transforms us into the likeness of Jesus so that His glory is seen in our lives (see 2 Cor 3:18).

(e) **The gifts of the Spirit.** We have seen already how the gifts of the Holy Spirit are gifts to the Body of Christ and not only to individual Christians. We may say that they are gifts to the Body which are manifested through individual believers. It is this truth which Paul emphasises when he writes, *'Now to each one the manifestation of the Spirit is given for the common good'* (1 Cor 12:7).

The gifts of the Holy Spirit really make no sense apart from the fact of the fellowship of the Spirit. Their operation should be a sign of the unity of the Body. The tragic fact is that so often the reverse is true. What God gave for unity of life and action has become the ground of division and pride. This was the sin at Corinth and it has been repeated, time and again, throughout the history of the Church.

(f) **The hope of the Spirit.** Faith and hope are the Siamese twins of Christian life. Where there is faith, there is hope. It is not true the other way round. Christian hope is not the hopefulness which the natural human heart seems to have such a capacity for. Sadly, this hopefulness so often turns into wishful thinking, and through Satan, gains such an opportunity in the lives of men and women by playing on it and leading them on into unreality. Christian hope is total because it is based on the work and Word of Jesus, and it is born out of faith. This faith is produced in us by the Holy Spirit: *'By faith we eagerly await through the Spirit the righteousness for which we hope. For in Christ Jesus neither circumcision nor uncircumcision has any value. The only thing that counts is faith expressing itself through love'* (Gal 5:5, 6).

Words like these make the point that the faith, hope and love which the Holy Spirit engenders within us are not merely individually experienced but are expressed corporately in our lives together in the fellowship of the Holy Spirit.

(g) The worship of the Spirit. Fellowship in the Spirit is a fellowship before the throne of God in worship. This is where our fellowship is most deeply expressed. This is the dimension of fellowship which is most affected when things happen which prevent brothers and sisters from meeting together. True worship finds its root in the work of the Holy Spirit. Paul makes this point in his warnings to the Philippians against those false Judaising teachers who wanted to insist on outward ritual: *'For it is we who are the circumcision, we who worship by the Spirit of God, who glory in Christ Jesus, and who put no confidence in the flesh'* (Phil 3:3). This fellowship we have in the Spirit is most profoundly expressed when we engage in worshipping the Father together through the Lord Jesus Christ.

Every one of these aspects of the fellowship of the Spirit leads us to a deeper appreciation of what we have been called into Christ Jesus. The fellowship of the Spirit is a living reality; it is found where believers relate to each other in love and truth; it is strengthened through love and loyalty and it is the most urgent challenge to be laid at the door of our lives today.

B: One in the Spirit

There must be a deep pain the heart of God when he sees how far short we fall of the ideals He has presented us with in His Son. He has laid the foundation of our fellowship in Jesus and He has given us the power to make it a reality through obedience and love in the Holy Spirit. The devil so often seems to succeed, however, in leading us into failure and pain.

Of course, at a practical level, we cannot *have* fellowship with every Christian in a deep personal sense, nor are we meant to. We are *in* fellowhsip with every true believer whether we like it or not, because we are joined together in the heart of God through the work of Christ. It is necessary for each one of us to discern our circles of fellowship, not in an exclusive sense, but in a way that will enable us to express and fulfil this fellowship with other Christians at a practical level.

In my experience these circles change through the years because of many varying circumstances. For example, geographical location determines fellowship to a real degree, and in our highly mobile society fellowship will change in intensity because people move from one area to another. Again, commitments and involvements in ministries change. God calls us from one area of service to another, and it will often follow that the people involved with us will change as well. We don't need to see this as a hurtful or wrong thing, but recognise the breadth of God's work and calling, and rejoice in the variety into which we are placed by the Spirit.

Jesus Himself operated with different circles of fellowship. Even within the twelve it is clear that there were three who had a special relationship with Him. Again, the home at Bethany seemed to have a special place in the life of Jesus that nowhere else could fill. Then there were larger numbers of disciples who were sent out by Jesus to minister and who obviously shared another level of fellowship with Him. Jesus seemed able to hold all these different circles in a creative relationship within His own life, so that the fellowship they expressed was fruitful on all sides.

(a) Fellowship is fruitful. The Psalmist expressed better than most what it means for people to be in fellowship with one another. In the beautiful Psalm 133 he highlights the reality of fellowship as far as God and man are concerned. He uses two profound pictures to express his feelings. First, Aaron's beard. This happened at the anointing of Aaron, where the special oil of consecration was poured over his head (see Ex 29:7). This was a sign of his being set apart to God and marked his special place in the service of the Lord. Second, the Psalmist says this unity is like the dew of Hermon falling on Mount Zion. The dews of Hermon are the source of water and life for the land: they bring refreshment and sustenance to the people. So it is with true fellowship. There is something precious here for the heart of God, and it is the source of refreshment and nourishment for Christians in their daily walk with God.

(b) Fellowship is creative. There are many areas in our Chistian lives where we cannot function properly apart from fellowship with other believers. Christian discipleship is, in the end, not an individual exercise but a corporate one. Most of the challenges we face arise because of the fact that we live in relationship with other people. Right at the beginning of the Church the reality of this fellowship was demonstrated in a very practical way when the Holy Spirit moved amongst the new believers in such power that they were united in heart and mind and shared everything they had together so that *'there were no needy persons among them'* (Acts 4:34). The same is true in the realm of the gifts of the Spirit in the Church. Peter urges his readers to exercise their gifts in terms of fellowship. Then there will be no poverty of spirit or lack of spiritual gift in the body, and everybody will be enriched and built up as we share our gifts together in mutual love and service (see 1 Pet 4:10, 11).

It is the same with faith and mutual encouragement. Encouragement is at a discount among believers today. Instead we would rather indulge in the party spirit and damn each other with faint praise. But this is not the Father's will. His will is for a generosity of spirit which recognises what is of God in each other and fosters it through mutual encouragement and help. The writer to the Hebrews highlights this when he says: *'Let us consider how we may spur one another on toward love and good deeds. Let us not give up meeting together, as some are in the habit of doing, but let us encourage one another – and all the more as you see the Day approaching'* (Heb 10:24, 25).

(c) Fellowship is costly. The fact is that when we open ourselves to fellowship with one another we are making ourselves vulnerable. We are far from perfect people and the cost of fellowship is that not only do we receive from each other what is of God in us, but we are open to every influence and natural trait that manifests itself in our lives and personalities. This is why some people find it hard to open themselves up to others for fear of hurt and misunderstanding.

We can see this vulnerability in the experience of Jesus and the men and women of the Scriptures. Jesus experienced in His spirit the devastation of betrayal by one of His inner circle of friends. Barnabas broke fellowship with Paul because of a disagreement about another person, John Mark. Demas forsook Paul because he loved the attraction of the world more than the service of Christ. Others preached the gospel out of selfish ambition and envy even while Paul was in prison for his faith. Paul's reply to the Philippians on this issue is a measure of how he understood the principles of fellowship in the Spirit and followed them within his own heart and life. The greatest pain in the life of fellowship is the pain of having to stand by and watch others whom you love deeply in the Spirit of Christ take actions or stances which you know will be unproductive or hurtful to themselves or others.

We should humble ourselves and allow the Spirit to search the thoughts and attitudes of all our hearts. Our gospel cannot remain credible alongside continual breakdown and spiritual divorce between true believers. The pain that such separation brings can often be the most debilitating factor in our lives and ministries. It robs us of confidence within ourselves and between each other and it provides the world with a major reason for rejecting our message. '*This is how we know what love is: Jesus Christ laid down his life for us. And we ought to lay down our lives for our brothers ... Dear children, let us not love with words or tongue but with actions and in truth*' (1 Jn 3:16, 18).

5: Ask and You Will Receive

I want to end where I began. The Holy Spirit is a Person. There is no doubt that He will have been speaking to you as you have read this book. His business is to make us open to God. He creates a thirst for God in our hearts. It is a thirst that God satisfies when we cry to Him.

Some people ask me how to receive the Holy Spirit into their lives, as though there were some magical formula. I always respond by drawing their attention to the words of Jesus in Luke 11:9–13:

> *So I say to you: Ask and it will be given to you; seek and you will find; knock and the door will be opened to you. For everyone who asks receives; he who seeks finds; and to him who knocks, the door will be opened. Which of you fathers, if your son asks for a fish, will give him a snake instead? Or if he asks for an egg, will give him a scorpion? If you then, though you are evil, know how to give good gifts to your children, how much more will your Father in heaven give the Holy Spirit to those who ask him!*

There is a sense, of course, in which the Holy Spirit is already there. Every born-again believer receives the Holy Spirit at the time of their incorporation into Christ through faith. Paul teaches us that in his letter to the Ephesians: '*And you also were included in Christ, when you heard the word of truth, the gospel of your salvation. Having believed, you were marked in him with a seal, the promised Holy Spirit, who is a deposit guaranteeing our inheritance*' (Eph 1:13, 14). But in the very same epistle Paul exhorts his readers to '*be filled with the Spirit*' (5:18). This filling is the source of daily power and strength for discipleship and witness. The actual meaning of the words in the original Greek is that we should 'go on being filled with the Spirit'. This underlines what we all know, that although we may have received the Spirit in conversion and although we may have experienced an initial 'baptism' in the Spirit, we need to go on being open day by day to the flow of the Spirit in our lives. I invariably find that the Holy Spirit makes us aware of our need of His power in our lives before we ever ask for it. If you know you need Him in your life, why don't you ask the Father to give you the Holy Spirit?

Don't be afraid of what God might do. Fear is not part of the work of the Holy Spirit. Love is the key to His work: *'For God has not given us a spirit of fear, but a spirit of power and love and a sound mind'* (2 Tim 1:7 J. B. Phillips). Open yourself to God. Let the wind of the Holy Spirit blow through you. Be open to receive all that He brings you. Let Him sanctify you through and through – spirit, soul and body. Let Him fill your life with God's power. Receive from Him the gifts He brings and learn how to praise, worship and witness in the power of God.

If it helps, and it probably will, get someone who knows what it means to be filled with the Holy Spirit to pray with you. But otherwise you can ask for yourself, right now. Use a simple prayer such as this, and the Father will hear you and answer you in the power of His Spirit:

Dear Father,
Thank you for this promise that whoever asks will receive and whoever seeks will find. I know that I need more of your power in my life. I know that I need more of the fruit of your Holy Spirit in my life.
Father, I confess my sin before you and ask for your cleansing in my life through the blood of Jesus.
I open my life completely to you. Please send the Holy Spirit into my life in power right now. In Jesus' name. Amen.